D

D0046184

A Mingled Yarn

Carpenter

Scott

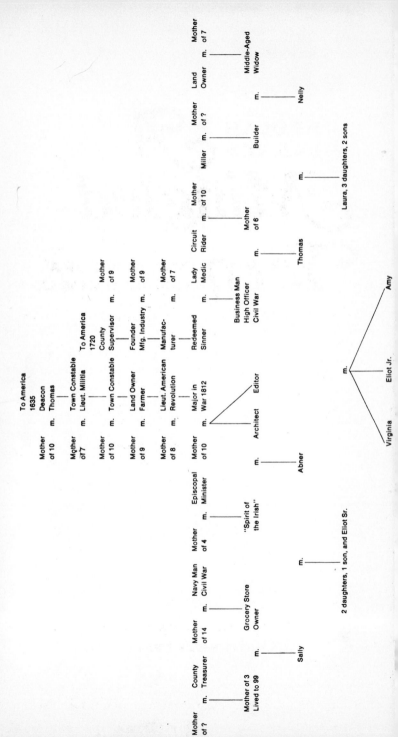

BEULAH PARKER "A Mingled Yarn

CHRONICLE OF A TROUBLED FAMILY

NEW HAVEN AND LONDON,
YALE UNIVERSITY PRESS, 1972

Designed by Sally Sullivan
and set in IBM Selectric Century type.
Printed in the United States of America by
The Carl Purington Rollings Printing-Office
of The Yale University Press.

Published in Great Britain, Europe, and Africa by
Yale University Press, Ltd., London.
Distributed in Canada by McGill-Queen's University
Press, Montreal; in Latin America by Kaiman & Polon,
Inc., New York City; in Australasia and Southeast
Asia by John Wiley & Sons Australasia Pty. Ltd.,
Sydney; in India by UBS Publishers' Distributors Pvt.,
Ltd., Delhi; in Japan by John Weatherhill, Inc., Tokyo.

The web of our life is of a mingled yarn, good and ill together.

All's Well That Ends Well

Contents

Introduction

This is the story of a family that began in piety and ended in disaster. Its pilgrim founder landed on this continent in 1635, and for a little over three hundred years, a series of solid and prolific descendants of two well-respected family lines participated actively and effectively in the growth and development of America. In the tenth generation, a daughter in one line and a son in the other met, married, and created together a home in which seeds for the extinction of both family lines took root and flowered.

This book deals largely with the offspring of that union and tells the story of their lives. However, I have written it primarily for the purpose of conveying a feeling for the kind of emotional overtones that pervaded the home of Laura and Eliot Carpenter, Sr., and of showing how the interpersonal atmosphere that they established laid a foundation for the destruction of their children.

In their early years, the Carpenter children were among the most fortunate people in the United States. They were born into a family neither too rich nor too poor. No daily struggle against mediocrity or the loss of social and economic security plagued their parents. They were not alien, not disadvantaged, not discriminated against. The Carpenter children were white

Anglo-Saxon Protestants, with a background of money
and social position honorably earned by their maternal
grandfather, and a tradition of solid virtue on both sides
of their family reaching back to the earliest days of this
country. Their father was handsome, brilliant, highly
successful in big business at an early age, and well-
meaning toward his children. Their mother was charming, well-bred, lovable, normally intelligent, and truly
devoted to providing what she felt to be in the best
interests of everyone. All three children were more than
ordinarily endowed with intelligence, talent, health,
good looks, and opportunity. Even at times of economic
hardship, they were never without a comfortable,
attractive home, a first-class private education, and some
of the luxuries that are considered basic necessities by
most upper-middle-class people. They had everything
going their way, but something went wrong. The lives of
all three were seriously crippled by emotional disturbance, and one became schizophrenic.

At the present period of history, more and more
people in the United States have become acquainted
with the word *schizophrenia*. Even those who have little
contact with the mental health professions are hearing
that a relative or friend is schizophrenic, or has an
adolescent child afflicted with this form of disturbance,
and are bewildered to find "insanity" touching their
own lives. Schizophrenic patients fill one-half of our
mental hospital beds and one-fourth of the beds in
general hospitals, costing the taxpayers millions of
dollars. Vast numbers of those suffering from milder (or
unrecognized) forms of this condition remain in their
communities crippled by an inability to cope realistically with their world. There is, therefore, an ever-
increasing desire on the part of the nonprofessional
public, as well as the members of the mental health
professions, to understand more about this form of
mental illness.

Schizophrenia is a disturbance of the emotional and thinking processes. It exists throughout the world, affects all classes of people, and has been extensively studied for many years from every possible point of view, psychological and physiological. Some theorists question whether it can be called a disease at all, suggesting that it is simply a process of adaptation to a reality that has become intolerable for the affected individual. A majority of those in the mental health professions accept it as a form of illness and are basically in agreement about most of its manifestations. However, there has always been, and continues to be, controversy about its causation.

For many years, schizophrenia has been thought to be transmitted genetically. Although there is no doubt that this disorder runs in families, more recent investigations have shown that environmental influences are extremely important in determining whether a disturbance actually develops, and that genetic heritage transmits at most a predisposing factor. To determine the cause of breakdown in any individual case, one must decide how much his or her vulnerability is due to genetic predisposition, and how much to the environmental climate in which developmental years are spent.

Many people believe that the most crucial environmental preconditioning factor in schizophrenia is defective mothering in earliest infancy, although it has been very difficult to pinpoint just what kinds of mothering are sufficiently defective to lay a groundwork for inevitable future illness. Within this group are those, including myself, who accept the fact that poor mothering may be an important factor in laying such groundwork, but who question whether even a good many preconditioned individuals would become actively schizophrenic in later life if exposure to destructive attitudes and patterns of thinking were not continued far past infancy.

In recent years, a number of clinical studies on the
families of schizophrenic patients have been published
in technical books and journals. All the families studied
have shown various forms of gross disturbance in the
way family members interact. To date, the studies have
all been concerned with families of men and women
who became ill at earlier ages than the individual with
whom we are concerned in this book, and one might
expect to find less grossly deviant influences within the
family that we are considering. At a superficial glance,
Laura and Eliot Carpenter, Sr., might not seem too
different from many highly successful people in our
upwardly mobile society, and the events that took place
in their family life are not much more bizarre than
things happening in many families where children may
grow up to be emotionally disturbed or delinquent, but
not schizophrenic. On the other hand, they created an
atmosphere in their home very similar in important
ways to that found in the families of patients who
became schizophrenic earlier—an atmosphere tending to
create marked distortions in the attitudes of their
children. For instance, members of the Carpenter family
had great difficulty in communicating what they felt in
a direct way. Although taking a different form in each
case, "communication deviance" has been characteristic
of all the families containing a schizophrenic member
that have been studied so far. Just what role this factor
plays in producing a schizophrenic reaction is at present
an important subject under professional investigation.
What role communication deviance played in creating
disaster in the Carpenter family may become clear as the
story progresses.

You are about to read the story as told by someone
intimately involved in it. Amy Carpenter is, of course, a
fictitious name, as are all the names used throughout
this book. However, she is a very real person—a

contemporary of mine and a colleague with whom I have been associated a number of times in the course of our careers in psychoanalysis and in developmental psychology, respectively. She has shared my interest in studying various aspects of schizophrenia and also shares my belief that more descriptive accounts of actual interactions among people under professional observation should be made available for study. These documents may supplement and give detailed data for theoretical points based on scientific research findings which are presented in technical journals.

Ten years ago I published a book in which therapeutic interactions between a psychotherapist and a young preschizophrenic patient were presented in the form of actual detailed dialogue. Not long afterward, Amy suggested that the story of her family, presented in a somewhat similar, fictionalized style, might be of value to those interested in studying schizophrenia. One of her siblings was the first person in ten generations of two well-documented family lines to develop an active form of this illness in adult life. Because she believed that students of the problem would gain insight from firsthand exposure to the kind of interpersonal atmosphere in which the children of her family grew up, Amy wanted me to write a story about it, even at the risk that those who knew us both might recognize her identity. She had tried to do it herself but felt too close to the material and really did not want to be identified with it. Since I agree that certain modes of family interaction are important contributory factors to the actual breakdown of those who may be predisposed to developing schizophrenia, I accepted her offer. I have set down her story in a form that I hope will convey our message to nonprofessional as well as to professional readers, adding only an occasional comment or question.

It is characteristic of the thinking that prevails in many families containing a schizophrenic member to ignore even the most blatant evidence of disturbance in order to keep from facing the fact that mental illness exists among them, and to avoid strenuously any contact with psychiatrists or psychologists. Many afflicted people and their relatives do not come to the attention of professionals at all, and even those who are forced into such contact by the need to hospitalize a patient are often unwilling or unable to cooperate with the professional staff in giving accurate information. Members of such families make poor subjects for study in formal institutional settings of any kind, and a true picture of how they interact when alone together is nearly impossible to obtain.

Amy Carpenter is both willing and able to furnish such a picture. She has decribed from behind the scenes what went on in a family whose members were not, and probably never could have been made, available for study. This account of their lives and the lives of their forebears is neither a technical treatise nor a work of fiction, but simply an attempt to illustrate in a graphic way their modes of communicating and the impact of such modes upon the way the children developed. Only two chapters of discussion contain any technical interpretation of the material.

Amy and I spent several evenings a week for many months talking about her experiences within the family and her views of all its members. In addition to her descriptions, comments, and opinions emanating from these discussions, Amy furnished extensive family records to supplement her memories—a genealogical study of her ancestry drawn up by a professional genealogist; innumerable newspaper clippings reaching back through several generations; family portraits; and memoirs written by both her grandmother and her maternal aunt during their later years. Records from her own generation include a long, partly autobiographical treatise by her brother, letters she wrote at various periods of her life, and a collection of her diaries, kept faithfully from the age of twelve into adult life. I have studied them all and used the information in depicting events and personalities.

From this story you may not get any clear answers to all the questions about *why* the tragedy occurred, but hopefully you will derive some feeling for *how* it came about.

Prologue

A.C. When I think of those early days, I get an immediate visual image of our house on St. Charles Place. I suppose I'm like the rest of my family, in that my first associations are always to the physical environment in which things occurred. Along with the rest of my parents' friends, our family left that neighborhood when I was eight, and I've never been back since. However, that is where it all began, and I can see the house very clearly in my mind's eye, right down to the smallest detail of its furnishings.

As a matter of fact, in fantasy I've often returned there as an adult, filled with curiosity and nostalgia. When I picture it in the fantasy, it is seedy and run-down. Trees that used to line the streets have been killed by blight or by gasoline fumes. Men in undershirts fan themselves with newspapers on stoops that never were intended to be used as front porches. I see a "Room To Let" sign standing in the window of our house, and am suddenly seized with an irresistible impulse to go in. All this is very vivid in my mind, and I can see myself standing on the street as it probably is in reality by this time (unless urban renewal has transformed it). From that point on, however, I feel confused about what happens. All I'm sure of is that sinister elements get a grip on me when I enter the house. I find myself witnessing a murder or overhearing a plot that involves me deeply in criminal activities. Somehow I am inextricably trapped there or, if the fantasy lets me escape, my life is at least permanently altered by having gone in. I returned there with an innocent interest in the past, intending to awaken only for a moment the memories hidden in my old home, but it doesn't turn out like that. If I come away again at all, it is not as the same person who entered so unaware of what would be found. I guess that house has become a symbol of everything that happened later.

Although the surrounding neighborhood was already beginning to decline, St. Charles Place was still a "good" street when we lived there. The high front stoops of its grey stone houses were decorated in spring with window boxes of red geraniums, and well-pruned elm trees before each house gave the street an aura of quiet elegance. Automobiles were scarce in those days, and the two little electrics belonging to my mother and Mrs. St. John stood out, the shiny black of their polished bodies giving tone to the whole block.

At the end of enclosed, iron-gated passageways beside each house, morning glories and nasturtium climbed the side fences of our back gardens, and snowball bushes grew along the back. In the center of our garden was a young maple tree, and although grass had temporarily given way to trenches dug by the neighborhood children for "going over the top" in emulation of national heroes, it was usually surrounded by a neatly clipped patch of lawn. However, even in the physical environment there was a discordant note, for across the block-long back fence common to all the gardens of St. Charles Place lay the littered, clothes-lined yard of a boarding house run by Ma and Pa Di Spaghetti, Italian people with an otherwise unpronounceable name, who belonged to another neighborhood. This other neighborhood, back to back with ours, was part of a world separated from us by far more than a picket fence, but it touched our lives as closely as that yard touched our garden.

Between the two rows of houses facing in different directions onto St. Charles Place and Preston Street lay a children's world, enclosed in the contiguous back-yards. The children of our street participated intensely with the children in back all during our neighborhood playtime. They crossed over into our world, were welcomed to it, and although they seldom invited us to their house, brought its essence with them. They were charming, devilish, and full of information about fascinating aspects of life quite alien to us. When I think about them now, I immediately see our back fence, on which one of them had chalked pictures from which I really learned the facts of life, presented earlier by Mother in distinctly different terms, and I can see Mother's horrified face the time I came in from a bout on the swing calmly announcing I had fallen on my ass. However, they were for the most part polite enough and clean enough to pass muster with our parents, and since there was one Di Spaghetti child the age of almost every child on our block, they infiltrated our homes and our inner lives, bringing an earthy touch that fortunately escaped complete censorship. Mother was glad to have them in our yard and playroom, and she frequently took one or another along on our excursions. They were part of us, and we of them. When the chips were down, however, the Di Spaghettis were kept in the backyards of our lives as well as of our premises.

Our mother, like most of the other St. Charles Place mothers, was a good Christian and a kind person. She taught us in no uncertain terms that all men are equal in the sight of God, that snobbishness is petty, and that it is wrong to look down on people just because they are

different. She was polite and friendly over the back
fence with the parents of our friends and would not
allow us to use in her presence the distortion of their
name, uttered by us without malice, and accepted
without resentment by the children themselves. Any
sign of disrespect for their parents was firmly dealt with.
Nevertheless, adults from the two worlds never crossed
the social line separating our street from theirs, and
when our mother spoke of these children, a barely
detectable change of tone passed on to us the unequi-
vocal knowledge that in her mind they really were not
quite as good as the children with whom we went to
private school in another part of town. While they were
welcome to play with us after school and all day
Saturday, it was clear that they really were not welcome
at our birthday parties. We were told it was because the
children themselves would feel uncomfortable with our
friends, and the few times we insisted on inviting them,
it turned out to be all too true. At this moment I can
see George, squirming miserably in his stiff corduroy
knickers and new yellow shoes, which stood out so
sharply against a sea of blue serge and black patent
leather. I can literally taste my own embarrassment and
shame mixed with pity for him. Even then, however, we
knew the real reason for Mother's not wanting them was
something else, and that this something else was part of
a bigger and more painful something that pervaded our
lives. I think this something else is a main element in the
core of despair lying at the roots of our lives—roots
which never quite shook off the soil of that backyard
no-man's-land.

Along with all the love and fun we had there in those
days, despair was there also, you see, growing up inside
us as we grew—despair caused not only by our inability
to reconcile discrepancies between the values of different sets of beloved people, but also by our inability
to reconcile diametrically opposed attitudes expressed

simultaneously by our parents themselves. We were confused when our father, in particular, expected us to follow rules that differed so much from the ones he seemed to follow. We wanted desperately to please our parents but despaired of ever completely doing so. No matter how hard we tried to accept what they said and do what they wanted, it was impossible to follow one line without rejecting another.

Dr. P. If you followed the spoken word, you had to disobey the wishes they transmitted more unconsciously.

A.C. Yes. Most of the time it was obvious that they absolutely believed that they felt certain ways, while at the same time different reactions came through so clearly by tone of voice or by involuntary sign. Whenever that happened, eddies occurred in the currents of our own minds. Even if we managed to please them, which I honestly think we did most of the time, we somehow never really felt good about ourselves. There was always a tug-of-war within us—a tug-of-war between love for our parents and anger at them for confusing us.

Dr. P. Do you think you were conscious of feeling conflict at the time or of the fact that you were angry about their unconscious hypocrisy?

A.C. No. I think we were just aware of vague discomfort and unhappiness, without having any idea why we felt that way. Our relationship to the Di Spaghetti children was a good example of how it worked. After knowing them—in spite of open encouragement from our parents to enjoy the spice and earthiness of this world—everyone and everything touched by spice and earthiness seemed slightly depreciated and forbidden, just as everything connected with those children was. At the same time, everything and everyone classified in our minds as socially acceptable seemed to lack gusto and sincerity.

Dr. P. Your relationship to the Italian children became symbolic of situations in which you felt assailed by irreconcilable forces.

A.C. I suppose that's why I started with them. There were so many things that couldn't be reconciled—so many discrepancies between what actually was and what seemed to be. The facts of our lives so often differed markedly from the "official version" of those facts, presented in euphemisms and cleaned up by eliminating unpleasant aspects of reality. Eventually the discrepancies wove such a confused pattern in our minds that we all approached the brink of disaster.

Dr. P. You connect these discrepancies with the development of mental illness in your family?

A.C. That, and the constant, meaningless chatter. There was a continual stream of anecdotal talk in our family, but it wasn't *about* anything. I don't know just how that fits in, but it seems important to me. Perhaps in the course of the story we'll see why.

Anyway, St. Charles Place is where it started, and by the time we left there, our characters were already pretty well formed. All of us spent the years of our basic development there, and the older ones were almost grown before the family moved. Jingo was brought as a small child to the house where Eliot and I were born five and ten years after her—Virginia was her real name, but for some reason she was always called Jingo. At the time we left, she was a young woman already in love, anticipating a year of finishing school in Paris before her debut and wedding. Eliot McIntyre Jr., who had only recently rebelled at being called "Brother," was approaching the time for prep school, and I was already old enough to ride my bicycle alone through the park to school. A new way of life was beginning for us all, but already there were rumblings of disaster.

PART I: THE BACKGROUND

1

Ancestors

A.C. I'm not quite sure whether to go on about us right away or stop and go back to the earliest days of my family. Ancestors aren't really a part of what happened to us, but on the other hand perhaps it all began with them.

Dr. P. Who knows where it all began? Ancestors must be a part of this story, not only because of the controversy over the relative importance of "Nature versus Nurture" in the causation of schizophrenia, but because of the way patterns of thinking and behavior are passed along from one generation to another.

A.C. Everything I know about the early ancestors comes from the genealogy book, although a few anecdotes did get passed along by our parents. Perhaps it would be better just to give the bare facts and then hurry along to the main story.

Dr. P. No. I think it might be important to catch the flavor of how information about your background came through to members of your generation.

A.C. All right. As you know, my family was thoroughly studied by one of those researchers who pick up documentary spoor left in county courthouses, church

registries, and graveyards, and eventually manage to
string together a fairly coherent account of major events
in the lives of people long gone and forgotten. A lot of
people put stock in that sort of thing, and as a matter of
fact, I myself think it rather fun to know the connections. I guess most people like to know where they came
from and to relate themselves to a continuity of
generations if they can. Anyway, a lot of not-very-
exciting facts about some quite unimportant people
have been unearthed, although the facts don't tell us
much about what anyone was really like as a person.

Dr. P. Even bare facts about main events can sometimes tell quite a lot about people. We can at least
get an idea of how well they functioned in the society
of their day.

A.C. So far as I can see, most of them were
appallingly solid citizens. In the direct line of paternal
descent, seven generations preceded our grandparents on
the American continent. The first immigrant, "a single
man and thirty years of age," sailed from England on
the *Mary Ellen* in 1635 "for a matter of religious
conviction" and settled on a farm in Massachusetts.
Shortly afterward he married, fathered eight children,
and died a rich man at the age of seventy-five, a few
years before his wife. On his tombstone these words are
engraved: "Here lyeth within this arched space the body
of Deacon Thomas Carpenter who was one of the
foundations of the church."

Our maternal ancestor did not arrive until two
generations later, in 1720, but he also farmed the land,
acted as supervisor of his township, and left an estate of
"£418.10.4, a fine stone house, and a grey or white
mare." I've always wondered why they couldn't figure
out what color that mare was. Anyway, it is jokingly
said within the family that although he was uneducated,
he married a literate woman, and from then on all the
Scotts picked smart wives. Mother used to add that the
Carpenters did too.

In the next five generations, direct descendants from the sons of these lines continued as husbandmen, constables, town government representatives, and fighters in the militia. One was an officer in the American Revolution, a few got rich, and a few lost what their fathers had accumulated and started again on their own. In all these generations, the women bore no fewer than seven children, raised most of them to adult life, even during eras of high infant mortality, and lived to see their grandchildren. There is nothing in the records of either the men or their wives to indicate that they were anything other than well-regarded citizens of their communities or that they behaved at all strangely.

There were no effete men or neurasthenic women. No artists, writers, or musicians—no "silk-coated gentry" or introspective dreamers. The men were pillars of the church, fought for their country, and took an active part in community affairs. The women busied themselves with active households and died at ripe old ages. With few exceptions they all worked hard to make a go of it, survived into their seventies or eighties, and were buried with respect. They were intelligent, reasonably well-educated, nonintellectual people of sound judgment and high moral purpose. It was the same with the generation born around the turn of the nineteenth century—the grandparents of our grandparents. As you can see from the chart, we know the occupations of nearly all sixteen of them and also have a good deal of data on the lineage of those who married into the two families.

Of that generation, only two individuals stand out in my mind as real people, probably because they were the only two ever mentioned by our parents. One was a Carpenter, the other was a Scott, and both were "drinking men." Perhaps this already says something about us, although I suspect it is also true of most people that they enjoy the idea of sober, upstanding relatives a little less than the artists, renegades, or rogues. Anyway, one of these great-great-grandparents of ours was an Irish lord—the only aristocrat in the whole bunch—who came to this country as an Episcopal minister in the southern states, and sometimes shocked his congregation by preaching "while under the influence." My father would tell it with a laugh, plainly delighted with the man who so mocked his own piousness. The other one, John Scott, was "left fatherless with considerable property at the age of thirteen, and came under evil influences which led him to drink and penury." In a fit of desperation, this man left his wife and family to join the navy under an assumed name but returned years later to redeem himself. The navy was no picnic in those days, and he had seen it through. Meanwhile his wife, who was hardly a shrinking violet either, took her two young sons by wagon train to the Midwest, studied medicine with her brother, and became "greatly in demand as a midwife." Mother was proud of them both but did the most talking about the redeemed sinner.

Dr. P. In him she had it both ways—an interesting sinner and a virtuous example for the young.

A.C. One so seldom gets anything both ways, but Mother often seemed to. Well, around the 1820s our eight great-grandparents were born. When he was grown, the Carpenter great-grandfather was the first to emigrate from New England to the South and as an architect and builder "erected many fine edifices" in a number of cities. Unfortunately, along the way he acquired a few slaves and fell into disrepute with his abolitionist relatives who severed all connections with his branch of the family. My father, who preferred to identify with the esteemed position of his Puritan ancestors, did not cherish his grandfather's memory and never had occasion to visit him. However, he loved the idea of his grandmother, the aristocratic daughter of the tipsy Episcopalian. He had never seen her, but we had a miniature of her, painted on porcelain, which hung with a lot of other family portraits in our parents' bedroom. Whenever he saw me looking at it, he always said the same thing—my father had a tendency to fall in love with his own phrases, which would come out reflexively whenever the stimulus was presented—"Ah, there's the Spirit of the Irish in her eyes, Amy, and it's in all the Carpenter women." Then he'd laugh with a kind of boisterous pleasure, and I always hoped it was in me too.

Daddy's grandfather also had a brother about whom we heard a great deal as children. He was a newspaper editor of fiery disposition who killed in a duel the editor of a rival paper who had libeled him in some way. For reasons that will eventually become evident, my father substituted him in fantasy for his own grandfather and set him up as a kind of hero for us. He became the prime example of someone who wasn't afraid to stand up for his own good name, and although our father extolled above all else the virtue of observing the law, it did not seem to bother him that duels had already been outlawed by that time, and that his great-uncle had been a fugitive from justice for a while until things cooled off. People of spirit were the ones he could admire, and it was not lost on us children that, in spite of all the talk about virtue, someone who had killed a man illegally remained in very high esteem. As I've already said, we began rather early in our lives to understand that what our father seriously thought he believed, and what he actually felt, were two quite different things a lot of the time.

Dr. P. As you said, most of us do have a sneaky admiration for the colorful rogue.

A.C. But with my father there was such a feeling of intense *pleasure* in violence—in such marked contrast to his constant harping on following the law. Anyway, his other grandmother lived far off in the Missouri mountains, and nobody in the family had ever seen her. However, she too became a romantic symbol of the hardy pioneer blood running in our veins. This great-grandmother actually lived only to the age of ninety-nine, but myth had extended her years into the hundreds. For years I myself believed she lived to the age of one hundred and eight, with "never a grey hair"—drinking strong coffee on her rustic porch and reading the newspaper without glasses until the day of her death. She undoubtedly was a vigorous old lady, and since my father's own hair was just getting a touch of grey at the age of eighty, maybe the whole tale is true enough. I only know that she became a legend, and that our picture of all these people is far more vivid than that of Mother's grandparents, even though Mother was the one who remained in contact with her family and cherished its connections.

Dr. P. In spite of their eccentricities, nobody you have described so far gives obvious evidence of being mentally ill, although of course there is no proof that they were not. Records of adequate performance in the ordinary business of living may be very deceptive unless one knows something about the personality and life-style of the individual. Were there any letters among the documents to give a flavor of what members of that generation were really like?

A.C. No. Only the genealogist's report and occasional vignettes that stood out in the minds of our parents, picked according to the selectivity by which a human being culls from many pieces of information only those that reflect something in himself. There are no data on the attitudes and personality characteristics of the people involved that could not be deduced from a chronological account of their lives.

Dr. P. Many a pillar of the community is known to be a gross deviant by those who can see and understand the inner workings of his mind. However, pillars of the community who raise large numbers of children, most of whom in their turn go on to be pillars of the community, would probably not be listed among the recognizably schizophrenic by any psychiatrist. Of course, with each new generation, new genes are introduced into family lines, and one can never be sure what combinations of inherited traits will create difficulties in subsequent offspring.

A.C. Don't you think it safe to say that a family is free from specific genetic defect if both sides of the direct lines of all the husbands and wives are without discernible flaw?

Dr. P. Usually. Insofar as it is safe to say that of any family, I think it could probably be said about yours in the adult generations before 1850. I assume there are more exact personal data in the records of the later generations.

A.C. There is a lot of firsthand information about the generation of our grandparents, partly written and partly passed on by word of mouth from those whom we knew. It spans four generations, and our grandparents' memories actually cover a one-hundred-year period between the birth of their own parents and ourselves. For instance, Mother's mother was born ten years after Victoria became Queen of England, and her conscious memory covers a time from the American Civil War, ranging throughout her school days, to the Second World War, which was just beginning when she died in 1939. When I think of all the changes that took place during that period in history, I'm not surprised that the family life of those in her generation got a little confused. Mother's parents were the ones we knew best and who, so far as we knew, affected our lives directly. In our family, Grandfather Thomas Scott was looked upon by everyone as a pillar of strength to lean on in times of need—a source of security never failing in

kindness and generosity at moments that might have
been far more frightening had he not been there in the
background. He was already a great man when we were
small, second in command of a mighty empire that
pretty much dominated industrial life in the United
States. We were very proud of him and felt personally
elevated by his greatness.

I'm sure children always tend to feel rather special
through relationship with someone who has that kind of
charisma, and he certainly had it. To love and be loved
by someone like that is quite awesome, and we all took
it for granted that we loved each other. Mother certainly
told us so often enough.

Our problem was that none of us really felt very
comfortable in his presence. Perhaps we were put off by
the inexorable and interminable morning and evening
prayer sessions that characterized his home. That same
suspiciousness that we had about all people who preach
virtue too strongly fell upon him too. I know that from
the earliest times I can remember I've felt that the
outwardly pious are probably not as godly as they
appear to be and have responded with wariness to strict
observers of religious ritual. We never questioned the
sincerity of our grandfather, and to this day I consider
him to have been a good and honest man. However, try
as we might to feel close to him for Mother's sake, we
found it difficult to perceive him as other than a rather
stern, forbidding figure. Had we known then, as we
learned later, that he did once actually fall rather hard
from grace, I think we might have loved him as much as
we respected him.

Dr. P. There we are again with that secret admiration
for the rogue.

A.C. I guess it's pretty strong in all our family. The
way I feel, anyway, the rogue is a lot more apt to be
sincere than the moralizer.

Grandfather Scott almost never talked about his

boyhood, either to us or to his own children. I suspect that the picture of his parents was as shadowy in his mind as it was in ours, and that he remembered them much as we remembered him. Nothing really seemed colorful enough to tell.

His father, brought at the age of eight to a small midwestern town by the enterprising midwife, had made his way steadily upward in society, serving as a high officer during the Civil War and ending as president of a thriving business firm. He was, however, a sober and unapproachable character. His mother, daughter of a circuit-riding preacher, kept a strict and uplifting home pervaded by devout Methodism and managed to raise five of her six children. The children grew up loving and respecting their parents, as it would have been unthinkable not to do. While the girls remained throughout their lives in the small town near their parents, all the boys went forth into the larger world to achieve brilliant success through hard work and piety. Two became captains of industry, and one a distinguished educator. In material terms at least, the most successful of all was our grandfather.

However, no anecdotes ever filtered down from this family to indicate that the slightest fun or humor ever lightened a serious and purposeful atmosphere. I recently asked my mother's cousin whether she ever heard any, and she said all the stories she ever heard came from her mother's side of the family. Apparently the Scotts married light-hearted girls, but none of them were very light-hearted on their own.

Grandmother Scott must have been quite gay and charming as a young girl. Through her husband's success she had been a great lady long before we knew her and even in old age retained an aura of dignity, but to us she was always an object of affection—a sweet, kindly, friendly grandmother who could chuckle at her own follies. When we were young, she brought us presents and read us stories. In her old age, she took an interest in our problems and listened tolerantly to our tales of woe between episodes of her numerous daily radio soap operas and evening mysteries. Whenever I think of her now, I can hear the buzzing of the "Green Hornet," turned up to full volume, and it is a pleasant memory. All of us lived in what Mother called the "House of Refuge" for varying periods of time during the four years that she survived Grandfather, and when she died, still alert and shyly humorous at the age of ninety, each of us felt a personal loss. We owe a lot to her—a lot that is good and constructive in our lives and in our characters—but while Mother called her home the "House of Refuge," we children called it the "House of Usher." I'm sure after a while you will see why.

Grandmother Scott's early life had been quite different from that of her husband. In fact, the stories she told were so intriguing that, when she was sixty, her children insisted that she write memoirs of her girlhood. These memoirs constitute a set of descriptions and anecdotes that would be fascinating not only to her descendants but to anyone interested in the life of a small midwestern town in the 1850s and '60s. Of course, they are of particular interest to me in terms of understanding the influences that played upon a young girl who later raised my mother. This is the first document we have that gives through someone's own words a feeling for her early personality. Although Grandmother was already approaching old age at the time of writing, she gave a clear impression of the small-town child who later entered a world of prominent people. I get the picture of a very cute, nice little girl, intelligent, obedient, and eager to be good. However, an outstanding thread running all through the material is one of innocent vanity and pride. Offspring to one of the small community's most prominent families, only child of doting middle-aged parents, pampered playmate of a married half-sister by her mother's former marriage, and honored little princess of the whole town, she graciously accepted the homage of everyone in her environment and fully considered it her due. She lost her father at the age of eight, but every memory of her life with him, as well as with her mother, gives the picture of a child well loved, indulged, and instilled with complete confidence that virtue would be rewarded. And it inevitably was.

As I said earlier, the environment in which we live has been important to all of us, and Grandmother's memoirs focus heavily on detailed descriptions of her physical surroundings. She obviously wanted her children to picture the styles in furniture and clothing of her period, but what comes through most clearly is her pride and vanity—pride in the "elegant" possessions of her family, and vanity over her own appearance and performance in various "recitations" and choral recitals where she received much approval and applause.

On the other hand, running alongside the pride and vanity is a clear thread of guilt. Pride and vanity were sins, and sin wasn't taken lightly in a town still influenced strongly by revivalist camp meetings and preoccupied with avoidance of eternal damnation. There is also a strong current of mysticism, born, perhaps, of her immersion in an atmosphere where religion featured the literal reality of miracles and supernatural influences.

Dr. P. Probably stimulated also by her struggles between pride and guilt.

A.C. I can't resist quoting one example, because the story was told so many times to her own children, who in turn passed it on with no apparent doubt that it had occurred just as told.

"Just before my father died, I had a dream that my sister was jumping out of a low window of her house to come to ours next door, which she often did in reality. She was dressed in a green gown covered by a grey wool shawl, and in her arms she carried her baby boy. The baby was dead. Within a short time, the dream came exactly true, and it frightened my mother that I had told it to her before it happened."

In later life, our grandmother Nell never laid claim to prophetic gifts, but she must have believed to some extent in the special significance of her own thoughts. This is important in view of what happened later in her life, and what in turn happened in the life of our mother because of it.

Dr. P. Do you think your grandmother's belief in the reality of miracles is out of line with the beliefs of Fundamentalist religion in general?

A.C. I don't know that much about Fundamentalist religion. However, I do have a feeling that supreme confidence in the importance of her own wishes was not too far removed from a belief that those wishes would influence events in a magical way. After all, they did influence a lot of events, although not by magic. Throughout her entire girlhood, Nelly had only to express a wish, and that wish was granted. The climax came when, at the age of eighteen, she wanted to move to California where her half-sister had already gone with her new family. Her aging mother immediately sold all her property and, pulling up stakes from the home where she had been happy for twenty years, accompanied her youngest on the long, arduous journey by boat through the Isthmus to California. There Nelly met Grandfather, decided to marry him the first time she saw him, and did so within a year. This handsome young man had already been appointed to take charge of a main office in his industrial organization, and his pretty, high-spirited young wife was about to take her place among leaders of a far more sophisticated society than she had ever known. That, of course, was where she felt she belonged—in a place she had no doubts about achieving.

Dr. P. Self-confidence of that caliber can work many a seeming miracle.

A.C. It did. You will see.

Our family grew up far away from the Carpenter grandparents and fortunately saw them only occasionally. (You will see in a moment why I say "fortunately.") All the children were fond of Granddaddy, whom we knew in our childhood as a kindly old man who loved children and had infinite patience with us. I was particularly attached to him and remember that when he spent one summer with us on our farm, I hardly ever let him out of my sight. It soon become clear, however, that our parents didn't hold a very high opinion of him, and this couldn't help but color our own as time went on. Mother never said a word directly against him, and the vibrations from her were not very strong. As a matter of fact, I suspect that she rather liked him, but she certainly didn't respect him, and the faintness of her praise came through as a clear negative. "Your grandfather is a very kind man, dear, but he isn't very forceful. He never really 'thought big' like your Daddy." Our father's contempt for him was, of course, beyond question. He was always scornful of anyone who couldn't "pull his own weight in the world"—that was one of those little phrases he used over and over— "A man who can't pull his own weight in the world is no use to anyone." It was quite obvious that Granddaddy Abner couldn't pull his, and that, with him, a long line of doers in the Carpenter family had temporarily ended. We were very fond of him, but from both parents we got the message that he was not to be admired, and we didn't admire him. We felt, in fact, a little bit guilty for liking him so much.

Dr. P. Self-reliance was the cardinal virtue with both your parents?

A.C. I don't know about Mother—actually she had pretty mixed feelings about that, I think—but certainly to Daddy. A dependent man was an object of real disgust to him, even if that man was physically ill, as his father was.

Actually, Granddaddy Abner had started out very bravely. Raised in the South by "Spirit of the Irish" and her architect husband, he had volunteered at the age of thirteen as a messenger boy for the Confederate Army. However, in one of the last battles of the Civil War, he was wounded in one lung and later developed tuberculosis, from which he never fully recovered. In those days, under those circumstances, one went west to seek a better climate. His parents had been impoverished by the war and could give him little help, so, at the age of eighteen, with their blessing and very little money, he started working his way across the South. Up in the Missouri mountains he picked up his bride Sally, daughter of the lady who lived so long, and then went on to the green, sparsely populated countryside near San Francisco Bay.

What happened to his personality along the way I don't know. I do know, though, that the "luck of the Irish" deserted him, and that he was never able to make more than an intermittent, largely inadequate living for his wife and the four children who started coming quite soon. This, to my father, was an unpardonable weakness, not excusable on the basis of poor health nor mitigated by the knowledge of what his father actually did accomplish. Granddaddy occasionally entered business ventures that paid off for quite a while. Sometimes, in fact, he showed an almost visionary ability to foresee the possibilities in neglected real estate that later acquired fantastic value. At one point, for instance, he bought up supposedly worthless mud flats on San Francisco Bay, mud flats on which San Francisco's whole Marina District now stands. However, a little later he sold them for a small profit to invest in a bicycle factory, just before the invention of the automobile made bicycles practically obsolete for any large-scale use. So it went. Through all these ups and downs, his family often lived from hand to mouth, a situation that neither his wife nor his children found at all palatable. My grandmother was one who made her opinions felt pretty strongly and I hate to think what their marital life must have been like during the periods when things weren't paying off.

The Carpenter men obviously liked women of mettle and short temper. Our grandmother had both and seems not unlike her husband's own mother, at least as the image of that mother was transmitted to me by my father. Grandmother also possessed an iron determination, along with an almost fanatic faith in the soul-saving efficacy of hard work and devotion to Fundamentalist religion. This enabled her to raise the children almost single-handed, while her husband relaxed in semi-invalidism and dreamed of great enterprises to come. Even though he loved children, I doubt that he got much to say about raising his own.

As you have gathered by now, events and people in my father's background took on a highly romanticized coloring which may or may not have coincided with the facts. In any case he could make me practically smell his mother's Irish stew, sparsely laced with meat but teeming with good, nourishing root vegetables and potatoes hauled from the country market by the sackful. My mouth waters when I remember his descriptions of corned beef and cabbage or tasty pig's feet with sauerkraut, although in actuality everyone in the family, except our father, loathed pig's feet. The food cooked by his mother was plain but plentiful and acquired considerable aroma in retrospect.

I picture very clearly an indomitable woman with her Bible propped at eye level above the washtubs, improving her mind and her morality as she scrubbed for three men and two girls. Money seldom came her way until her oldest son started at the age of nine to bring it in, but her children were at all times clean, well-mannered, and intensely imbued with the value of obtaining a fine education by whatever honest means they could. They were also kept far too busy to get into any sort of mischief.

Every day after school was filled to the brim with chores and homework; the Sabbath from morning until night was devoted to religious instruction. Grandmother had a particular fear that her boys would get mixed up with girls of inferior background, and she saw to it that they had no opportunity. Poor as they were, the children were deeply impressed with the fact that they came of good stock and that, if their mother had anything to say about it, they would all grow up to be ladies and gentlemen. They all did, too. Their mother died of pneumonia at the age of fifty, before the younger ones were grown, but by then her work was done and her influence indelible.

Although our father had an inordinate admiration for his mother, our own mother was scared to death of this woman who accepted her as a daughter-in-law because of the distinguished family from which she came, but who despised her personally as a useless piece of fluff. We never heard a word of this directly, but all of us knew it from an early age. I know, too, that my sister, who was old enough to remember her, shared Mother's anxiety in her presence. My father's mother has come down to me as harsh, humorless, and preoccupied with the avoidance of evil. It was lucky for Mother, as well as for us, that geographical distance kept her pretty much out of my father's life after his marriage.

Dr. P. Since she may have had an important part in laying a groundwork for the mental illness which afflicted her son's family two generations later, we have to wonder whether she introduced genetic defect into your father's family line.

A.C. I don't suppose we can say no to that question, although ancestors of both her father and her hardy, long-lived mother can be traced through generations of industrious, respectable Scotch-Irish country folk, back to the earliest migrants from Kentucky to the middle-western South. Her genes must have been pretty dominant because all of her own children, as well as many of her grandchildren, looked just like her and had the same tendency to be intensely aggressive. My grand-mother's children had plenty of cause to feel aggressive, of course. But if she carried genes bearing schizophrenia, why didn't this show up somewhere else in the nine generations that preceded her?

Dr. P. Perhaps there can be no answer to that question. On the other hand, perhaps we don't need knowledge of her genes to explain her part in the chain of events that took place. Maybe we don't even need to know whether her own unbending character was the result of her earliest family relationships, the influence of tough rural life in her youth, or her indoctrination with fire-and-brimstone religion. It seems enough to say that, when a woman of her personality makeup was faced with the frustrations of life alongside a man like your grandfather, she was unable to show maternal tenderness. That inability seems to have been largely responsible for the driving, exacting, fanatical atmos-phere in which your father grew to manhood, and which must inevitably have influenced his own attitudes.

A.C. I've always suspected that the trouble started where my father's character and personality were formed. How much do you think the problem stems from attitudes and behavior passed on from parents to children throughout the generations? How much must we blame on our genes?

Dr. P. At this point in the story, it would be nearly impossible to say. I don't think that the evidence for genetic influence is prominent in your family. On the other hand, the personalities of all your grandparents—and the great divergence of personalities of husbands and wives—suggest that problems might very well develop in the next generation of both families.

2

The Early Days of Laura and Eliot

Dr. P. You have said that everyone in your family talked a lot, Amy. Did your parents tell you much about their own youth?

A.C. Very occasionally Daddy did, but I think you will see as the story progresses that he had other things to talk about. Mother, of course, talked constantly about hers when we were little, always telling us what had happened to her at any age we happened to be at the time. When I was a little girl, I think I knew her childhood far better than my own, and I know I liked it better. The life she lived as one of six rollicking children seemed the kind of life that could only happen in heaven. I think it was, too. However, it was very real to me, as it was to Mother as she told it.

There were a million stories about the House on the Hill. There were Maggie Maloney, the cook, and the nurse Annie, who joined the family when she was sixteen and later married the butcher's delivery man. Later there was Joe, the Chinaman, who stayed for many years because he'd had his queue cut off as the result of a fight over another man's wife and was in disgrace back home in China. Conchita, the Chihauhua, was brought home in their father's pocket, and there

were kittens named Adelina Patti and Enrico Caruso, for
whom they made clothes out of their mother's best
petticoat. They played wonderful games that I tried to
get my friends to play and made up fantasies I knew so
well that I sometimes confused them with my own. To
this day I don't know whether "Jennie Jones in Bricks"
was an old witch of my own concoction or Mother's. On
second thought, though, she must have been Mother's.
That whole childhood picture was a magic circle, and I
doubt that she ever stepped out of it.

It sounded as though the house was continually
ringing with laughter and music. Grandmother played
the organ and sang in her beautiful contralto voice,
while Grandfather took the tenor. All the children sang
and played instruments. Mother's was the violin, and
although she begged me not to, I had to take it up
myself for a while until I was forced to see she was
right. You couldn't be really good at it without years of
dedication to practice. However, I had always imagined
her playing like Fritz Kreisler right from the start, and I
wanted to do that too. I don't think it ever occurred to
me to wonder why she so seldom played for us and
seemed so inexpert when she did. I guess I thought she'd
just lost her touch over the years.

When they were little, they had a stage built across
one end of their attic where all the cousins and
neighborhood children joined them in putting on plays.
I grew up on tales of the "Sleeping Princess," with
Mother as the fairy who said "I give her purity" in such
a mumbling voice that nobody could hear. When they
were teen-agers, they dressed every evening in pretty
puffed-sleeved dresses and high button shoes to wait for
callers in the parlor. When the young men came, as they
always did, in droves, how they all laughed and shouted
at their silly games and taffy pulling. I tried to pull taffy
myself, but somehow it always ended up as a sticky
mess, not at all as delicious as theirs had been, and the

waltz and the polka, the mazurka, schottische, and quadrille in their dancing school were a far cry from the two-step I was laboriously learning. The boys always ran to choose the Scott sisters from among all the other pretty girls, and it ended with a grand march that sounded very grand indeed. I could see those four sisters kneeling down in their ball gowns before setting off to dance the night away, and I thought even *that* must have been intriguing, in spite of my own revulsion over those prayer sessions at Grandfather's house. Mother and her sisters were all "belles of the nineties," and anything they did must have been a very splendid thing to do. Their debuts were outstanding events of their various seasons, and I had newspaper clippings to prove it. How I longed to have a debut myself.

Dr. P. How much of all that was really true?

A.C. Most of it, I think. Years later I read the memoirs of Aunt Ginny, written in her sixties just as her mother's had been, and in them found the same stories I knew so well. Here and there, however, were a few details I had never heard or, anyway, never heard that way.

I had known that Aunt Hattie was out of school for a year when she was ten and had had a marvelous tricycle that all the girls took turns riding. I had not been told, however, that she'd had St. Vitus dance, which a doctor later told Aunt Ginny must have been merely a form of extreme nervousness, like her own migraine headaches in childhood and the "nervous prostration" she had for a few months shortly after my mother's wedding. Mother had spoken in passing of her own "bilious attacks" as a child, and of course we all knew how horrified Grandfather had been when his oldest son showed early evidence of being an artistic dreamer, but I had to be far more aware of the meanings of things before putting all this together into the question, "What was going wrong in that gloriously happy household?"

As a matter of fact, not until this exact moment have I
ever asked myself why those sisters were going to balls
and leading such a worldly life when their father was
supposedly such a strict, pious Methodist? What kind of
split was there, even in the generation before ours,
between what was said and what was actually done?

It shouldn't have taken so long to ask those questions, because we have always known that of those six
children, five had unfortunate marriages, and four died
in early adulthood. Uncle Charley, the poet and painter,
contracted tuberculosis from a "scheming girl who
snared him into marriage" and died within six months
of his wedding. Aunt Hattie married an adventurer who
told her on their wedding night that he was homosexual.
When Grandfather discovered what the trouble was, he
had the marriage annulled and brought her back home.
However, after a few years, during which she studied
palmistry and astrology, secretly controlling her "nervousness" with sedatives, she suddenly dropped dead of
a heart attack on the street. Uncle Paul, the most
charming, shot himself at an early age in shame and
despair over his inability to resist a predilection for
alcohol, and beautiful Aunt Amy, who eloped at
seventeen with a traveling salesman, "died of a broken
heart" when she discovered he was keeping a mistress in
the next apartment. All of them were childless. Only
Aunt Virginia, the angry and irascible intellectual of the
family, had a reasonably happy marriage—this by virtue
of her remarkable sense of humor, coupled with enough
good sense to marry a gentle, unexciting, stable man
who loved her. Laura was our mother, and you will hear
what happened to her.

Grandmother really brought up two families, the first
group of three born in the early years of her marriage,
and the last group born in her thirties, when their father
was approaching the peak of his career and she the peak
of her social ambitions. All the children loved, respect-

ed, and stayed close to their parents as long as they lived, idealizing their mother and worshipping their father. They did it from a distance, however, particularly the younger three, which included our mother.

It was only late in our lives, and certainly not from our mother, that we learned what woefully neglected "poor little rich children" they had seemed to their aunts and cousins. Only then did we begin to think how much they had lived in a children's world, bringing themselves up with the somewhat dubious assistance of Maggie Maloney and the sixteen-year-old nursemaid while their mother was busy having beautiful gowns fitted by Madame Armand, the French dressmaker, or driving out with horse and carriage to make calls. When she was home, she sang with the children in the evening and read to them sometimes, but many, many evenings she was out at dinner parties or balls.

Dr. P. She had no concept of their inner lives?

A.C. Nobody in that family thought much about their inner lives, and if they did, they certainly never discussed it.

Grandfather was a more dominant force in the family, ever the center of everyone's awareness during those twice-daily prayers, but he wasn't really close to them either. They all respected him tremendously, but he demanded a degree of strength and virtue that was apparently felt to be unattainable, particularly by the boys who, even in their earliest years, must have given up on the idea of ever meeting his ideals for them or approximating his greatness. The girls, no matter how bright, were not expected to achieve much except a good marriage, but he hoped to see his sons rise even higher than he and pushed them inexorably to that end. However, he also believed that everyone must make his own way from the bottom, so both the boys started at the bottom of his mighty organization. They worked at grueling, menial physical labor, which literally killed the

delicate oldest and so undermined both the health and
morale of the youngest that he took to drink. Both sons
tried desperately to please their father and despaired
when they could not. Grandfather never forgave either
of them for their weakness and, after they died, never
mentioned their names again.

Dr. P. He had the same attitude toward weakness as
your father.

A.C. I imagine that's how you become a captain of
industry. He didn't seem that harsh as an old man, but
by then a lot had happened to him which you will hear
about later.

I never heard anyone in the family admit that
Grandfather had a favorite among the children, but I
have never had a single doubt that there was one, and
that it was Laura. You couldn't possibly hear those
family stories without knowing it. Although it was clear
that the older siblings treated her as a rather silly little
doll, her father obviously enjoyed her cuteness, in spite
of his tendency to worship strength and intellect. In any
case, she had a talent for getting around him, much to
the discomfiture of the others. There was the time he
came home from a directors' meeting announcing that
they had started giving ten-dollar gold pieces to everyone who attended. Laura piped up promptly to say that
she just happened to be collecting ten-dollar gold pieces,
whereupon Grandfather, with a wry little smile, shoved
his across the table to her and continued to do so after
every meeting thereafter. By the time she married, she
had quite a nice little nest egg. Aunt Ginny laughed
when she told it but even after so many years her teeth
were quite noticeably clenched. Perhaps this, and similar
incidents, accounted for the "nervous collapse" she had
when Laura was first of the four to marry. We children
always enjoyed stories like that. If Mother was silly, she
was silly like a fox, and in any case she was undoubtedly

very cute about it. Our mother was, and remained throughout her life, very cute and endearing. All of us could empathize with Aunt Ginny's envy, but perhaps you would have had to be a sister to hold Mother's little wiles against her.

Whether she was also Grandmother's favorite is hard to say. Certainly they were very congenial later in life, and Grandmother told with a chuckle endless stories about Laura's youthful vanities, which were so much like her own. There was never a doubt in anyone's mind that they were close, but by that time a lot had happened to draw the two women together. I suspect that early in life my mother's focus was almost entirely on her father. Perhaps it was a wish to remain his little doll that prevented Laura from ever growing up, or maybe there was more to it. I don't know, but I do know that she wasn't satisfied with any man until she found one exactly like her father. So it looked in the beginning, anyway.

Believe it or not, Laura Scott met Eliot Carpenter at a dance. The way we children told it for years, he was a poor little newsboy in shiny new pumps who had somehow mysteriously gotten into her dancing school. Actually, she was close to eighteen, and he was a member of an eminently respectable fraternity at the university, even though he had only come for one year as a "special student" and was working his way through.

Our father-to-be had first ventured into the business world at age nine as an after-school newsboy and had fought for his corner according to the rough-and-tumble laws of the jungle which governed the newsboys of his time. Day after day, week after week, he had learned how to protect his territory and outwit competitors in order to bring in enough money for his mother's peace of mind. Step by step, he rose to be in charge of all distribution and, as the end of his schooling approached, was doing well enough to be a major source of support for his parents and three younger siblings.

Knowing that opportunities for future education would be limited after high school, Eliot nevertheless appreciated the importance of having a college background to aid his future career. Surely, therefore, it was with no difficulty that he persuaded the authorities to let him spend his last high school year attending the university's freshman class. Our father seldom had difficulty convincing anyone that whatever he wanted to do was right. Anyway, he was given the proper permission, and I'm sure nobody could have gotten more out of that year. Not only did he learn what he could, but he made lifelong friends of his fraternity brothers, friends who remained loyal to him much longer than one might have expected in view of what followed. When he left to become a promising young reporter, he was also already engaged to an extremely eligible young lady, with the blessing of a very important and powerful father-in-law-to-be.

However, from here the story changes, and it does so in a way that tells a good deal about what was to come in the future. Sent back east on an assignment by his paper, Eliot Carpenter got an excellent business offer and just didn't return. There is, in fact, considerable reason to suspect that he more or less forgot all about his engagement. To be sure, his fiancée received occasional notes in response to her long, loving letters, telling of his business progress and his hopes for future advancement. I wish I could believe that those notes also told Laura how much he loved her and couldn't wait until they would be together again, but I'm afraid I can't. In view of what I have come to know about my father, it is likely that those notes were very much about himself and his own activities, but it is also likely that, between the lines, Laura read all the messages of hope and promise that she wanted to see there. In fact, I'm sure she did see them there.

Her main worry was that before Eliot left the engagement had been announced at a big party, with much newspaper publicity. She had been given a large collection of porcelain engagement cups, one from each friend, as was the custom of her day, but she had no ring and no potential bridegroom for anyone to see. After two years, this became increasingly hard to bear. She had complete faith in Eliot, but her friends were beginning to wonder, and it was getting harder and harder to persuade them that he was due back any day. Finally it was her father who decided enough was enough. He took it upon himself to call the young man during one of his trips east and asked whether his intentions had been honorable. Within a few days, a beautiful ring arrived, and shortly afterward the young man himself. Of course his intentions had been honorable. How could anyone have questioned them? He had just been very busy, that was all.

The wedding day dawned dreary and overcast, but the church was packed with the most fashionable people in town. They were subdued at first, like the weather, but began to brighten at the eagerness with which the young bridegroom walked part-way up the aisle toward the bride in his impatience to take her from her father's arm. Just as the minister pronounced them man and wife, a shaft of sunlight burst through the stained glass window to fall on the happy couple; everyone gasped, and there were tears in many eyes—tears of awe and joy to note the spring in Eliot's step as he proudly pranced up the aisle with his wife on his arm.

That's the way it was always told, and I'm quite sure most of it was true, although I've wondered a bit about that shaft of sunlight. About my father's pride and eagerness and happiness I never had a doubt, because the capacity for that was always in him, vying with his ability to forget all about you.

Years later, I asked my mother's cousin about that wedding. Did the sun really hit them at just that moment? She looked at me rather quizzically and replied, "It might have. I really don't remember. I'll tell you one thing for sure, though. Never in the whole world was there a more handsome, buoyant, promising young bridegroom than your father."

At that point I broke down and cried.

Mother never talked about her early married life. That should have made me suspicious, I guess, because she talked so much about the rest of her youth, but I really never thought to wonder about it until my sister mentioned an anecdote from those days, after we were both grown. Mother had apparently told Jingo stories that seem heartbreaking to me only because they throw light on so many things that happened later.

Right after the wedding, Mother and Daddy went to New York where Mother expected to be the sort of junior society matron she would have been in her own bailiwick. Apparently she spent a good deal of her time preparing for calls from Grandmother's prominent friends, but whenever one of them came, something always went wrong. It makes me ache to think about it, partly because the whole thing seems so silly to me, and yet I know how much it meant to Mother to "do things right." For instance, she never got over the fact that someone called while she was unpacking and had excelsior all over the living room. Another time, when she had a luncheon using all her new wedding presents, the Swedish maid forgot to wash the goblets she had taken out of a barrel, and Mother caught one of the ladies smiling as she held one up to the light and saw a rim of dust on top. Mother nearly died of mortification.

I know how absurd it sounds, but she couldn't see anything funny in something like that. She felt disgraced, and I'm sure she wouldn't have felt any worse if she'd had a baby six months after the wedding. She got no sympathy from Daddy either. A lot of his friends were rather bohemian newspapermen who couldn't care less how things were served, and her feelings were completely incomprehensible to him. He'd call up an hour before dinner to say he was bringing four or five cronies home with him, and when Mother said she hadn't enough food in the house, he'd just say, "Oh, put a little more water in the soup, Laurie," and laugh. That was his idea of a joke, but it was no joke to his proper little bride.

When I think about it, I feel so torn I can hardly stand it. Knowing Mother, I ache for her, and yet so many things I hear make me realize how awful it must have been for him. I can remember how I felt about her fussiness over little details, and I particularly remember how El felt one day when he told her some college friends were dropping by for lunch the next day and then found she had stayed up most of the night preparing a real party, with flowers on the table and her best tablecloth. When it came my turn to encounter such a situation, I rebelled and literally forced her to serve just soup and sandwiches. She did, too, but they were cut up fancy around the edges and had strips of pimento crisscrossed on top. The worst part was that my friends adored them. They all loved Mother because she was so cute and quaint and said they wished their mothers would take the trouble to make sandwiches look pretty. I was consumed with guilt for days, pitying Mother for having such unappreciative children.

Anyway, to get back to those earliest days, she obviously found Daddy's friends boors, which they were compared to the people she had grown up with, but she tried to be nice to them and couldn't understand why

things went wrong there too. Once a particularly
impecunious reporter came to dinner on a snowy night
without an overcoat, and as he left, she offered to give
him one of Daddy's. He got very red and refused most
rudely, and as my sister told it, I again felt sorry for
Mother. Can you imagine how Daddy must have felt,
though? She had the best intentions in the world, too.
That's what makes it so gruesome.

There were so many things like that—times when in
retrospect I feel such sympathy for a childlike, confused
young bride suddenly confronted with a world she'd
never known before, and at the same time, I think what
it must have been like for a young husband from my
father's kind of background to be faced with that kind
of nonsense. I feel exasperated myself, even though I've
been brought up to share many of her feelings about
"making things nice."

For a short time just after Virginia was born, they
lived in the South, and Mother was terrified most of the
time because she had never seen "colored people"
before. She was afraid in some nameless way that her
baby would be upset, and I suppose for that very reason
Jingo cried most of the time and wouldn't nurse, until
an old cook took over the feeding for a while and got
her on a bottle. Mother had the whole house carpeted
and made everyone whisper for fear of waking the baby.
Can you imagine the effect that must have had on an
exuberant young man? And believe me, he was exuberant. Jingo insists that her first memory is of hitting her
head on the ceiling when he tossed her in the air, and
although she does exaggerate wildly, it could have
happened. I remember being tossed around myself, and
how scary it seemed. Had the baby's head hit the
ceiling, Daddy would have been sick with remorse, I
know. He never wanted to hurt anybody.

All in all, it seems almost incomprehensible that two

such different people could have made it together even through the first two years.

Before I get into telling about us, I think I ought to describe Briarpatch, because, in a sense, Briarpatch was part of us all. It was so important in our early lives that I sometimes wonder whether it wasn't actually a major influence on all our personalities. Certainly it was responsible for the way my brother and I responded to natural beauty. Speaking for myself alone, I'm pretty sure it was the cornerstone of a fortress to which I regularly retreated when I felt my life endangered.

Dr. P. Did it also become a symbol of what happened there, like the house on St. Charles Place?

A.C. Not exactly. It just infiltrated us, gave us a certain capacity to experience the outer world in a deeply emotional way. I can't really describe its influence better than that.

It all began in the early days of my father's career, when he came out on the wrong end of a land promotion deal. Such a thing didn't happen to him very often, and when he found himself stuck with several thousand acres of apparently worthless land in the middle of nowhere, it was obvious he wasn't going to stand by and do nothing about it. If there was one thing our father couldn't tolerate, it was coming out on the wrong end of any deal at all. And anyone who knew him assumed that he could turn the deal to his advantage. He did, of course. He came up with an ingenious plan to turn loss into profit and wasted no time in putting his ideas into effect.

The large acreage falling to his share of the deal lay in the heart of the middle-western north woods country, where early-day lumbering had left a wilderness of rotted stumps. However, new growth was well under way; already woodland patches of thin-trunked trees

dotted the area with very pleasing effect. Along clear
streams and muddy rivers, a dense growth of reeds and
shrubs appeared between the few stands of large trees
inaccessible to the lumbermen, while wild flowers
bloomed between clumps of sweet fern and berry vines
trailing over rocks. Birds, butterflies, and dragonflies
abounded. There was a haunting, wistful beauty in this
rejuvenating countryside, still unspoiled by civilization.
To the unimaginative eye, however, the general effect
was one of desolation, and before people would be
interested in buying the land, they would have to be
taught to appreciate it. Eliot was just the man to teach
them, and he set about showing what could be done by
someone who was more than ordinarily endowed with a
keen imagination.

His plan was to show prospective buyers the possibilities inherent in this kind of property by building a
model farm close to the nucleus of a simple resort area.
He planned a kind of place that would attract families
of white-collar workers, commuting by overnight lake
boat on summer weekends from dreary low-echelon
desk jobs in big cities; a place to raise chickens and grow
vegetables, while children ran free, breathing the soot-
free air and riding in horse-drawn buggies over dusty
roads to swim in a clear lake with a white sandy beach.
He would invite such workers to come up in groups, and
when they saw how lovely it all could be, they would
rush in droves to buy a few acres each. Everyone would
be happy, the workers with their nice little plots of
land, and Eliot with his nice little profits. His business
ideas always tended to be tinged with humanitarian
idealism and brightened with a generous coloring of
romanticism, but that is how he looked at it, and that is
what he went about accomplishing.

The model farm was intended to be exactly the kind
of little farm that a city worker would want for his
family's summer living, but of course it didn't really

turn out that way. It was impossible for Eliot to think in terms of anything small. The owner's cottage came first, and that was small enough, perched on the bank of a little trout stream flowing through a narrow ravine to feed a patch of swamp down the road. The barn was enormous, however, and then came pigsties and cow sheds, potato cellars and apple houses, and that wonderful, dark, cool, mysterious edifice housing massive chunks of ice to last through the summer. Before much longer there were rows of neat white houses for setting hens, there were incubators and brooders, and there were fourteen hundred white leghorn chickens with yellow legs and bright red combs, hopping, pecking, and hiding their eggs behind bushes over several acres of land. There were four or five acres of vegetables too, row after row of peas, beans, carrots, potatoes, and squash—yellow, white, and green. Best of all, there were rows of melons—muskmelons, honeydew, and watermelons, big green ones with white stripes, lying hidden among the lush vines. Prize vegetables, thousands of eggs, prize farm stock—this beehive of activity became the cynosure of all eyes, just across the sandy road from an old white farmhouse that became the main dining-lounging area of a multi-cottaged inn. Soon, in fact, the whole complex became a poor man's dream and a rich man's plaything. It also became a children's paradise, particularly after the dam broke.

At some point, Daddy decided to have a dam built across the little stream flowing before his cottage, probably intending to increase the size and usefulness of a little pond beside the inn. Engineers wagged their heads and wasted words of advice, knowing that a wooden dam sunk in the ravine's sandy banks would not hold, but Daddy had decided there would be a wooden dam, and so there was. There was, that is, until it went out, creating a roaring flood that cut through the ravine, nearly washing away the cottage on its banks and completely draining the pond it was supposed to improve. The building of the dam was a complete disaster, just as everyone had predicted, but for children it created a fairyland of beauty and joy.

The old swamp had been a vast lowland morass, croaking with frogs and shining with the black backs of mud turtles sunning themselves on rotting logs, a place where timbermen had not been able to penetrate. Giant, primitive trees still stood there, trunks entwined with woodbine and the black berries of deadly night-shade. Alder thickets and tangles of berry bushes covered the muddy ground, and in among them stagnant backwaters green with spirogyra waited to trap the unwary. A lovely and mysterious sight to see, but perilous ground on which a child would hesitate to set foot. After the flood, all that was changed. White sand piled in deep drifts around the bases of the trees, and everywhere the high bushes of blackberry and raspberry stood with their roots as if in bowls of sugar. Little sandy-bottomed creeks ran among the thickets, with deep pools ideal for swimming, and in them sheltered islands on which a child could build a house or a little secret nook. There were long sandy stretches where one could put up a tent and cook wienies over a fire, an intricate network of paths on which to track like an Indian exploring the ancient forests, and in among them all, the frogs and turtles, still croaking and sunning themselves, unperturbed.

The swamp in all its mysterious glory became the center of paradise, but all around was heaven too, a world of watermelons picked juicy, pink, and still warm from the sun, of egg hunts and butterfly chases, of wild flower collecting, of jumping in the hay barn, and of day-long picnics on the lake shore.

This was Briarpatch, beloved by all our family—the place where we summered for many years and where we sunk roots before the acres were all sold off. It was a place where everyone was happy until paradise was sliced up like a pie and made into little patches of the mundane world for weekenders from the city.

PART II: CHILDREN

3

The Carpenter Family on St. Charles Place

Jingo

A.C. Jingo came along two years after the wedding—a very much wanted child who, according to the way Mother talked about it later, sprang from the womb fully mature and ready to engage in fascinating conversation. Jingo was, in my mother's eyes, the most precocious, charming little girl ever born, one who exuded an aura of sprightly intelligence which more than compensated for any degree of conventional prettiness she might have lacked in her early years. Not that she was ugly at all, even during the long period when wire braces were cemented on her teeth. She was graced with the white skin, thick black hair, and full red mouth so characteristic of all Carpenter women, and Mother made it very clear that Jingo always gave promise of being a very attractive woman at a later stage. However, her looks were usually soft-pedaled, and it was for her extraordinary verbal gifts that she was really known from earliest childhood.

As soon as she could talk at all, this vivacious little chatterbox talked to everyone and made friends wherever she went. Her clever repartee never failed to amuse adults, bringing smiles to the faces of complete strangers. One story in particular was told often—how she had started chatting with a woman on the trolley car and had everyone on the whole car laughing. Perhaps it says something about me that I can't remember just what she was supposed to have said that was so funny, but I have been assured she was always a refreshing addition to any group. Mother's friends all loved having her brought to call, as many of them have told me themselves, and although I gathered that their children were not always quite so pleased with her wit, that seems to have been no loss to Jingo. Children are notoriously unreasonable about other children who are held up to them as models of perfection, and in any case the adults surely made up for any coolness on their parts.

Even many years later, the image of this fascinating child was still fresh in the minds of everyone who had known her, as I myself can testify after hearing at every stage of my own development how interesting Virginia had been at the same age. I heard it not only from Mother but from grandparents, aunts, uncles, and all the teachers that we both had as we passed through the early grades of the same school, and I received the distinct impression that nobody, before or since, ever had so much to say or was more generally appreciated. She was obviously born to be a famous raconteuse and was on stage most of her early years before her many admirers.

Dr. P. Exploited to the hilt by every adult in the environment.

A.C. Undoubtedly. I'll tell you a really pathetic story about that. Jingo used to get quite violent every time she told it in later years, and she told it very often indeed. It makes me feel violent to hear it too.

Daddy was, of course, full of tales about her witticisms. Undoubtedly everyone at his office was ready to retch at hearing how precocious his daughter was at four, but his boss was intrigued. He was a very rich, childless man who later gave our father a bad time, but at that point they must have been friendly because he invited Jingo to dinner *alone.* I guess Daddy was flattered to have her asked and actually took her. Imagine subjecting a child to something like that! There she was, delivered up to a strange butler in a large marble foyer, and then two strange adults in evening clothes came and led her to the middle of a long refectory table where she was supposed to start being funny. Before dinner was even served, she had vomited all down the front of her best dress and had to be mopped up by the butler in the kitchen. When Mother came to get her, she burst into tears at the first sight. Jingo always insisted it was only because she had disgraced the family, but I know that wasn't true. Mother was undoubtedly torn to pieces with shame and guilt and sympathy for her child, but I'm sure the sympathy was most prominent. With all her feelings about propriety, Mother's children came first in her mind, but you couldn't convince Jingo of that. I suppose there were a lot of ways in which she was exploited, and she had a right to her outrage, but in later years, Jingo did tend to forget everything except the worst aspects of anything.

In any case, she was always presented to me in terms of how interesting she was, and I suppose I envied her beyond words. All I know is that I never even tried to compete with her in anything, and it was years before I knew that she hadn't surpassed me at every step along the way.

Let me tell you about her imaginary companion. Stories about that seem to stand out in my mind because I heard them so often when I was a child.

Virginia wasn't always talking to other people, but that doesn't mean that she stopped talking for very long. Sometimes on Saturdays she would spend hours walking along the top of the long fence which connected the gardens of St. Charles Place, balancing herself like a tightrope walker, and chattering away as though in deep conversation with an invisible companion. As she went by, the neighbors would laugh to see her talking to herself, but they had never met Little Billy, so how could they know that he was right there beside her wherever she went?

Jingo shared Little Billy with Mother as she shared everything else, without reservation or inhibition of any sort. These two confided in each other a great deal, because except for Little Billy and each other neither of them had anyone to talk to a lot of the time. Daddy often stayed late at work or went away on business trips, and Mother, being a rather prolific chatterer herself, was very glad to have a companion with whom she could converse. She worried some about Little Billy at first, not knowing quite what to make of him, but as time went on with nothing dire seeming to happen, she accepted him pretty much as one of the family. Periodically she felt called upon to remind Jingo that this was an imaginary friend, but it was hardly necessary—Jingo knew that of course he was imaginary. He therefore had his own place set at the luncheon table, got a taste of all her food, and when Mother read *The Wizard of Oz* aloud as they ate, there sat Little Billy listening as intently as Jingo herself. Often he inserted a comment on the story, mediated by his friend, or told Mother what was all right for Jingo to do and what was not. He even stayed around for quite a while after Eliot Jr. was born, and when I heard about him later, I got a strong feeling that at times Mother almost saw him too. When an imaginary companion is so firmly entrenched in a child's mind, does it indicate that she was particularly disturbed?

Dr. P. Oh, no. Imaginary companions are quite common among perfectly normal children. As a matter of fact, such companions are apt to be created by unusually bright, imaginative children and usually fade away when no longer needed. Sometimes it means the child is lonely, but one also sees them in cases where a child feels too close to his or her mother; the imaginary companion is a kind of buffer who creates a little distance.

A C. That would certainly fit in Jingo's case. It seems hard for me to imagine that she was ever particularly lonely, even as a small child, for although she was often in the company of adults, she always had plenty of children her own age to play with too. From the time she was brought to St. Charles Place she had one very good friend named Susan, who played with her from the time she was very small, and when she was old enough to be out around the neighborhood by herself, she had plenty of friends who liked her as well as the adults did. Jingo was undoubtedly a very likable child, but nevertheless, throughout most of her youth her closest friend was Mother, who treated her more like an adult companion than like a child. It was Mother who was lonely, not Virginia.

By the time Eliot was born, Jingo was already five years old, enjoying an excellent progressive kindergarten, and had been well prepared for what was going to happen. Her Scott grandparents and Aunt Hattie lived nearby at the time, and since she had frequently stayed overnight at their house, there was little disruption of her routines during the actual birth. After her brother arrived, Mother shared him with Jingo as much as Jingo had shared Little Billy with her, and as El got a little older, I suspect Jingo considered him just one more appreciative member of her audience. I'd be willing to bet that her communion with Mother was not much altered by his arrival or by any of the events that preceded it, which I'll tell you about in a minute. There were always maids around to take care of the baby while Jingo and Mother went shopping or calling on

Mother's friends, and I imagine Mother prattled to Jingo about whatever was on her mind at the moment, and that Jingo felt very important to her.

However, the advent of her brother did create one major alteration in her life that I think had very far-reaching effects. This alteration was that Daddy, who had previously been one of her most enthusiastic admirers, turned his attention almost completely toward the little newcomer, demonstrating unequivocally that a "Son and heir" was of far greater worth to him than even the most entertaining little girl in the world.

Dr. P. To someone whose whole experience had been at the center of everyone's stage, your father's absence from her audience must have come as an overwhelming insult, particularly since, at the age of five, a little girl is apt to be very much aware of her father's interest.

A.C. It seems to me that no matter how many other people entered her life to fill the breach, the wound made by Daddy's unforgivable desertion never really healed. That is the only way I can explain the core of anger at him which was her most striking characteristic later in life, even at times when he didn't seem to deserve it.

Dr. P. As you well know, anger like that is often a measure of intense early love. Nothing can create greater bitterness than disappointed expectations.

A.C. At building up disappointed expectations, my father was a master.

Jingo was already ten years old when I was born and first appears in my memory as a sweet, peppy young girl of about fifteen, who had recently acquired the status of womanhood by putting up her hair and appearing in her first long party dress—pale blue chiffon with bunny fur around the hem and sleeves, as I see it now. To me she was always one of the adults with whom I had little contact. However, she was a heroine I worshipped from afar—one whose life seemed to me in every way suitable to the life of the "perfect girl." This idealized view, strengthened by euphemistic descriptions passed on to me by my mother, remained imprinted on my mind for many years, and even now I have difficulty readjusting it. On the other hand, later in life, when she had already been embittered by all the terrible things that had happened to her, Jingo painted to me a picture of her youth that really had to be too black and was contradicted even by my own distinct memories. Just where the real truth lies, I can't tell you.

My guess is that she grew up fairly uneventfully on St. Charles Place, troubled by the usual things that trouble a growing girl, but actually having rather a pleasant time of it—an existence dominated by close companionship with her mother, enjoyment of her schooling, and active participation in the social life of her peers. True, she had a series of problems with her health, and true, she resented her father. However, he entered her orbit only at the dinner table and actually interfered very little with what went on in the lives of his children. He always used to say jocularly, "Mother is the boss of the children. My job is to bring home the bread and butter." Nobody ever had to ask him for permission to do things, and even our allowances came through Mother. Jingo had some moments of anguish that were very poignant, but on the whole her life flowed along rather evenly.

When the family was ready to move to another part of town, she was a lovely young woman of eighteen, free at last from disfiguring braces on her teeth, and fully realized in her potential for striking appearance and charming manner. Along with other daughters of distinguished families, she had planted her sprig of commemorative ivy along the weathered brick wall of a fashionable school yard, said her tearful farewells to admiring teachers, and graduated into a broader environ-

ment well liked, well respected, and well satisfied.
Ahead lay the prospect of Paris where, in the company
of four congenial friends, she was to live for a season in
the home of a cultured French woman—to study,
explore, and find ready introduction to that segment of
Parisian society which opened its doors to well-bred
American girls. The future looked rosy indeed. A taste
of international living had always been her dream, and
she already had a fairly fluent grasp of French with
which to contact foreign friends and add them to a large
domestic collection. All those new personalities, all that
world, and all those experiences would be hers to savor.
All Jingo asked was an opportunity to bring them home
for discussion and development with her childhood
sweetheart Alex. There were many things in Jingo's life,
but Alex was the center of it.

Alex, scion of a wealthy and prominent family, had
been informally engaged to Jingo since the age of fifteen
and was considered by everyone to be an infinitely
"eligible young man." Not only was he socially eligible
and potentially well able to support a wife "in the
manner to which she was accustomed," but he was an
interesting, promising young writer who already, at the
age of twenty, had to his credit a short story published in O'Brien's annual collection of America's "best."
To top it off, he was charming, lovable, and as much in
love with Jingo as she was with him.

From the day these two met, they had shared every
thought, every idea, every plan. They had read the same
books, all those fine literary works that a good writer
must emulate in style and breadth of vision. Together
they had mulled endlessly over the ideas and characteri-
zations depicted therein and adapted their own thinking
to that of each author in turn. Whenever Alex wrote
something, he first brought it to Jingo for criticism and
approval. Whenever she met someone new, or had an
interesting experience, or heard something funny, she
converted the event into an anecdote and brought it to

him for subject material. Since the days of their early adolescence, Alex and Jingo had shared every aspect of their lives, from their innermost thoughts to their most superficial encounters. They had the same background, the same tastes, the same friends, and the same view of life. They were as alike as two peas in a pod, and nobody in either family could find a single objection to the idea that after Jingo's "coming out" season these two well-matched young people would announce their engagement. Daddy wanted Virginia to go to college before marrying and made this a condition of her European trip, but even this rather unwelcome demand threatened no permanent stumbling block to her ultimate goals.

At the point of her departure for Paris, therefore, Jingo faced the brightest prospects ever faced by an attractive girl on the threshold of a fascinating and sophisticated world. Nothing predictable stood in the way of smooth progress toward a happy and secure life at the side of a man she truly loved, a man almost certainly destined for a brilliant career through his own efforts and abilities.

Perhaps this is a good time to tell you about the little episode I hinted at earlier—the time that Grandfather Scott had his single lapse from grace. It happened five years after Mother was married, when Jingo was around three, and in my opinion everything that resulted from it had a monumental effect on all our lives.

Dr. P. Did you know about it as a child?

A.C. No, and I doubt very much that Mother *ever* knew. If she did, she certainly never breathed a word of it to her children or to anyone else. It was only many years later that Grandmother herself let something slip out to Virginia while Jingo was confiding her current marital problems. Grandmother said she understood very well, because at one time her husband too had had an affair with another woman. What's more, he thought he had contracted venereal disease from her and, although later this turned out to be untrue, was firmly convinced that God intended him to be punished. Quite rightly so, of course. His God did not make allowances for human weakness, so Grandfather not only confessed all to his wife but vowed never again to have "carnal connection" with any woman, including herself. So far as Grandmother knew, he had kept his vow, but in any case he did so as far as she was concerned. From then on, he devoted himself to his work and to Bible study exclusively.

Grandmother said no more than this, but it makes understandable what we as children had always wondered about. Grandmother had only to express the slightest wish, and Grandfather would jump to fulfill her whim. His image as a mighty man was never disturbed by a word or hint from Grandmother, but one couldn't help seeing that he wasn't really the boss in his own home, no matter how powerful he was in the business world, and even as a small child I wondered why. Once, I remember, she wanted to go on a cruise around the world. She never said so openly, but pretty soon little travel folders appeared on the library table, and then one day Grandfather said, "I've always wanted to go around the world. Why don't we go this spring?" And Grandmother was delighted, just as though he had dreamed it up all by himself. It was perfectly obvious she had tricked him into it, and although such "womanly wiles" were accepted tolerantly by my parents, I think I resented them even then.

All this might be irrelevant to our own story were it not for the fact that, almost immediately after discovering his transgression, something rather amazing happened to Grandmother. Suddenly, without any warning, she became totally blind, and nobody could find out why. All the most eminent eye doctors were called in consultation, and not one of them could find the cause of Grandmother's trouble.

Dr. P. Perhaps they would have been more successful had they consulted with specialists from another profession, or had all this taken place in our modern, post-Freudian era.

A.C. Perhaps so. For all I know, those doctors may have hinted there was something Grandmother did not want to see, but if they did, nobody in the family was able to hear them. Everyone simply accepted the fact that the most eminent ophthalmologists available for consultation in the early 1900s were able to find no cause and effect no cure. They kept Grandmother in her room with the shades drawn lest any light falling on her sightless eyes reduce her chances for recovery, but after many months her doctors sadly announced there was nothing more they could do. The situation was quite hopeless.

For nearly a year Grandmother sat rather calmly in her darkened room and thought. She also talked to many sympathetic visitors and listened to all the sundry and contradictory bits of advice that are handed out gratuitously by people who are helplessly trying to be helpful. Finally one day, she raised the shades in her room and said she had had enough of blindness. She was going to cure herself by Christian Science. Nobody was going to tell her she had to remain blind, because she wasn't going to do it. And she didn't.

Gradually, over a period of several months, her eyesight came back, and it came back so completely that she didn't even need reading glasses. At the age of ninety she was still reading with glasses ground only for magnification.

Dr. P. This is what you meant about her faith in the magical power of her own thoughts?

A.C. Yes. It seems to go a little farther than faith in the power of prayer, don't you think?

Dr. P. Perhaps. But real, deep faith in anything has a lot of power, you know. Even the most scientific psychiatrists and psychoanalysts don't really know how big a role faith plays in psychological cures, most particularly in cures of hysterical conditions, such as this one seems to be.

A.C. I don't know whether the two miscarriages that Mother had during the period of her own mother's blindness were caused by the upset over that. I do know, however—at least I'm very sure in my own mind—that she was deeply affected by the whole thing in at least one very fundamental way. When Grandmother converted to Christian Science, our mother converted along with her. That was just a little while before Eliot Jr. was conceived.

Eliot Jr.

A.C. Eliot became the Christian Science baby, conceived in joy and born in "knowledge of the truth." That's how Mother described it to herself, and that's the way she told it to others over and over again. Without the need for anesthetic or medication of any sort, she was able to be fully conscious throughout the delivery and for that very reason was able to save his life. At a certain point, the doctor found the cord to be wound around the infant's neck and begged her not to bear down until he got it disentangled. She was able to cooperate and to deliver completely without pain a "perfect child." Mother looked upon the whole incident as a "manifestation of Divine Mind."

Dr. P. The baby had no anoxia due to pressure on the cord?

A.C. Absolutely not. From his first moment in the word, Eliot was pink and beautiful, healthy and happy. He nursed well, slept well, and charmed everyone with "deep throaty gurgles of pleasure." For the first years of his life, apparently everything went smoothly with his development, and he never gave his mother or anyone else a day of worry.

Dr. P. You don't think this ideal view was distorted in any way?

A.C. I have no reason to think so. Everyone in the family corroborated it, and I can at least attest to the fact that in his baby pictures he looks like a happy little cherub. There were simply no early problems that anyone knew about. In him Mother had fulfilled her ideal. At the age of thirty, with a charming girl and a handsome male to carry on the line, she had completed her family and was content. And for five years it stayed that way.

Of course, my own memories of El don't start until he was nearly ten. I have some spotty memories of the time before I was five, but not many of him except for a feeling that he teased me rather viciously from the time I was very small. He didn't ever tell me much about his views of his early childhood either. In spite of all the talking we have done throughout our lives, we seldom reached a level of telling how we felt about events in our youth, although we reminisced endlessly about things we did and people we knew. The whole picture of what he was like before he was graduated from college is rather shadowy in my mind.

The sky was blue* and soft sand already warm in the

---

*This sketch of a day when he was five has been adapted by the author from an autobiographical short story written by Eliot Jr. Throughout the rest of the book, all other sections about his experiences are based on material obtained from his autobiography and from conversations with his sister Amy. Other sections appearing in italics throughout the book are paraphrased versions of Amy's own accounts of her life and relationships, supplemented by information obtained from her diaries, and one letter from Eliot Jr. to his sister.

sun as Eliot Jr. slammed the porch door of a cottage by the creek and stepped out into a summer day. He was dressed in an Indian suit, with a string of gaily colored feathers hanging down his back, and carried a paper bag containing two peanut butter sandwiches, an apple, and a small Hershey bar with nuts. The world was before him, the whole of a vast cutover timberland in which to roam at will on his pony Happy, and the day was his for the asking with nobody to question or limit his choice of territory. The pony, no larger than a big dog, seemed to the boy a mighty stallion, and his heart was filled with pride as they galloped over sandy roads and fields of interminable stumps or picked their way delicately over fallen leaves on the forest floor. Only the occasional whistle of a bird disturbed their solitude. With Happy to keep him company, the boy made his way throughout a pleasant day, with never a thought of loneliness.

Summer at Briarpatch was a series of such days, a time of happiness and serenity for the little boy. Some days, feeling a need for human companionship, he sought his mother to join him in butterfly hunts or wild flower and berry picking walks, but most of the time he felt no such need, wandering free to do as he pleased until evening, with no danger of interference from anyone. Sometimes he chose the swamp, picking up the line a tracker of snapping turtles comes to recognize in the sand. Broader than that left by the tail of a mud turtle, it was exciting to find, leading soon to that stinking old fellow himself, lumbering along on scaly, clawed feet with a rolling gait and dragging a heavy black shell over the muddy ground. Many a snapper he grabbed by the tail just before it could slide to safety in the murky waters and held high in triumph before letting it go again. Never did he destroy one, however, although the meat is very good to eat, not because he was a humanitarian, but because he had no idea how to go about either killing the monster or cutting away the flesh. Nobody had ever taught him things like that, and Eliot was not at all a real woodsman. Completely on his own in the countryside, he was as baffled by the practical aspects of turtle hunting as he was by the practical aspects of everything else around a farm. He loved the chase, just as he loved watching the farmers round up cows for milking, but he would no more have considered asking how to extract turtle meat than he would have considered learning to squeeze milk from bulging udders. He was a watcher, chatting sometimes with the men about their work, and hearing them say that one day he too could do all these chores. All his participation was in the realm of thought, however, and remained totally remote from what was actually going on. The boy was a dreamer, not a doer, and at the age of five liked very much to be just that way. Dreaming about the farm offered infinite pleasure, and in his dreams no task was beyond his power to perform.

Only one place in the entire world of Briarpatch was closed to Eliot, and this not by parental prohibition but by a nameless fear brewed in some dark corner of his own inscrutable young mind. That place was the "Forbidden Road," and he would no more have entered it than he would have eaten chipped beef in cream. Adults could argue that it was just another road in the woods he knew so well, just as they told him chipped beef was good, clean, and nourishing, stirred with butter into pure milk and the same flour bread is made of. To Eliot, creamed chipped beef was still unclean, and the Forbidden Road forbidden. Every other patch of wood and field was his, however, and the days were endless for exploration and discovery.

One happy day toward the end of summer, men from the barn were off for haying, and Eliot with them, high aboard a hayrick in the dew of early morning. Such trips were gala events, and his nose quivered in anticipation as the fat old work horses began kicking up the dust of a road lined with sassafras bushes and oak branches. Suddenly, however, he realized in terror that they were turning into the Forbidden Road. His heart thumped so loud that surely everyone must have heard it, but farmhands are not ones to be tolerant of nameless fears, so there was nothing to do except close his eyes and say his prayers. By the time he opened them again, a brand new world was opening out beyond the patch of woods.

They were coming into river bottom land, where dry dung smell and dust were supplanted by a breath of sweet grass and the odor of mud. In the clearing, a meadow of hay swept far ahead, a deep rich wilderness of razor-edged grasses filled with fragrant wild flowers. Not too far away lay the river itself, lined on either side by rows of mighty trees left untouched by earlier lumbering. Rosy clumps of Jo-pie weed stood between them, and in a sunny pool of the backwater a large black snake whipped swiftly through the lily pads. Eliot was calmed a little by the scene's beauty and further comforted not long afterward by surprises found in his own pail as everyone sat down to lunch. He was still in a restless state, however, and soon wandered off by himself toward the ancient trees. Picking his way aimlessly through the thicket, he passed gradually away from the men with scythes, from turtles, water snakes, and mallard mothers with ducklings, out of the world he had known into the secret world of a darkened forest.

On this forest floor there were no leaves. Only mud was there, black mud laced with twigs and fallen branches strewn among the bases of huge trunks. These trunks with their sprawling roots were dark and gnarled, with deep ridges bitten into their bark, and from above fell the shadow of heavy boughs with leaves like basalt. Everything was dark, dark as far as the eye could see.

However, even in the muted light there could be seen flashing far and wide the bloody spikes of countless red cardinal flowers. Everywhere the boy looked were flowers—flaming, brilliant flowers, with the curious curve of their petals shining in the gloom. Then as his eyes grew accustomed to the scene, he saw in the distance a light—no common light, surely, but something of strange import luring him forward from log to log, over crackling thoroughfares of twigs making a sucking sound beneath his feet. Before him, a lone sunbeam penetrated the night of the woodland, falling through the gloom in a shimmering shaft, and where it struck, produced a marvelous sight. Instead of black murk, a small pool of water jumped into view, and blooming from it were the starred petals of white and yellow water lilies, delicate and airy above the bronze of their pads. That sight was in an instant set in the boy's memory as a vivid jewel destined to remain forever clear.

Later, Eliot, writing of the boy he once had been, described it as a moment touching on the miracle of life, something of infinite richness beyond the province of a mind to understand, with origins lying in a world of marvel and another plane of experience. He felt that in some way his life had been indelibly marked by what he felt in the mysterious aura of that secret woodland, before he turned away at last to rejoin farmers who were finishing their lunch.

When his son was a grammar school boy growing up on St. Charles Place, Eliot Sr. was at the height of his prowess in the business world, as almost anyone could have guessed just from looking at him. A handsome man, wearing black suits and ties set off by flaring, white batwing collars, he was the epitome of confident exuberance, emitting a sense of power with every movement of his vigorous body. To a boy watching through the window, eager to greet his father first, Eliot Sr. appeared as a veritable titan, striding down the block with springing step and head held high, a man who must indeed rule the world practically single-handed. "Our Father, who art the breadwinner" his son sometimes muttered mockingly, but in actuality it was no joke. In the mind of Eliot Jr., the distinction between Father and God Himself was very thinly drawn.

The picture of his father as he neared the house, still fired, as he was, with excitement from the day's battle against odds—that, and all the feelings that went with it—remained clearly imprinted on his son's mind for the rest of his life. Later on he wrote of those times, trying also to see a picture of the boy he used to be, and searching with his mind's eye each room of his boyhood home. He was looking for a pretty normal little boy, doing well in school, playing games, and in love with a girl named Alice, who at a party once honored him with a heart-studded paper hat. But closing his eyes, all he could see was his father, filling every room with his presence and so dominating the scene that all else lay in shadow. Memory could produce the boy only as a disembodied wraith, hearing his father's voice and experiencing a total absence of self.

From half-past five in the afternoon, when he first stepped through the front door, Eliot Sr.'s voice pervaded the atmosphere, reverberating from the walls and penetrating the farthest reaches of upstairs and down. It was at the six o'clock sharp dinner table, however, that his impact was really felt. There, night after night, year after year, he presided, and night after night, year after year, he corrected table manners and held forth on the subjects of Reason, Manhood, and the Good Life. Eliot Sr. worshipped reason, and he worshipped it with the adoration of a man himself highly emotional, engaged in activities where reason actually played a far less important part than intuition and a shrewd ability to appraise the extent of potential folly in each of his fellow men. He also worshipped Manhood and was determined that, whatever else he did or did not do in life, he would make a Man out of his son.

From the time Eliot Jr.'s high chair was discarded in favor of a chair seat elevated by Webster's *Unabridged*, his father prepared him for his masculine role—taught him what a Man did, and the standards, approaches, and attitudes by which a Man achieved his ends. He spoke about the business world where one rolled up one's sleeves, spat on one's hands, and the devil took the hindmost. That was the world a Man lived in, and later his son saw it all—the huge polished desks, the wire baskets filled with important papers, the deferential typists tick-ticking their monotonous lives away. All that could be his, and more. He too could be ruler of a Man's world, because to him would be offered opportunities for achieving the "finest development." He need only follow the path great men had trod before him, and the rest would follow as the night the day. "Just train your mind, Mac. Train your mind. Elbows off the table, Mac, and sit up straight like a Man. Train your mind." So it went, night after night, year after year, at the dinner table.

Eliot Sr. had risen the hard way, but he saw in those who had had "advantages" evidence of the "finest development" attainable by human beings. He saw it in his first boss, a graduate of Harvard or Yale, a man rich and cultured who ruled a mighty empire with the power and influence presumably derived from this kind of education. He wanted to see it in his son too and, from babyhood on, indoctrinated him to that end. One might say that he indoctrinated his son, without letting up for one moment, from six o'clock until bedtime, seven nights a week, for thirteen years, and his ideas did not fall on stony ground. Eliot Jr. loved his father, admired him, and listened to him. He listened to his father seven nights a week for thirteen years and believed every word he heard to be the gospel truth.

Eliot Jr. heard and knew absolutely that those who could not meet deadlines were slackers, and incompetents were no better than bums. Those who lost big accounts deserved the sack, for a man must stand on his own two feet, and if he didn't cut the mustard, he was nothing but deadwood to the organization. Eliot heard it over and over, and the more he heard, the more he worried, and the more he worried, the more his own two feet slipped out from under. Gradually and inevitably a certain knowledge grew within him, knowledge that no matter how he tried, he could surely never make it and must forever remain ignominiously among the deadwood and the bums. In spite of infinite feats of exhibitionism to prove his masculinity, Eliot Jr. knew without a doubt that failure stared him in the face. Well before the onset of his teens, he was already quite certain that he was not, and never would be, a Man.

Perhaps it was the accident when he was twelve that finally tipped the balance in his mind. The end began with a broken leg, splintered when a delivery van hit his bicycle. There were no other injuries, but the break was a bad one, and Eliot lay for a long time with his leg hanging from a frame by ropes and pulleys. People came in, of course—friends, family, and a tutor to help him keep up with his work. He had books, and games, and special treats—birds to feed, the dog to pet, and white rats in a cage. He also had plenty of time alone to think, and the weight of ideas lying upon that twelve-year-old boy was equivalent to a ton of stones. By that age he had listened to his father's doctrine for many years, and lying in bed with nothing else to think about, he "digested the poison [his] father had fed him."

Eliot Sr.'s son had been asked to accept certain things, and he accepted them. He accepted the fact that a "good life" was totally extroverted, unfeeling, cultured, and dominated by reason. Dreams, beauty, and idle fancies had no place in the life of a Man, and a side of life which brought to him only terror was the "finest development" of which man is capable. To be weak in that was to fail utterly. He would fail utterly because there really was no choice. The "good life" simply wasn't for him, so right then and there he stopped trying. That is what seemed to happen as hour after hour he lay there brooding on his inadequacy as a male, and by the time his leg had healed both mind and emotions were almost totally paralyzed. That's the way he saw it in retrospect, anyway, and that's the way it felt at the time. Before he left St. Charles Place, Eliot Jr. "had begun the long, slow descent into Dante's Inferno, where the lowest pit is a lake of ice."

That is the phrase he used to describe it. The way I see it, he was simply blown out like a candle at the age of twelve and not rekindled until adult life.

Dr. P. Obviously Eliot was in for a terribly difficult adolescence, and I gather that Jingo had troubles at a somewhat later stage of life. How did you manage to escape all the problems?

A. C. I didn't. I also hit adult life messed up in many ways, but in order to understand how my experience differed from that of the others, I'll really have to start back at the time of my birth. What I know about it I heard from Mother herself, and always in a framework of love and gratitude that God had given me to her as such a pleasant surprise. I'm sure I first heard it at an early age, because it seems I have always known that my birth was an accident, and in all the years of my growing up, it never occurred to me to doubt what she said about being glad to have me. However, I know now that it came as an overwhelming shock when at the age of nearly thirty-four our well-satisfied mother again found herself with child. Virginia was already in the fourth grade, Eliot was completing kindergarten, and Mother was deeply involved with their various activities as well as with charitable causes suitable to her station in life. Whatever in the world was she going to do with a little baby at that point? For a moment she was thrown into a panic, but only for a moment.

Amy

Laura did not let "mortal mind" overpower her for very long. She was brave and had infinite faith in the "rightness of things." Laura knew that if she merely held the "good thought," everything would turn out for the best, and she instantly realized that she wanted that baby more than anything in the world. It would be the most welcomed, the most prepared-for, and the most cherished baby ever born. Satin-lined bassinets, dainty hand-embroidered dresses, and quilted silk blankets began to arrive and to dominate every family conversation. The whole house reeked of sachet and baby powder. Daddy wasn't home very much to share her enthusiasm, but the other children were around, and they heard of nothing else for at least eight of the nine months waiting time. Laura herself went around with stars in her eyes, and everyone marveled at how well she looked.

Then the day came closer. Kind friends who came to tea started wishing her luck against all the possible mishaps that might befall, mishaps that Laura had never even heard of and which her kind friends considerately described in painstaking detail. The "good thought" began to slip away from Laura, and as she lapsed into panic with increasing frequency she turned temporarily back to a more familiar god outside her own mind. Pacing the floor night after night, she prayed that no terrible thing would be the matter with her child, and the "Good Thought" receded ever farther into the background. Finally after such a night, and in a state of near exhaustion, she went into hard labor at three in the afternoon and after seven hours delivered Amy.

Amy turned out to have only one head after all, not such a bad little head at that, and her other body parts were also quite intact. This ungrateful child, however, refused to take from her mother what little milk the anxious breasts could summon up. Stubbornly she turned her head away, demanding nourishment from a less anguished and reluctant source. In despair the disappointed mother finally had to admit defeat and, after six weeks, delivered her youngest into the care of a highly trained baby nurse.

It must be said emphatically that she by no means rejected this infant in her heart. Every morning for five years she met with the nurse for an hour, heard everything that had happened the day before, and outlined in detail every moment of the current day's program. When she could, she played with her child— sang her lullabies, talked to her, and read to her. Those two often had exceedingly good times together, in fact. However, a true feeling of oneness with the infant during a period when oneness with a mother is very important—this she could not furnish, much as she wanted to, and her child missed it very much indeed. Amy, in fact, having acquired with others some feeling for what it might have been like to be really close to her mother, tried throughout most of her life to achieve this state of bliss.

When Amy was placed in the loving arms of her nurse at the age of six weeks, she and Alma were ensconced in *a fine, sunny bedroom on the third floor of the house—sole residents of an area removed from the noises and intrusions of family life. A large, well-equipped playroom at the other end of the hall was not intended for their exclusive use, but although the other children often played there, it was in actuality the living room of an apartment where Amy and Alma lived in virtual isolation from everyone else and spoke together in German, which nobody else understood. Throughout her first years, Amy even had most of her meals in this nursery world and saw her parents for quite limited periods in the day. To the outward eye she appeared contented in this peaceful atmosphere, and so far as she herself was aware, Amy actually felt contented.*

It was only in the night that she occasionally felt unhappy—this usually after a particular dream which had already come to her several times before the age of five. When it came, she felt guilty about the fright it induced, because she knew it was only a dream and shouldn't be taken so seriously. She had been told so repeatedly, not only by her mother but by Alma herself. On the rare occasions when these two agreed on something, that something was established in her mind as incontrovertible fact. Amy tended to believe the words of people who loved her anyway, because those words usually stated what turned out to be true. However, she couldn't always feel the way she knew she should feel, no matter how hard she tried. Since the dream inevitably upset her, she felt guilty about letting everybody down.

The site of the dream was always the dining room, although the room looked a little different from the way it did in reality. The heavy mahogany sideboard crowned with a silver tea service was still there, and so was the round central table. Instead of chairs lined up against a side wall, however, there was a narrow cot covered with Indian blankets on which Amy lay.

*Through red velvet portieres drawn back to reveal the
living room, she could see her mother sewing, as she
often did, on a window seat at the far end, her head
silhouetted against the light which filtered through the
elms outside, making patterns on the Persian rug. Amy
would put her hand down between the cot and the wall
but would immediately withdraw it in terror as something snatched at it. Jumping up and throwing back the
blankets, she would uncover a wicked witch who began
chasing her around the table. She knew if she could only
break out of the circuit and run across to her mother
everything would be all right, but she couldn't make it,
and the chase went round and round. All the while her
mother smilingly continued to sew, completely oblivious to what was happening.*

*Events following the dream were always the same.
Waking with a scream, Amy was picked up and held on
Alma's lap. After being reassured and comforted with a
glass of warmed milk, she was tucked into bed again and
kissed goodnight. Amy would drop off to sleep immediately, but almost at once would come another dream,
the grey one that was not terrifying but brought with it
a heavy sense of cold loneliness that was usually gone
before she woke again. In the grey dream there was no
action at all, just the visual image of a washed-out lake
bed, its swampy bottom covered with grey ooze through
which protruded grey stumps of a once submerged
forest. The sky all around was grey too. That was all,
and then she woke.*

*Amy had no idea that years ago she had actually seen
such a sight. It had been imprinted on her brain in
connection with a sense of panic, panic transmitted to
her in some mysterious way by fearful adults, as is so
frequently the case with babies, and it reappeared later
as a pictorial representation of her own bleak or
frightened moods.*

She had seen it in Briarpatch, a place associated in her

waking mind primarily with sensuous pleasures, the smell of sun-warmed pine needles and a taste of milk fresh from the cow; the feeling of soft sand between bare toes, and of milkweed silk sliding between her fingers. Her memories were of fun with her mother, of constructing sand villages and castles complete with moats and drawbridges, and of gazing from an upstairs window onto the garden lit with gaily colored Japanese lanterns for evening Red Cross benefit shows. Wild flowers and berries from the vine, chipmunks in the woods, and red-winged blackbirds in the fields—these were her memories of Briarpatch. They had built into her mind a source of comfort and tranquillity to be forever after derived from contact with the out-of-doors.

In Briarpatch Alma assumed protective custody only on walks across fields and woods far from home or during occasional quiet suppers in the large upstairs room that was also relegated to them in the summer cottage—a little world of their own away from family and guests. There Amy ran free around the farm, tagging after children who were invited up in groups from the city's slums for a week at a time, following indulgent farm workers in the round of their chores, or participating in many-peopled picnics on the beach of Sapphire Lake. Memories of all these people, and no terror or loneliness, came to her mind when she thought of Briarpatch in daytime.

There was, however, a connection between this pleasant place and very disturbing emotions, a connection registered in her mind at the age of nine months and which lurked there out of awareness from then on. The connection was made when a terrified mother carried her in the grey dawn from a cottage already beginning to slope perilously over the banks of a brook that had become a raging torrent when the lake dam broke. Somewhere in the deep layers of her still

*wordless mind had been stamped a picture of the
drained lake along with a feeling that her mother's sense
of helplessness and her own were one. None of this was
in her conscious mind at any time.*

*On a particular winter afternoon when Amy was five,
Alma was having a cup of tea with the couple in the
kitchen. After returning from an afternoon at the zoo,
she had left her little charge upstairs, absorbed in a game
of paper dolls, and was not aware that, moments earlier,
Amy had crept under the cloth-covered kitchen table by
the door.*

*"It's a crime, when that woman neglects her so for
the older ones. What ever will become of her?"*

*Mrs. Koch made clucking noises and got up to test
the cake with a broom straw. Ernest grunted and
shuffled his big flat feet, feet on which Amy regularly
rode in the morning, holding onto his leg while he ran a
carpet sweeper around the downstairs rooms. She knew
from the tone of their voices that things were not as
usual, but beautiful smells intensified for a moment as
the oven door opened, and she was quite happy thinking
only about the good dessert she would later enjoy.*

*Amy did not feel she was doing anything wrong by
being where she was. She knew full well that had she
elected to come down with Alma everyone would have
welcomed her to the party at the table. In fact she probably would have been given a tiny loaf of bread baked
especially for her. However, earlier in the day, through
an already well-developed set of antennae for picking up
emotional vibrations, Amy had obtained a message that
for once even her devoted nurse would like to be free of
her presence for a while. Nobody had ever implied, by
word or deed, that Amy wasn't wanted at all times. In
fact, Alma often invited her along when she went for a
"day out." On this day, however, Amy somehow knew
that her friends wanted to talk without having to think*

about her, and in this hidden place she could be close to them without having to be included in the conversation. She didn't resent their wish to talk, nor did she particularly wish to join them at the moment.

Amy didn't feel guilty about eavesdropping either, since she hardly noted the words or reacted to them. She heard what they said and knew they were talking about her; she was rather pleased to be the subject of adult attention but did not really understand what it was all about. If she had, she would have been completely bewildered. Amy did not regard herself as a neglected child, nor did she question her mother's love any more than she questioned the love of these three who cared for and pampered her. At the time their words did not register more than a note of sympathy which was pleasant and warming.

Suddenly came the sound of the front door closing, and a booming voice extinguished the late afternoon quiet. Amy crawled quickly out from under the table, crossed a dining room at the moment unpopulated by witches, and ran happily to greet her father. With a leap she was on his shoulders, and he seemed happy too, tossing her into the air and laughing boisterously as his son, arriving two seconds later, gave scowling evidence of his frustrated rage. For once, Eliot Jr. had lost the daily race for the funny papers and was forced to wait impatiently for the Adventures of the Katzenjammer Kids *while Amy slowly looked at all the pictures, covertly eyeing his displeasure with smug satisfaction. He would take it out on her later, of course, when nobody was looking, twisting her arm or pinning her spread-eagled on the floor until her yowls of agony brought an angry Alma flying to the rescue. At the moment, however, Amy forgot all that and basked in her triumph while Mother and Virginia appeared, all pink and scrubbed for the evening. In a minute Daddy* went to wash his hands, Jingo played "It's a Long, Long Trail A-Winding" on the piano, and for fifteen minutes peace reigned before the onset of chaos at the dinner table.

At that stage of her life, Amy did not participate in the daily war. She sat at a small table beside her mother, only the top of her head reaching a level where others were eating adult food. Mother wished to spare her the frustration of craving what she was not yet allowed to share, and Amy had accepted her close-but-apartness here, just as she had accepted living upstairs with Alma in isolation from the rest of the family. Separatism had its compensations, especially when Daddy's voice started almost at once to sound angry at one of the older children, rising to an increasingly high pitch, while Mother's sounded so distressed in unsuccessful attempts to mediate between the different sides. At that period of her existence, Amy did not have to worry about keeping her back straight or using the correct utensil. As Mother leaned over now and then to talk gently with her, she ate her dinner obediently, totally unaware of feeling in any way left out.

After dinner, Jingo wound up the Gramophone while Mother found a record of Alma Gluck singing "Carry Me Back to Old Virginny." Daddy sat down with Amy and her brother to play one game of *Pit* or *Big Casino*, and there Amy shone, partly because Eliot Jr. was still too distracted to think quickly. She was, in fact, rather advanced for her years and surprisingly sharp at card games, much to the delight of her father. He had been known to tell people in her presence that "this one should be the boy," so Amy knew if she remained quick and clever at intellectual tasks, she would hold the center of her father's interest. After the game, she held the center of everyone's interest for a few minutes, engaging in a wild romp with Ito, the Japanese spaniel.

She was still in a state of hysterical giggles when Alma came down to sweep her back to their little private world on the third floor.

For what remained of a rather pleasant day, Amy spoke Alma's language, which came more readily to her tongue than that of her family, and sitting enveloped in a crisp white apron heard fairy stories about witches, elves, and woodcutters in the Black Forest.

A.C. That day stands out clearly in my memory because it was just a little while before my comfortable, self-contained little world with Alma was abruptly shattered.

4

The Beginning of the End

A.C. Before going on with the story, I think I should stop for a moment and tell you about an important aspect of my relationship with Mother, not only during that early period but for many years afterward too. In a way it's representative of everything that was wrong between her and us children throughout our lives, and to me personally it was certainly a primary bone of contention. I'm referring, of course, to Mother's preoccupation with Christian Science which, I think, lay at the core of our eventual destruction.

It wasn't just the direct effect that bothered us, although that was pretty destructive in itself. It was what Christian Science stood for in our minds. Somehow it became the focus for most of our rage, our resentment, and confusion because of the double-talk and euphemisms that kept everything between Mother and us on a plane of unreality. It wasn't the religion we minded so much, although all of us thought the jargon was so much gobbledygook; it was its effect on her, the way it made Mother impervious to any real contact except on rare occasions.

Dr. P. I can see how it would affect you that way, cut off as you were from contact with your mother anyway, but did the others feel as strongly?

A.C. All of us felt strongly, but perhaps for different reasons.

When Mother succumbed to "mortal mind" at the time of my birth, she lost a battle but by no means lost the war. Inability to nurse her baby was part of the defeat, but as I began to thrive in the arms of Alma, Mother realized that "everything turns out for the best." Before long, the "good thought" was reinstated as a guiding principle, and "infinite mind in its infinite manifestations" took over again with a force stronger than ever.

This is not to say that she was really a religious fanatic. In actuality, Mother was quite a practical Christian Scientist. When El broke his leg, she called the doctor immediately and cooperated absolutely with all his orders. Although God does the actual healing in such cases, it is only good sense, after all, to help him out by having the bone fragments placed in proper juxtaposition. Likewise, when I split open my chin in a fall from the icehouse roof, she didn't hesitate to have a few stitches put in. As a matter of fact, she didn't even like it when I tried to bite the doctor. Doctors are God's helpers on this earth and should be given every cooperation in their efforts to correct mechanical impediments to healing.

Mother accepted the value of prophylactic hygiene and also acknowledged the justice of sparing others the fear of "error" against which they were not armed with "good thoughts." She took all of us regularly to the dentist, and when public health regulations demanded some recognition of spots and swollen parotids, she was quite willing to follow instructions and nurse us back to our usual state of being. She was, in fact, a rather tender nurse who could make an ill child very comfortable.

Dr. P. She had a remarkable facility for rationalizing any act which, on a deeper level of awareness, she recognized as necessary.

A.C. To a point. However, ailments of obscure origin like headaches or stomachaches were "manifestations of mortal mind" which had "no life, truth, nor substance," no matter how severe these manifestations might be, and Mother tended to ignore the reality of their seriousness. She herself suffered from headaches and could always dispel them after a day in bed spent concentrating intensely on "the truth." During the last years on St. Charles Place, Jingo suffered from a series of stomachaches which Mother treated with "good thoughts," although Alma sneaked in with ice packs and aspirin after extracting an oath of secrecy. Those without faith might wonder which of these agencies were responsible for the fact that an acute infection of the appendix subsided after a period of slow leakage into the abdomen, leaving some rather troublesome adhesions that caused more stomachaches in the future, but in Mother's mind there was no doubt that she had driven "error" away.

Dr. P. Jingo was lucky to get off with just some adhesions.

A.C. She was pretty bitter about it in later life. However, Mother really needed her religion. She needed it very badly as a shield against the thoughts and feelings which might have overwhelmed her had she been without such protection. She wore it as an amulet to ward off pain and anxiety and found that the abstract God of Mary Baker Eddy furnished a more effective repellent to evil than the anthropomorphic God of Methodism, who made her feel more helpless and less in command of her own fate. Submission to a totally dominating force in human form already threatened to crush her, and a firm hold on the reality of "divine mind" dispelled the dangerous reality of her very mortal anger, frustration, and despair. By preserving against all attack her "knowledge of the truth," Mother found it possible to maintain her illusions, cope with the emptiness of her daily existence, and sustain life with our father for the first twenty years of her marriage.

Dr. P. It is a little surprising that none of you children accepted what she believed so fervently.

A.C. I wish I could say we recognized her need and went along with what was so important to her, but it just wasn't that way. All of us, so different in so many ways and so often in opposition to each other, presented a completely united front against Christian Science from the earliest years of our childhood on into our adult lives and made frontal attacks upon it whenever we could.

What's more, I don't think ours was the usual conspiracy of children against parental values. There was something very specific about it. We all loved our mother and wanted to see her happy. After a while, we could even understand how unhappy and vulnerable she was beneath a brittle but impenetrable surface. The whole situation made us sick at heart and tore at our emotions in a terrifying way. To one and all, however, Christian Science was a palpable presence that had to be resisted at all costs. Mother's immersion in this particular creed posed a dire threat to each of us, because it struck at the core of each one's emotional life. To each of us the danger lay in a possibility of further destruction to an area already felt to be in jeopardy. To Jingo, the threat was directed against her physical body. This was already the site of her greatest vulnerability, for whenever tension built up in her, an infection ran rampant, her skin broke out, she stumbled, fell, or cut herself.

Dr. P. In other words, illness, accident, or dire physical distress appeared whenever sorrow, fear, or anger rose to a volume that caused overflow from the channels of verbal expression.

A.C. I guess so. And to El the threat was against what he most valued too. To him beauty was the essence of life itself, for without the sights, sounds, smells, and touch of beauty to stimulate his emotions, he had none. He could hardly breathe, in fact, and every time he entered the sterile, unadorned, little Colonial-style meeting room designed to minimize sensuous stimulation, he felt himself walking into the cold of a tomb. That's what he told me later, anyway. A more emotional form of religion might have touched a very responsive chord in his sensitive nature—a religion expressed through Gothic naves, stained glass windows, incense, and a giant organ's roll. A religion, however, which denies reality to all sensual responses violated every cell in his mind and body.

Dr. P. And to you the threat was further loss of emotional contact with your mother.

A.C. Yes. If it hadn't been for that, I think I might have responded rather happily to the plain, cheery Sunday school room smelling of soap and fresh white paint like my own nursery. However, at an early age I had somehow picked up the knowledge that this building—these monotonous, uninspiring hymns, this dull little paper-covered lesson book, *A Key to the Scriptures*, all somehow represented The Enemy. In some mysterious way it became symbolic of whatever came between me and my mother to prevent the warmth, closeness, and real emotional contact without which I couldn't thrive. Mother's religion came down like a glass wall between us, and I spent a good part of my life trying to break it down. Sunday school became the target of my efforts, and every week there was a pitched battle to keep from having to go. Every week, year after year, I continued to fight relentlessly. Finally, in my adolescence, Mother got tired of fighting and ceased to force the issue.

Dr. P. Nobody else put up a struggle?

A.C. Not really, although they offered moral support. Jingo didn't enter the battle openly because all her fire was directed against Daddy. El did his best to bring up reinforcing troops, but he just didn't seem to have the energy. I fought alone, and I never gave up. I never really succeeded in breaking down that wall of glass, but fortunately I was able to make quite a few cracks through which humor, companionship, and mutual understanding seeped slowly through from both sides.

Dr. P. So far as I can see, nobody else crashed through either.

A.C. No. In some ways Mother remained a rather unreal person to all of us, in spite of how much we all cared for her.

I was nearly six before Alma left. Mother had told me some weeks earlier that I was too old to have a nurse, and that although Alma would come often to see me, she would soon be living somewhere else. Mother was always very good about warning us ahead of time when major changes were going to occur. What's more, I don't think she gave me the spiel mothers sometimes give their children in situations like that—the one about how baby nurses have to go on to other babies when their charges are no longer small. I'm sure she knew how important Alma was to me and tried to soften the blow as much as possible. No matter how she herself felt about Alma, she never consciously interfered with our relationship in any way and, in fact, openly encouraged my loyalty to her.

I have no memory of how I responded to her announcement at the time it was made, but in view of what followed it is clear she might as well never have spoken.

During the weeks before Alma left, Amy's life went on as usual, except that Ito, the beloved dog, died and was buried with ceremony under the backyard maple tree. Amy mourned with the rest of the family and then proceeded in the even tenor of her ways. On the day her nurse actually left, Amy kissed her good-bye and immediately afterward ran out to play with the Di Spaghetti children. She made no protest, and she did not cry at all. She seemed quite content with the assurance that Alma would come to visit and accepted her incipient independence with some relief.

Alma kept her promise, too. She visited quite frequently, and Amy was always glad to see her. Meanwhile, she saw far more of her mother, who now took her to and from school and on long rides in the electric around the big city which she had never really seen. She rather enjoyed this and won the approbation of her teacher by building a city model in the school sandbox. However, Amy did not laugh any more and rarely even smiled. She didn't talk much either, although when she did it was no longer in inverted word order. She only got thinner and thinner. Her eyes got bigger and bigger in her tight little face, and her mother became more and more worried.

Finally one day, Alma mysteriously reappeared, saying she had missed Amy so much she decided to come back for a while. Amy was pleased to know this and glad to have her around again. However, being so much bigger now than she had been when Alma went away, she wanted to be on her own, playing in the yard or on the street with the other children. School was absorbing, and by now she had learned to dress and undress herself with minimal assistance. Alma occupied herself largely with keeping things straightened up and spent most of her time with the couple in the kitchen. Amy put on a little weight and smiled more often, but she still didn't talk much except to the tigers.

The tigers were three real tiger-skin rugs with stuffed paws and natural heads, which had always graced the playroom floor. Amy had sometimes patted their heads and had often used one or the other as a pillow, but at this period of her life, they assumed very distinct *personalities. They were known to her as the "good tiger" the "bad tiger," and the "neutral tiger." Amy already had a good vocabulary and knew just what* neutral *meant. Sometimes she would play that a tiger was an island where all her toys for the day had to be collected in advance, because she couldn't put her foot into the surrounding sea until it was time for dinner. Sometimes she merely lay on one, her cheek pressed against his smooth fur, and talked to him. However, she always had a very definite idea of which tiger was the tiger of the day and couldn't be deflected in any way from staying where she belonged at that particular time. Most of the time, she gave wide berth to the "bad tiger," rather fearful of his fierce expression, but in actuality he was the one she loved the best.*

Many years later, when Amy had long forgotten about all this, she went to the home of a friend who had before her fireplace just such a rug. The emotions that welled up in her would be hard to describe, but she was irresistibly impelled to go forward and lay herself full length upon that beast, with her arms around his neck, and to burst into an uncontrollable flood of tears that lasted many minutes. The poor friend hardly knew what to make of it, and neither did Amy.

Life went along like this for a year or so. During that period Amy had one scary experience—an encounter with the janitor next door which returned vaguely to her mind in later years as something shocking and exciting, but unclear in details. At the time it happened, she told nobody, and soon forgot the episode completely. Meanwhile, she was becoming better friends with Eliot, who was pinned to his bed with all sorts of contraptions and could no longer pinch or pummel her. In fact, he seemed really to enjoy playing with her when she came in with the checkerboard or Parcheesi to keep him company, and she looked forward to it herself. They didn't talk much, but both seemed to understand

*that they shared some kind of secret that the others
didn't know. When he got on his feet again, she was a
little apprehensive at first, fearing that things would go
back to the way they had been before, but they didn't.
He still liked to play with her, and now they would
often look together at pictures in books from the library
shelf. A favorite was Fox's* Book of Martyrs, *and they
liked to talk together about which of the various
tortures would be the most excruciating. Eliot's choice
was the rack, and hers the Iron Maiden. Both of them
felt a little excited by discussing what exquisite pains
such devices must induce, and Amy often acted quite
lively afterward. Everyone was glad to see her recovering
her animation. When Alma left a second time to get
married, Amy didn't show any of the previous signs of
strain, and her mother was enormously relieved that
things had straightened out so well.*

*As the family began making plans for moving to
another part of town, Amy busily helped her mother
pack. She was excited about the prospect of a move
and, when the day arrived, watched eagerly out the
front window for the big car hired to carry them all
away. Now she stood on the front doorstep, taking a
last look at the almost empty house.*

*Suddenly a look of terror came into Amy's eyes.
Without a word she turned and ran back into the house,
back through the living room, the dining room, pantry,
and kitchen. Down the back steps she ran and into the
yard where the maple tree stood dropping yellow leaves
onto the drying autumn grass. At its base she flung
herself full length upon the ground, arms tight around
the trunk of the tree, and there she began to sob wildly.
She thoroughly watered the base of that tree with her
tears, and as she wept she talked.*

*Amy was not going to go off and leave Ito. He would
be too lonely. You cannot just go away and leave people
who love you, because they will be too lonely and sad.*

It would be cruel to go away from Ito, and she wasn't going to do it. The rest of them could go if they wanted to, but she wasn't going anywhere. She was going to stay right here with Ito. Ito loved her, and she loved him. She was not going to abandon him when he needed her, no matter what anybody else decided to do. She simply wasn't going to, and that was that.

Her mother listened and tried to talk to her. She understood very well how sad it was to leave one's home because she felt sad herself. However, soon they would both be happy in their new home, and they would soon have another dear little dog to love and care for. Everyone had loved Ito, and he had known it, too. He had loved us, but that was quite a while ago. He was happy now in another state of dog consciousness and had long ceased to miss us.

Amy merely tightened her arms around the tree trunk and cried harder than ever. Her mother tried gently to loosen her arms and got kicked for her pains. She felt frustrated and helpless, and for a few moments she began to be angry at this child who had thrown a monkey wrench into an otherwise smooth operation. For some reason that she could not have explained, however, she suddenly got the message that her daughter was in the grips of something her mother could not understand—something nobody else could under-stand—and Amy would have to work it out in her own way before anyone could budge her. Several times during Amy's lifetime her mother got a message like that, and this was one of them. Anyway, Laura finally went to tell the rest of the family to go on. She and Amy would come later. Then she came back to sit beside the maple tree with her baby.

Laura didn't know what to do, and she'd already said everything she knew how to say, but she sat there anyway, and from time to time she patted Amy's heaving little back and said, "There, there." Amy didn't make any response, and she didn't even seem to know her mother was there. Gradually, however, she wept away three years of accumulated rage, sorrow, and panic over her own abandonment and spent her emotion on Ito's grave. In spending it, she recovered for a while her ability to feel and react. Gradually, as her arms grew limp and dropped away from the trunk of the maple tree, she allowed her mother to comfort her and take her to the taxi which bore them from St. Charles Place into a new, more fashionable world.

Nobody knew then, of course, what had been going on all this time in the world of business, nor did anyone realize how soon an impact from that world would shatter the one they were entering.

A.C. I suppose the trauma connected with Alma's loss is one reason I've never revisited St. Charles Place.

Dr. P. It is clear by now that all of you had some very traumatic experiences in early life, and I begin to get an idea of how the personality problems of your parents affected each child in a different way. If I didn't know the end of the story, however, I would find it hard at this point to predict which of the children became mentally ill.

A.C. Do you think it's possible to say that any of us were already destined to become ill by the time we left there? Perhaps we all had the potential, but it seems to me so much depended on what happened later.

Dr. P. I can't really answer that question. Although the seeds may already have been sown, one never knows what it will take to make them flower.

A.C. As I see it, the horror that followed for us all was related very directly to the complex, contradictory, egocentric personality of my father, although for Jingo it started somewhere else.

Throughout her days in Paris, Jingo was in constant lengthy communication with Alex. Almost every evening she sat down to write the exciting events of her day, and every morning she eagerly awaited the mail which brought his equally detailed comments and declarations of love. This flow of correspondence was interrupted only when Mother went over to take her for a two-month tour around Italy and Great Britain as a grand finale to the European venture. While on the move at that time, they were unable to receive mail from home and arrived at New York in a fever of anticipation.

Daddy and I met them at the dock, and I was completely unprepared for what was going to happen. I'll have that day burned into my memory forever, because it was the only time I ever actually saw my father in tears, and the only time I can even imagine that he shed tears for the sorrow of another. When we all returned to the hotel, excited and full of elation about the trip, it fell upon my father to tell Jingo that one month previously, in the course of a drunken house party at college, Alex had eloped with a girl he had known for approximately three hours. That was the news with which he had to greet his daughter on her happy homecoming, and that was the news that brought tears to his own eyes.

With all due respect to Alex, let it be said that this elopement was carried out on the impulse of a moment, and that before many days had passed he was very sorry indeed. In fact, he would have done anything in the world to undo what he had so carelessly done, but it was too late.

In those times, and in the circles in which he grew up, marriage was a sacrament not to be taken lightly. "He who marries in haste repents at leisure," especially if his young bride becomes pregnant on the first night. After an interview with each of the irate fathers, Alex had faced a clear choice. Either he would accept responsibility for supporting his new family, or he was out on his ear without a dime. There would be no divorce, no annulment, nothing. His college education was over. He would "be a man" and take care of his wife, or he could wash his hands of any help from the family and any chances of future inheritance. His father was willing to arrange that a bookstore be set up for him in London, and he could manage that or find something else for himself, but if he chose not to get a job, he was on his own. Forever.

I do not know how Alex felt about that choice, but I do know that he and his bride had packed up for London and were gone by the time Virginia reached home. She did not see him, and she did not hear from him again for a long, long time.

What came next didn't help her much either; in any case, the girl who returned to the Middle West after receiving that news would never again be the same girl who had arrived in New York three days earlier.

The destruction of Jingo went hand in hand with the destruction of the Carpenters as a family unit. In order to explain that, however, I have to go back and tell you a little more about my father. By that time he had already made a million dollars—in fact, had made it before he was thirty-five—and I think that very fact is part of what happened to our family.

As I see it, the man who starts out from scratch and winds up making a million dollars has one quality above all others. He is in love with the process of making money. There are those who have this quality and fail to make a million, usually because they aren't smart enough, but I've seen very few successes in this pursuit who are without it. It isn't necessarily that they love money itself. Often they have rather simple tastes and hardly know what to do with what they earn. Long after they have enough, or more than enough for every conceivable need or desire, they go right on making money because there seems to be something in them that drives them to do this.

Dr. P. A need for the heady excitement derived from this process creates an addiction just as powerful as the addiction to heroin and often comes from much the same sources lying deep within the personality structure. Such an addiction overrides all other needs and loves. A man so addicted will put the process of making money above all else—above home, wife, family, in fact, everything that gives other men a reason for living.

A.C. Such a man was my father. He had that kind of love, and he had the energy and genius to make it pay off. This is not to say that he didn't love his home, his wife, and his family. I honestly feel that in his way he did love them. It's only that they were quite secondary to the satisfaction of his deeper, more fundamental need, and that when he was in the process of feeding his addiction, he simply thought about nothing else. He didn't know that anything else existed; in fact, nothing else did exist for him except his preoccupation of the moment.

Daddy had no idea he was this kind of a person. To the end of his days he believed he had a deep concern for his family and for the future of his children. He believed that he loved his wife dearly and devotedly, that all his hard work had one purpose only—getting her what she wanted and making her happy. When he was away from her, he didn't even notice the separation, so intent was he upon this goal of making her happy. He had no idea at all that she was not happy about the separation or that anything was going wrong in his family.

Dr. P. He was simply oblivious to the feelings and needs of others.

A.C. Well, he was and he wasn't. Theoretically he cared a great deal, and when he focused on something—

like that time with Jingo—he did feel for others. When his mind was on something else, however, he just didn't notice.

Daddy was a man with a heart who didn't like to see people suffer. He could be deeply moved by a pathetic story. If one of us started to tell how a little boy's dog had been run over in front of the house, he would spring up in his nervous manner and try to brush it away.

"Don't tell me, Amy!"

"Mac, don't tell me things like that!"

So we tried to be very careful not to tell him things like that because, when he got upset, he was apt to begin a barrage about our table manners. We didn't know for a long time that these barrages meant he was near the limit of his endurance. After a while we learned this, but it didn't make the barrages any easier to bear. Before that we didn't recognize that if he didn't let off steam in this way, he would explode from an accumulation of angers and tensions.

He had been poor in his youth and didn't like poverty. To be sure, he had little use for any man who allowed himself to remain in a state of poverty, but at the same time, with quite a separate part of his mind, he realized there was a lot wrong with the way the world was run and wanted to do something about it. Sometimes on a Sunday morning, he would take one of us on a walk through the city's slums. He wanted to show us some of the things that were wrong with the world and tell us that certain kinds of conditions degraded a man's soul. Striding forcefully down the seamiest streets, in his black suit and stiff batwing collar, trailed breathlessly by a boy in blue serge or a girl in dotted swiss, he would point out these conditions in his booming voice. "See how these people have to live! Isn't it terrible? Terrible! Terrible!" And he would be almost in tears. All eyes would be upon him, and we would cringe and cower under the hostile stares. He himself would not notice the hostility, however. He was thinking how to improve things for these people, and he could see nothing else.

Dr. P. He would become emotional about them, but his concern seemed to be largely an intellectual abstraction.

A.C. Yes, but because of it, his way of making a million dollars was to create a business in which people could buy their necessities for less money. Of course, there is no contradiction between making a million and saving a dollar for the workingman, as Henry Ford knew, and a good many other men as well as my father.

His particular business, however, was ahead of its time. I wish I could tell you about it, but I can't go into details without disclosing just what it was. Later on there were many like it, but his was the first, and it stepped on the toes of many very powerful interests in the business world. Those very powerful interests had very powerful political connections, and when father's profits began to cut into theirs, harassments to his business began. As they increased, the dinner table barrages were stepped up in intensity, and discourses on the "good life" were supplanted by shouts and imprecations against dirty politicians and corrupt business interests.

Eventually, somebody instigated a lawsuit, charging that his business did not have sufficient assets to cover its obligations. This was completely untrue and never had been true. However, it was difficult to discover what the assets were because of the complicated way in which his business was set up. There was wild publicity about it on the front pages of every newspaper in the city, with charges and countercharges.

This was The Case, and it was the beginning of the end for the Carpenter family. The publicity brought to light many facts that nobody in his wildest dreams could have foreseen and led to events that nobody could possibly have imagined. The children who were old enough to know what was going on were shaken in ways that had far-reaching effects on them, and the whole way of life for everyone was irretrievably altered.

Daddy was a man who liked to run things his own way and often found it cumbersome to have business associates who might argue with him. He didn't like anyone to argue with him, so why not ally himself with someone he could count on to sign wherever he pointed a finger, without question or concern? The obvious answer was to make his wife a high officer in this vast, complicated, highly technical organizational structure. He knew he wouldn't ask her to do anything wrong, and she knew it, so why clutter up his operation with someone who might ask questions or try to organize things by less sweeping and imaginative methods than his own? There was no legal reason why she should not have a title in this monumental company, so he made her treasurer. Mother, who could probably go no further in mathematics than to add a shopping list correctly, was the top officer of his financial setup.

Dr. P. I suppose it never occurred to him that she or anyone else might suffer from such a situation.

A.C. I'm sure it didn't. If it had, I'm certain he wouldn't have done it. She did suffer, however, and so did her children. If the charges brought against the business should happen to be substantiated, she technically had as much responsibility as he and she was just as apt to end up in jail. Absurd as this idea might be to anyone who knew her, that's the way it looked to the world, and that's the way it looked to her family.

Dr. P. Is that the way it looked to her?

A.C. Nobody will ever know. Certainly she never admitted to the slightest fear that "good" would not triumph. She held her head high and acted as if nothing was happening.

The older children, however, again had occasion to

cower and cringe. El had just managed to live down a
very midwestern pompadour with which he had arrived
at his fashionable eastern prep school and found it
almost unbearable to wonder whether his friends knew
about the situation and pitied him. Jingo's suffering had
a particularly poignant edge; not only was she right on
the scene to see exactly what was happening, but the
whole thing broke practically on the eve of her debut,
threatening to collapse the social structure upon which
her whole life, and that of her mother, was based.
Among the people they knew, it was permissible for
one's name to appear on the society page, but acquiring
public notoriety in any other form simply wasn't done.
Anyone who did so might very well expect ostracism,
and both Jingo and Mother feared it very much, despite
all appearances to the contrary. Protectiveness toward
her mother, plus outrage over what had been done to
the whole family, fanned the embers of Jingo's resentment, and hatred for her father burst into a hot flame
along with fear for her own entire future.

Dr. P.   Did that aspect of it get to your father at all?

A.C.   Yes, and he was very sorry about it. Just the
same, he knew he was in the right and expected his
children to have the guts to hold up their heads without
a qualm. In the end it turned out he was in the right,
too. When they finally untangled the intricate structure
of his business, the courts ruled that everything had
been in perfectly good order and dismissed the charges.
That was a good many years later, however.

Dr. P.   He had done nothing the slightest bit illegal?

A.C.   If he had, any number of people would have
been more than happy to lock him up and throw away
the key. No. Throughout his life our father was very
careful to abide by the law. He taught himself a great
deal about it—more, in fact, than many of his lawyers
knew. He was a master of the myriad loopholes through

which things can be accomplished legally. Nobody, in the course of many ventures and many years, was able to show that anything he ever got involved with was wrong in the eyes of the law. But that didn't keep a lot of people from trying.

Dr. P. What was the timing of all this in relation to Jingo's abandonment by Alex?

A.C. The first publicity broke about six months later. However, she had lived through the abandonment, and she lived through the beginning stages of the The Case. Whether that particular ordeal was harder on a young girl whose lover had just jilted her than it would have been on someone else, I'll leave you to decide. However, she took it very hard, and, as I have already said, it made her very bitter. The intensity of bitterness toward our father seemed, in fact, to prevent the development of any real bitterness toward Alex, who seemed to fade from importance in her mind as The Case progressed.

Dr. P. She displaced all her feelings of abandonment onto the one by whom she had felt abandoned in early life.

A.C. I'm sure that was a big part of the fury she felt toward Daddy, in spite of all the reality aspects of it. Anyway, she carried on with her plans to "come out" at a small tea rather than a dance, but her bitterness festered, and it was directed almost entirely against her father for what she felt he had done to her mother. Six months later, she was engaged to a young man from the East who had come to town as an usher at a friend's wedding.

Sid was the son of a New York banking magnate, and you can well imagine that all his relatives were a little worried that he might have picked up some hick fortune hunter from the Corn Belt. They planned to turn out in full force for the wedding to see what kind of background this hastily acquired fiancée came from, so Mother really gave them something to see.

While nobody knew from moment to moment whether Father and Mother would be criminally indicted, Jingo and Mother got busy. Invitations went out, flowers were ordered, and caterers interviewed. Jingo's arms broke out in a horrible rash, and she got a badly infected pimple on her chin, but she covered everything up with calamine lotion and carried on with the show. Presents arrived by the hundreds from all Grandmother's loyal friends, and all Mother's loyal friends, and all Virginia's. I only remember a large marble statue of Cupid and Psyche sent by Alma, and sixteen silver trumpet vases for a single flower, but there was all manner of sterling silver, crystal, fine china, and monogrammed linen—enough to fill several rooms lined with trestle tables. A trousseau was gathered to rival that of any princess. Everything looked splendid, and if anyone in the family was worried about anything, nobody showed it.

Early in the game, Daddy had expressed himself rather forcefully to the effect that "marriage is a serious business" and that this whole thing was being pushed through too fast for the young people to know what they were doing. After noting the look in his daughter's eye, however, he had for once decided to say no more, and if he thought any more about the situation, he did not tell anyone. He was so preoccupied with what was going on downtown that he barely had time to come to the wedding anyway and would certainly have been the last one in the world to worry about whether any of the local gentry would be snobbish enough to snub his family because of what they were reading in the daily papers.

We'll also never know if Mother worried whether anyone would show up, because such thoughts were relegated to the regions of "mortal mind" where they most surely would be vanquished by "the truth." If Jingo herself worried, she did not breathe it to a soul. For all anyone knows, things were pretty much as they seemed, with nobody thinking about anything except the practical details of preparing for a wedding.

Unlike the day on which a sunbeam brightened the dull October weather for another bride, Jingo's wedding day was graced by an unexpected snowstorm in the middle of April. The caterer almost didn't get there because of a skidding accident, some of the flowers arrived frostbitten, and the minister sprained his ankle. However, at the actual moment of the ceremony, everyone was there. Not only did the caterer make it, and the florist, and the minister, but almost everyone in town who received an invitation was there to honor Jingo and to wish her well. Whatever they may have thought about her parents, nobody punished Jingo for their shortcomings.

If anyone pitied Virginia for what had happened to her before, nobody showed that either. I was the only one who cried at that wedding. I could hear everyone whispering about how sweet it was to see a little girl so sorry to lose her sister, but the facts of the matter were otherwise. I wept not because I was sorry to lose my sister, or even because I was sorry *for* my sister at that particular time. I cried because my nose was seriously out of joint. At the age of nearly nine I was too young to be a bridesmaid and too gangly to be a flower girl. I cried because I felt terribly out of things. However, I was the only one among the guests to show distress of any kind.

That was one time when the Carpenters really pulled themselves together and functioned at a moment of crisis. Jingo was married with pomp and circumstance. All Sid's relatives were satisfied that she came from a fine family and prepared to welcome her with open arms. Whether our own mother was happy about the whole situation I don't know, but I do know she had the satisfaction of feeling she had carried off a monumental project with aplomb. She could at least breathe a sigh of relief that nothing had gone wrong.

I also don't know whether Jingo herself was happy at that moment. At least she sailed off on the arm of her new husband with a gay smile and a light step. What she was stepping into she had no way of predicting, but in her mind nothing the future held would even remotely approach the horror of what would face her if she stayed behind. She therefore made her exit in dignity and grace from everything that had given meaning to her previous existence and never looked back.

Throughout that entire period nobody really explained to me what The Case was all about, but I could hardly have failed to sense that something pretty upsetting was going on. Everyone was talking about "publicity," and I knew that publicity was something bad and unfair that was happening to Daddy. However, I was busy at school where nobody said a word about it, and it didn't really affect me personally until a few months after Virginia's wedding. That was when I had my first big adventure. I saw it then as one of those serial movies I used to attend with Alma and El on Saturday afternoons at the vaudeville house near St. Charles Place—thrillers where the heroine was always being pursued by bad men, and each installment ended just when it didn't seem there could be any possible escape. The next week it came out all right, of course, but I could never imagine ahead of time that it would. I couldn't imagine the end of my adventure either.

One evening after an ordinary day at school, Amy was just about to go to bed when Mother appeared in her room and said quietly, "Get your coat on quickly and don't stop to ask questions. You and I are going to take a trip, and we'll get our things later." At almost the same moment, someone started to pound on the front door of the apartment. While Jingo stalled by repeatedly saying, "Wait a minute until I put on some clothes," Amy and her mother got out the service entrance to a side street where Daddy waited in a taxi.

The next thing Amy knew she was on a train, with Mother telling her they were being chased by "bad men" called process servers who wanted to make trouble for Daddy by forcing Mother into court. Mother would have to stay out of reach until Daddy had time to make them understand everything was "in perfectly fine shape" at his office. It was all very exciting and Amy loved every minute of it.

A few days later, they had to escape again from a hotel in New York because the "bad men" had found out where they were. By that time, however, Amy and her mother had visited the Statue of Liberty and seen scarabs at the museum— wonderful scarabs that forever after remained associated in Amy's mind with the delights of salmon in aspic eaten beside little brooks in the Japanese Roof Garden of the Ritz Hotel. Imagine brooks and fountains coming out of rocks on a roof in the middle of a big city. Nothing like that had ever entered her life before—that or anything so marvelous as the Chateau Frontenac, a palace such as she had seen only on postcards from Europe.

It was late autumn when they got there, a time of cold winds across the Plains of Abraham, but all the maple leaves were still in wild color. Amy had the time of her young life. Sunny days were spent walking along the ramparts or collecting leaves to press and show her teacher. When it rained, she could spend hours jumping up and down on the couch in their hotel room, imagining herself a horseman riding to battle with Montcalm and Wolfe. Her mother looked a little frantic at times, and when the jumping had gone on pretty long, she would suggest it really wasn't too good for the

*couch's springs. However, she never scolded and only
some time later decided to get a "cozy little place" in
the residential district of town, where Amy could use up
her excess energy roller-skating in the quiet streets
where a child wasn't particularly noticed. When the time
came, Amy hated to leave that lovely hotel, but she
didn't fuss. Mother was obviously worried enough about
the "bad men" who were chasing her.*

*Amy knew she already worried her mother by eating
nothing except boiled potatoes with catsup. She had
really tried to stuff down cinnamon toast with her tea,
but it was a terrible effort, and the very thought of meat
made her want to vomit. She wanted to please her
mother, but she didn't want to get sick and be a bother.
A bother was the last thing Amy wanted to be, because
she was so grateful to her mother for letting her come
along and so happy to have Mother all to herself.*

A.C. Of course, that was before I knew this was just
a prelude to the time I would have Mother completely
to myself for quite a number of years.

A.C. Shortly after we got back from Canada, El went
off to boarding school, and I moved with Mother to
New York where Daddy expected to join us within a few
months and make a fresh start in a new community. It
wasn't long before Thanksgiving, and we had no doubt
he would be with us by then.

For some mysterious reason, however, his move
didn't come off quite according to schedule. Somehow
he was just awfully busy. Of course, he did find time
nearly every week to write a one- or two-page note
telling Mother the current status of his affairs, and in
about one out of every three such notes he promised to
rejoin us very soon—"by the end of October," "in a few
weeks," then "surely not later than Christmas." Those
were the regularly recurring promises, and those were

the things I'm sure he truly believed would come about just as he said. Termination of his affairs in the Middle West was taking a little longer than he had anticipated, that's all. However, as soon as he tied up some loose ends, the family would all be happy together again.

Somehow his affairs didn't ever quite get wound up, though. The Case, through no fault of his own, stretched out into three or four years of court battles, recriminations, counterrecriminations, attacks, and counterattacks. All this was featured in detail by the newspapers, and the publicity led to so much trouble that it took his every minute trying to straighten out the disruption it had caused. One large tabloid, making prime copy of the whole situation, pounded its readers month after month with sensational running commentary on all the alleged illegalities of the business. Most of what it printed was unsubstantiated insinuation, but nothing could be done to stop it, and it caused Daddy a lot of trouble. Readers ate up the insinuations and, considering them facts, stopped patronizing the business. The more ruin stared him in the face, the harder he worked, but it did no good, and his business went steadily down the drain. All this took a great deal of time, as you can well imagine.

As it became more and more evident that he would soon be bankrupt, our father became more and more angry, more and more frantic. There was nothing he could do, however, except rant and rave and try without avail to save a business that had been perfectly sound and legal but was now on the verge of collapse. When the court eventually decided in his favor, acknowledging that the business had indeed been sound and legal, the tabloid failed to mention a single word of the outcome. There was nothing anyone could do about that either, because we have a free press in this country, and a newspaper does not have to publish any news it does not want to publish. All he could do was rant and rave some more.

Daddy was about to explode from the pressure within him. At last he got a break, however. That powerful tabloid, quite by accident, did something that powerful tabloids almost never get caught doing. Somebody in the editorial department made a colossal blunder and printed a statement committing outright, legally action-able libel. They probably failed to insert the words "it is alleged" in front of some outrageous statement. I don't know, but what they came out with was indubitably libelous, and our father had them exactly where he wanted them. In fact, he had them where he had wanted them for a very long time, and nobody in the world was more prepared to do something with a situation like that than Eliot Carpenter Sr.

His money was almost used up by the protracted series of court battles, but by now he had a legitimate case against one of his persecutors, and that persecutor was one of the most solvent tabloids in the entire United States. That newspaper, with its unfounded insinuations, had ruined a million-dollar business. It had threatened the moral reputation of its founder and humiliated his family. Our father was going to get retribution for everything everyone had suffered, and he was going to get plenty of it. He was a very happy man indeed.

Dr. P. Nothing makes a man happier than an oppor-tunity to get just retribution for wrongs suffered through the malicious unfounded attacks of others.

A.C. That was just what he was going to do. The owner of that tabloid knew it, too, and he was scared. He well understood the spot he was in, because his whole battery of highly paid lawyers undoubtedly told him about it. He also had a pretty good idea of what kind of tiger he had by the tail, because as soon as he knew what had happened, he sent emissaries unofficially to approach the man who had been wronged and to sound him out on whether he would accept a quiet settlement of several hundred thousand dollars. Each emissary sent in with such an offer was greeted with a shout of derisive laughter, so the publisher knew he was going to be sued for several million dollars which, in an unbiased court, his victim had an excellent chance of collecting. Of course, it can only be surmised that this is what he thought, but this is what he had good reason to think, because this was indeed the situation.

Under the circumstances, there was really only one thing the publisher could do to save himself, and if what I have heard is true, he did it. He began calling on his vast network of political friends to start paying back past favors. Before long, someone was found who could persuade a minor stockholder of the recently ex-onerated company to charge our father personally with embezzlement. This would entail another long series of court battles and in all probability would cause the libel suit to be deferred indefinitely. Naturally, there had been no publicity about the charge against this paper by any other newspaper in the entire country, and if Daddy was busy trying to save his own neck somewhere else, the publisher could cease to worry. It probably seemed very simple to solve the problem that way.

That is what our father believed happened. That is also what most of his family believed, and oddly enough that is what a lot of other people believed too—many of them people who did not even know Eliot Carpenter personally and had no reason to believe a word he said. These were people who were willing to help him because they knew something about the machine in which he found himself caught. In any case, despite the libel which every lawyer in town admitted had unmistakably been committed, there was one delay after another. While Daddy was fighting in other courts for his honor and his very freedom from prison, his attempts to get the libel suit before a court were delayed for a very long time.

Everyone, including his own wife, advised him to make a deal with that publisher. Everyone advised him to say he would call off the libel suit if the embezzlement charges were withdrawn. However, those who thought he might be persuaded to do that didn't realize the kind of man they were dealing with. Our father was a man who had brought up his children on the slogan, "If you are wrong, admit it and take your losses. If you are right, stick to your guns at all cost." Our father was a man who had grown up venerating a great-uncle who had killed someone in a duel for committing libel against him. Eliot Carpenter Sr. was not about to be a quitter. He stuck to his guns, even though the cost was considerable.

People thought he would surely run out of money to continue fighting such a case, but they were mistaken about that too. They didn't realize that a desperate man in the heat of passion will call upon everyone he knows to help him fight a righteous cause. He will call on his father-in-law, his fraternity brothers, his daughter's new relatives, and everyone with whom he is even remotely connected. He will even call on the eminent father of his son's prep school roommate, whom he knows only slightly. What's more, a lot of people like that will put money into such a cause, at least for a while. Nobody realized either that when such a man is fighting a newspaper known the world over for its corruption and its iron-fisted control over city and state politics, many a liberal young lawyer will offer his services free in the hope of striking a blow for idealism. This was in the early 1930s, but they were doing it even then. In spite of our father's ranting and ravings about "dirty Jew lawyers" and "dirty Irish prostitutes in the judiciary," a lot of young lawyers, both Jewish and Irish, rallied to his cause. So the fight went on.

That is what delayed my father in his plans to return to the bosom of his family. That's the way I heard it, anyway, and if the story seems vague to you, I can only say it seemed a thousand times more vague to me at the time and still isn't very clear, even though by now I know some of the details. Most of the time I knew nothing at all, except that Daddy was due back at any moment, and somehow wasn't able to make it just yet. Ten years after Jingo's wedding, the fight was still going on, and we were still waiting for him.

PART III: YOUNG PEOPLE

5

Growing Up

Amy

Dr. P. During those ten years that your father was fighting in the Middle West, did he have any direct contact with his children at all?

A.C. I think he occasionally wrote my brother about some plans he had for him, but with both him and Jingo the contact was mainly indirect. Indirect as it was, however, its effects were devastating, in spite of his good intentions. Thank goodness, he had no contact with me at all. Sometimes I attribute my survival to that fact.

The memory of my own life during that period is pervaded by a heavy feeling of depression in the pit of my stomach that descends upon me whenever I think about it. Later I became aware of the degree to which I was split into two different people then. I reconnected with a very undepressed side of my adolescent self as well. However, even now when I think back, it is the apathetic, half-alive self of summertime New York that comes back to obliterate the rest. Depression to me is practically synonymous with humid air and sizzling pavements, even though I rarely spent more than a few of the really hot weeks in town. When I turn my thoughts to those years, I immediately think of an evening around the end of June that seems to represent the whole of my relationship to Mother at the time.

I was about fourteen, and the day had been excep-
tionally hot. Mother and I often spent a few hours after
supper taking a ride on the open top of a Fifth Avenue
bus, where there was at least some movement of air,
hoping that our stifling little apartment would cool off
enough to allow sleep by midnight. There we were on
this particular evening, dressed in the dark print foulard
dresses and white kid gloves without which no "lady"
would have been seen dead outside her door in those
days, and I was hatless only because my long hair was
still wet from an afternoon swim at the Y.

*That wet hair symbolized a privilege gained at
considerable cost to both Amy and her mother. Laura
strongly disapproved of using public swimming pools,
feeling that "people who have not had certain advantages" often don't have the same habits of cleanliness as
those more gently bred, and have even been known to
"do things" into such pools to make them anything but
sanitary. She wished her daughter to defer swimming
until she got to camp and could not understand at all
her refusal to make this minor sacrifice. Amy didn't care
much for the Y herself, since in summer it was
overcrowded and heavy with eye-stinging chlorine, but
she would have been willing to swim in a pool of
completely undiluted urine if it had been the only place
to practice her diving. After all, at that point in her life
she did not have the "advantages" of a country estate
with private swimming pool like many of her friends. It
had seemed necessary for her to fight and win the battle
of expediency versus gentility and hygiene, although the
battle drew blood on both sides.*

*Amy had developed into a good natural athlete,
excelling with seemingly effortless grace at almost any
sport she undertook, but actually she put a lot of hard
work into perfecting the skills that earned her many*

honors. That year particularly, she was desperately anxious to win the camp diving meet, and although she was quite confident of having no serious competitors, practicing for this event was of paramount importance in her life.

This issue also had paramount importance to her mother, however. Faced for the first time in her life with relative poverty after a life of considerable afflu- ence, she was determined to bring up her younger daughter in the traditions of her family background, and "maintaining high standards of taste," despite a tempor- ary lack of financial security, was an effort to which she devoted a good deal of energy. When she saw her daughter display a "lack of discrimination," Laura suffered.

Amy, who was devoted to her mother, found it very painful to insist on something that she knew would cause her pain, but there were times when she felt she simply had to, and this had been one of them. Thinking about the sacrifice her mother was making to let her have a whole glorious summer at an expensive camp made Amy consider herself a selfish pig for not giving in on a little thing like going to the Y, but she had been impelled to stick to her point until it was conceded.

If you had asked her why it was so important for her to practice when she was sure of winning anyway, she would have told you that it doesn't pay to be overcon- fident, because you never know what is going to happen to upset your expectations. If she considered you a friend in whom she could really confide, she might also have told you that unless she had taken the trouble to make her actions practically automatic, she often bumbled just when it was most important to succeed, because the very wish to succeed made her tense up. Amy was not without insight into some of her own motivations and tried hard to be honest with herself. However, if you had asked her why winning was so *important in the first place, she would have expressed amazement at the idea that such a wish required an explanation. It would never have occurred to her that the intensity of her wish indicated any lack of self-confidence, and she would have laughed at anyone who suggested such a thing. She would also have been quite unaware that the importance of this issue went beyond the immediate situation into an extended fight against her mother's attempts to cling irrationally to a far-gone past and her mother's tendency to act according to fantasies of what life should be like. Amy carried on this fight instinctively, and her insistence on permission to swim at the Y had been but one of many lifesaving maneuvers designed to correct for herself the unwitting distortions of reality perpetrated by her mother. She was not conscious at all of striving to save her own capacity to be rational.*

Amy and Laura had been living together in New York for the past five years. On that particular evening, the "Battle of the Y" was behind them, and as they settled back to enjoy their bus ride, both were in a good mood. Amy was happy because she would soon be leaving the hot city for a lake in Vermont, and Laura because she had been lucky enough to find a good summer tenant for the Park Avenue apartment. By moving for two months to a small hotel on Lexington, she would clear enough to cover the cost of Amy's camp and to slipcover the living room couch in the fall. She was chattering on about her plans as the bus ran down the avenue.

"So don't worry at all about me, dear. I have lots of things to do, and Kate will be in town too, you know."

Amy, grateful to her mother for reducing her guilt about going away for so long, was very much relieved to hear this. Kate was the only real friend her Mother had in New York, among a number of quite superficial social acquaintances, and they got along famously. An erst-

while southern belle, Kate was married to a rich man twice her age who had been expected to die years ago but was still hanging on in his eighties. She was slightly on the loud side but enormously good fun to be with, managing to keep not only Laura but also Amy well supplied with belly laughter about her endless adventures with all kinds of men. A most unlikely friend for Laura to have found, but they had been drawn together in the unaccountable way of complete opposites and never tired of each other's company. Although Amy sometimes guiltily wondered what Kate saw in her prissy little mother, Kate was obviously fond of the delicate doll who was such a good audience for her tales. She lived in a vast Louis Quinze apartment at the Park Lane Hotel with her senile spouse and was apparently delighted at every opportunity to get out of it with an undemanding companion. The two women spent hours window-shopping together and never seemed to run out of anecdotes to tell each other about the glories of their respective pasts.

It suddenly occurred to Amy that her mother and Kate might actually be glad to have her off their hands for a while, and her relief became tinged with distress. Much as she hated the idea of having her mother dependent on her for company, she hated even more the idea that her mother might not need her at all. This thought she immediately put out of her mind with conscious effort.

"I do wish you could get out of town a little, Mother. Couldn't you spend some weekends with Jingo? At least you'd get some fresh air."

"Well, perhaps I will now and then. But you know, dear, married people really prefer to be with their own friends. I always love to see Jingo, and she is very hospitable, but we have an entirely different way of doing things, and I think we are both happier if we lead our own lives in our own way."

This was Mother's way of saying that at Jingo's house on Long Island there was far too much drinking and smoking for her taste, and Amy knew this was how she felt. She herself thought Jingo and her friends too glamorous for anything and adored visiting there where everyone considered her clever and amusing and treated her as though she were very sophisticated. She understood that the whole atmosphere made her mother uncomfortable, however, and the suggestion was only a way of expressing concern. Her mother, who recognized this, went on with her own prattle.

"Anyway, you know your Daddy's plea will be coming through very soon. He said in his last letter he'll probably be ready to come east before the middle of August."

"Oh my God, Mother!"

"Don't swear, dear, it really isn't becoming to a lady, you know. You don't have to take God's name in vain because you don't like something. Anyway, Amy, I really can't understand you. You don't seem to have any faith in your father. I have always said that loyalty was one of your most admirable qualities, but the one person in the world to whom you owe the greatest loyalty, you treat with nothing but contempt. Your poor father has been working his fingers to the bone for seven long years, just trying to get things straightened out so his family can have the very best of everything, and you act as if he were some kind of a criminal. You really aren't being very understanding, honey. Your father has been through some terrible times, and he needs the love and support of his children, not this supercilious attitude you all have toward him. I don't know what gets into you."

By that time, Amy had lost all pleasure in the ride. Her head had begun to ache, and there were knots in her stomach—anger interlaced with pity, exasperation, and despair. Why couldn't Mother see? Was she going to

*spend the rest of her life in a state of suspended
animation, waiting for someone who would never come?*

*Amy could remember very clearly the first time it
happened, soon after their own move to New York. He
was to arrive that night, and they were both so excited.
Mother had nearly killed herself fixing up the apartment
and preparing all his favorite things for dinner, and there
they were, Mother in a beautiful blue dress and Amy in
black velvet. It was just like that awful scene in* Stella
Dallas, *when nobody came to the party, except that
finally somebody did come—a boy with a telegram.*

*By the third such occasion, all the love in Amy's
heart for the handsome, exciting Daddy had turned to
cold hatred. Jingo just shrugged her shoulders and said,
"What did you expect?" but Amy's fury was of a
different magnitude—the fury of a woman scorned,
although she sincerely believed it to be born purely
out of compassion for what her mother was going
through. She felt misery and loathing for the father so
unconcerned about his family's feelings. However, right
along with those feelings went something even more
painful to tolerate, for she also recognized a good deal
of anger and disgust toward her mother who was already
a victim, and Amy hated herself for feeling that way.*

*She had come to experience the sense of helpless rage
that all feel who think themselves rational and find
themselves up against someone with impregnable, blind
faith, based on little else than a strong wish. If her
mother had screamed and raged, Amy would have been
for her all the way. If she had admitted defeat, given up,
and divorced her tantalizing husband, Amy would have
accepted the situation and given every possible ounce of
support, but this absolutely ridiculous, stubborn insistence on denying the obvious reality was beyond bearing.
At times Amy had flown into a frenzy in which she
literally beat her head against her bedroom wall or
chewed holes in her pillow, but no amount of rage and*

frustration could change the situation. Such outbursts usually took place in private, but there were times when her feelings were simply too strong to be contained. Then, in full awareness that she was only making things harder for her mother, Amy had to say something, piling guilt upon an already intolerable burden of emotion. Like now. Of all times, when she most wanted to be nice to her mother, she had let loose and said "My God" starting all this. She wanted very badly to undo what she had just done, but unfortunately it seemed that the bitter, underground side of Amy was in the saddle, because her conciliatory remark came out like another accusation.

"O.K., Mother. O.K. Perhaps this time he will come, and we'll all have to admit we were wrong. After all, he did manage to get you out of that mess he got you into, which was nothing short of a miracle."

"That mess he got me into! Really, Amy. He certainly did get me out of what you so charitably call his mess. It got cleared up just as soon as the court understood how your Daddy had things organized. You know, dear, people sometimes don't understand how your Daddy's mind works."

Here a rather wistful note crept into Laura's voice.

"Your father is a genius, you know, and people like that think big. They can't always be paying attention to little details and have to depend on other people to see that their ideas are worked out properly. You can't expect ordinary people to understand. But his own children should be more understanding. You should know better than to be so bitter against your father. You are understanding enough about everyone else. He is one of the kindest, most hard-working men in the world and would no more break the law than he could fly. You will see, mark my word. He is going to recover damages for those vicious, unfounded attacks that wrecked his wonderful business. Any day now it may

come through, and we will be back on our feet. Then we won't have to depend so much on the generosity of your grandfather."

Amy was thinking she would rather have a father who was a human being and not a genius, but by now she was sufficiently in control not to say it. A moment later, she found to her surprise, and much against her better judgment, that she herself couldn't help feeling a spark of hope that maybe the money would come through after all. It could happen, even if it wasn't likely. Feeling slightly heartened, she used her customary ploy of attempting to lighten the atmosphere by changing the subject, and as usual she was successful. Good humor was restored, and as the bus started to travel the home route, they chatted about trivialities and felt very companionable. Gradually Laura changed the topic.

"You children have always loved the country so much. I've been thinking about the possibility of getting a little house not too far from New York, where we can get in for some of the advantages of the city but be away from all the dirt and noise. Of course, I expect your Daddy will soon have his settlement, but just in case there are any more delays, what we pay for rent would probably buy us a nice little place somewhere. Virginia says she has a friend who knows about an old Colonial house near the Berkshires that may be coming up for sale, and we might be able to get it for a rather small down payment. It's a real farm too, and we could raise vegetables, just like the old days."

So they have already been planning definite possibilities! Amy got an immediate image of her mother in overalls, hoeing the cabbages, and broke into a broad grin. It was a nice thought, though. She was just about to make an enthusiastic response when she suddenly felt sick at the realization that she would have to change schools. The light went out of her eyes, and a kind of *dullness settled upon her. Mother would never have considered this if the money situation hadn't been pretty bad and had obviously made up her mind to do it as soon as she found a suitable place. It was just a matter of time. There was no use saying how she felt because it wouldn't do any good, and her distress would just upset her mother. She might as well start getting used to the idea, but the thought of changing schools was pure torture.*

At that point in her life, there were two Amys. One was a quiet, conflict-ridden girl who spent evenings and weekends isolated with her mother in a small apartment and who tried, in spite of occasional blowups, to make as few waves as possible. The other was a lively, vital girl who lived and had her being at school or camp, where she kicked up a great deal of dust and enjoyed every minute of it. She had achieved a position of leadership among her contemporaries by assuming the role of group clown, while at the same time managing to endear herself to most of the surrounding adults by maintaining an excellent academic record and showing an alert, intelligent interest in people and activities. It was true that the faculty members were often hard pressed to control her mischievous behavior, but Amy was fortunately enrolled in a first-class private institution, where each girl received understanding and individualized handling. The kindly, efficient schoolmistresses of those days were not familiar with terms like "behavior disorder," but when they saw one, they certainly did recognize a "high-strung, sensitive youngster who is having trouble at home" and were well aware that she needed their patience and forbearance. Actually, they often found Amy's pranks amusing and showed this in spite of attempts to maintain a properly stern attitude. "Attention-getting behavior" was quite understandable in "one who has lost her father" and did not really make them angry most of the time.

Those tolerant and warm-hearted ladies did not understand that Amy's ceaseless attempts to get herself scolded and punished by those who gave evidence of caring about her was a form of love-play which aroused in her a considerable degree of erotically tinged excitement. They recognized only her obvious quest for mothering and responded to it according to the intensity of their own individual needs to mother someone.

When an adult who needs to be motherly connects with an attractive child who wants to be mothered, strong attachments ensue. With her peculiar radar, Amy had been guided toward two particular adults with such needs, and she had been able to sense not only the exact degree of dependency each could comfortably tolerate but also just how much affection and what kind of entertainment each needed in return. Both at school and at camp she had attached herself to a loving, intellectually stimulating woman who found her not only eager for affection but interesting, companionable, and mature in her understanding of people. Both these women had offered her sincere friendship, and from each of them Amy received life-giving transfusions of down-to-earth good sense, humor, and intellectual integrity whenever her blood tended to become vitiated by an overdose of euphemisms. Their respect and admiration counteracted her sense of innate badness, and being able to share her feelings freely with someone who understood and even reciprocated with confidences of her own was the main source of nourishment for her emotional life. The thought of being separated from either one of these auxiliary friend-mothers was almost more than she could bear.

Since leaving the Middle West five years earlier, there had been no men in Amy's environment except the husbands of Jingo's friends who kidded her along and enjoyed making a brief fuss over the little sister. She had met no boys her own age, and although she concealed it very well by talking knowingly of sex with her sister and her own peers, Amy had become very shy with males, avoiding any situation where she might be thrown into contact with a member of this now-alien species. All her intense feelings were concentrated on her three mothers who were the center of her universe.

It would be impossible to explain such a split in loyalties to her own mother. All she could do was choke on her sorrow and hope nobody would notice. In a rather small voice, packed with as much ersatz pleasure as could be mustered, she said, "That sounds lovely, Mother! I don't suppose it will be right away, though, will it? You know, I have a good chance of making the basketball varsity next fall."

"Well, honey, I don't suppose we will actually move for at least a year. I've only begun to think about it, and of course we will have to find just the right place. But I know no matter where you go to school, you will soon be on the varsity. Daddy and I are very proud of all the things you do so well."

Amy knew that Daddy had no more idea of what she was doing than the man in the moon, and that if he was proud of her, it was because of some image in his own mind that had nothing to do with what she was really like. If Mother wanted to pretend, however, it was all right. Maybe it made her feel better to think he cared about what his daughter was doing. Mother herself didn't know a basketball from a Ping-Pong ball, but she clearly wanted Amy to be happy and was usually pleased with anything that seemed to make her so. Anyway, it looked as though there would be a reprieve before the ax fell, and Amy firmly willed herself to put it out of mind so that it wouldn't spoil her summer.

By the time they returned to the apartment, the suppression of her unhappiness was reasonably success-ful, and Amy was able to enjoy the nightly ritual of

*crackers and milk with her mother before going to bed.
She had trouble falling asleep, though, and could
accomplish this only after indulging in a fantasy that
gave her a warm glow and was eventually relaxing. It
was about a girl in a reformatory being beaten into
submission by a cruel schoolmaster. Or was it a
schoolmistress? That part wasn't quite clear in her mind.*

A.C. A year later, I started a three-year stretch in the
prison of a fashionable girls' boarding school, while
Mother made preparations for a move to New England.
That school was a disaster area as far as I was concerned,
and I just barely managed to survive. For the whole
three years I wrote pretty regularly to my friend Marty
because I was so starved for affection and shaky in
self-esteem. However, in college I picked up another
loving family who restored my feeling of being human.

Dear Mrs. Marten,

I always mean to start the New Year by writing
you immediately, but as usual I haven't had time.
Now I'm writing in study hall, which really isn't
the school's idea of being a "good example to the
younger girls!"

I came back after the holidays utterly discouraged, really thinking I couldn't stick out the term.
I had such a marvelous time visiting in New York
during the week of the "Metropolitan" dance. It
was really the first time I ever got rushed, and boy,
did I love it! At the end, on Long Island, it was
especially great. The people there, at least the ones
I come in contact with, live just the kind of life I'd
adore! (Mother says it's all so superficial, but I
think it's gay, which is more than things are around
home, I can tell you!) I do suppose going out every
night might get tiresome, as Jingo says it has, but

you could always stop if you wanted to, and it's so much fun while it lasts!

Well, that's over, and school has begun again for fair. I went to see Miss Elder yesterday about my report card. She was sweet, but the whole thing made me very uncomfortable.

She said my work was excellent, and that I was very intelligent, but that I seemed to have no sense of school spirit. (Grrrr! School spirit! I *hate* this school!) Anyway, I should be "a model" and could be such a "good influence," so why do I act like such an ass? (Of course she didn't say *that*! She's much too "refeened," but that's what she meant.)

Dear Mrs. Marty! I wish I could talk to you! You always sound so sensible and matter-of-fact! Maybe you could help me to understand why that's the only way I feel I can get by. Everything seems to stand in the way of my being natural and acting the way I know I ought to act at the advanced age of seventeen, so I end up continuing to be cutup, and everyone laughs and thinks I'm funny when really I don't feel funny inside at all.

I wish I could talk to Miss Elder, but she just makes me feel foolish. Her parting remark was, "We all feel your charm, but charm is not enough. You have to take responsibility." I really wish I could, but most of the rules are so ridiculous that the only way I can keep from blowing up is to make fun of the whole school.

What is charm? She says I have it, and I guess I must have something that makes people like you able to stand me, but I can't imagine what it is. I hope I don't let compliments like that make me nasty and conceited. Sometimes I wonder just how much flattery a fairly strong but not extra-reinforced character can stand! I want people to like me, but it seems revolting to be looking for admiration so much of the time. Ugh! What a mess I really am!

Don't stop letting me talk to you, though! Somehow I always feel better after I've written to you. How I wish I'd never had to leave the Academy!

Love,
Amy

Dear Mrs. Marty,

Another gym meet is over, and exams will soon be beginning, so I'd better write while I still have a chance. I can barely believe I have only one more term! I've tried to pull myself together and act more like a senior, but I'm sure everyone just thinks I'm sick or something!

Last night a bunch of us got into a terrific theological discussion, where nobody had any real idea what they were talking about, but it made me realize I'm quite at sea. What on earth do I believe?

Apparently there are a good many fatalists, led by Eileen, who think everything is planned out ahead of time, and our every motion is foreordained. That seems to me a most unambitious way to think! Why should anyone make an effort to get ahead in the world, or work to become someone, if they know their destiny is planned ahead and nothing they can do makes any difference? I asked Suzie if she believed that we were ordained from aeon zero to be walking up a hill pulling a sled on February 28 of this year, and she wasn't quite sure. She said she guessed the little petty things weren't really fated—only matters of birth, death, etc. How can anyone be so contradictory? If the important things are planned, why not the trivial ones? I hate people who don't make sense! (Except, of course, I don't either!)

Personally, I think you are given your life, but your character and place in the world are made by yourself and your ancestors. When one man has worked himself up—fought the world, and overcome difficulties, I suppose his children are better situated than those of one who had no ambition— but your own character is made by you, don't you think?

Is it just ignorance to be an atheist? I've grown up in such a sticky, narrow religious atmosphere that I know I'm inclined to rebound in the other direction, but there seem to be plenty of intelligent people who feel as I do. The difference, of course, is that they know why, and I have no idea at all. I can't seem to believe in any person-like God who rules one's life. It seems to me that belief in God has grown up around the need of human beings to worship something they can speculate about, to have someone they think can cure all their troubles. I wish I could believe, because I sure need a lot of things cured, but it just doesn't make sense to think of any kind of mind that would be able to keep track of every little detail that's going on everywhere, all at the same time!

And afterlife? If the soul lives on, what becomes of it? Does it take another body, as the Indians believe, or just fly around loose? People that would scorn believing in ghosts and spirits do actually think that only the body dies! Mother, for instance. She does a lot of talking about "divine mind," and "mind never dies," etc., but she doesn't even try to explain what becomes of it. God! I hate to be so in the dark about so many things!

Suzie and I also talked a little about companionate marriage. Marriage of any kind terrifies me! I can't imagine ever loving anyone enough to "go the limit" with him! The whole idea revolts me! Everybody does it, so I suppose it must be natural, but I do wonder if I'll ever love anyone that much. If I did, I don't think I'd want to think we could split up any time we didn't agree on something.

You must love Uncle Dan like that, because I assume everyone who stays married must like it. It makes me feel a little queer to mention such things, and I probably couldn't do it if we were talking face to face. There is some value in having to write letters instead of talk, I guess. (But not much! I'd much rather see you and can't wait until summer!) Mother says we probably can afford to let me come to Maine for a visit if you really want me! Are you sure you do, and weren't just being kind because you know how much I want to? It was such a beautiful suggestion, but I don't want to be a pain in the neck to you and Uncle Dan.

If you have managed to plow through a letter this long, you are a wonder. Well, of course you are!

Dearest love,
Amy

Dear Mrs. Marty,

We start College Boards next week, and this will probably be my last chance to write. All I can really think of to say anyway is Whoopee! Whoopee! Whoopee! In less than a month I'll be out of this rattrap forever, and nobody will ever again be able to give me a demerit for talking in the hall between classes or whispering in study hall!

Mother and Jingo came up for the senior play, and everything is all sweetness and light again with Miss Elder. She told Mother I'd "matured" more in three years than any girl she'd ever had, and Mother was very happy with her baby child! Jingo left early—she was going out with the friends she is visiting and said she was too recently out of school herself to prefer a school punch to champagne. Mother, of course, was all rattled at having her put such ideas into my head!

As a matter of fact, Jingo gave me the impression that she was utterly bored. She must be disgusted with me, or doesn't approve, or something! She wasn't listening half the time and obviously couldn't wait to get away. I can't imagine what I've done to make her mad, unless it was a remark I made to some of her friends that I thought we were really in different generations. They thought it was funny, and I can't see why she should mind that so much, but something is certainly bothering her. Ah me! Time Heals All, I guess! See you soon!

Love,
Amy

A.C. At the time, I didn't know about Jingo's troubles. When I finally heard, I was hurt for a while that she hadn't told me, but one gets used to not being told things.

Eliot Jr.

A.C. From the time we left St. Charles Place, I saw almost nothing of my brother until after he graduated from college. Even during summers we were usually in different places, and at times like Christmas or Easter vacations we met only in passing. Although at high school and college ages we sometimes went to the same parties, our friends were entirely different, and, as a matter of fact, I specifically asked him not to dance with me more than once or twice during the evening for fear people would think I was "using" him to keep from "getting stuck," as some girls used their brothers. I knew almost nothing about his life until years later, but I can give you a fairly accurate account now of what happened to him.

I've already told you that he went to boarding school shortly before Mother and I moved to New York. How that ever came about, I can only hazard a guess.

As you know, in the 1920s admission to certain long-established prep schools was not readily obtained, especially by boisterous entrepreneurs from the Middle West like our father. Men who wanted their sons to attend the particular school that Daddy picked out for El were apt to enroll them while they were still infants and even then were not sure the school would accept them when they reached an appropriate age. Daddy managed to enroll his son, however, even though Eliot Jr. was already a little past the usual age for admission. Perhaps it would be more accurate to say that Mother managed to perform that miraculous feat, because I'm sure that's who put the deal across. Her father had the influential friends who wrote glowing recommendations, and I'm sure it was her gentle charm and obvious good breeding that mesmerized the austere and dignified headmaster. How she did it I don't know, but she

obviously persuaded him to disregard very grave reserva-
tions about taking a boy whose academic decline had
been so marked in the previous year. She probably had
him sharing her belief that the whole problem was
"growing pains." Whatever she did, however, it was her
husband who produced the motivating force. In any
case, a miracle was performed somehow, and Eliot
Carpenter Jr. was admitted to one of the most exclusive
institutions of learning in the entire United States.

Dr. P. The same school that had been attended by
your father's first boss?

A.C. The very same. That was where one could attain
the "finest development," and that is where he wanted
his son to go.

El himself felt by no means at home amid ivy-covered
walls and tolling chapel bells. However, to the best of
his knowledge at the time, he was fired by a wish to
please his father and make the most of a fine opportunity. So far as he knew, he wanted to be like the boys
with whom he studied and played in those exalted
surroundings. He wanted so much to be like them, in
fact, that he systematically set about erasing in himself
any trace of individuality, and he managed so well to
accomplish this goal that he erased every trace of "self"
that had survived his accident. Eliot Jr. became the shell
of a boy, a well-polished, stiff, rather ornamental shell
who, although colored like the others, bore in reality no
resemblance to them at all.

Dr. P. In other words, he became a caricature of
everything he thought they stood for.

A.C. He became an arrogant, intolerant, impossible
snob, which I suppose is saying the same thing.
Nevertheless, he managed to survive, and throughout his
prep school years he encountered no one discerning
enough to recognize that he was dead inside.

Dr. P. I suppose the other boys gave him a bad time
of it.

A.C. On the contrary. Except for the usual teasing and hazing, El found reasonable acceptance among members of his class in spite of his dreamy bumbling. Except for occasional sarcastic ribbing from a games master unable to comprehend a boy who so inevitably tripped over his own feet, he also got from his teachers a puzzled tolerance and passing grades. Even he himself was not aware of his alienation from the whole scene and, if asked whether he had any problems, would probably have said merely that he was not particularly interested in his work. He had wanted to take chemistry, but Daddy made him take Greek instead.

Dr. P. Nobody in his environment understood the tremendous force of inner resistance against which he had to work or the tenacity with which he was unknowingly seeking self-defeat?

A.C. No. He covered up pretty well, and in those days the masters in schools like his were not very psychologically oriented. By the time of graduation, he had even achieved a modicum of recognition for creating one very creditable piece of sculpture in the classical tradition and winning the school poetry prize for lyrical verse inspired by Keats. However, he had learned very little except how to suffer in silence and was admitted to the university of his father's choice largely because almost anyone from his school was automatically accepted by any college he wished to attend.

Throughout his first university years, the pattern remained essentially unchanged. Masquerading as a participant in the life around him, El maintained a place in the clique of sophisticated boys who went from his school into the most exclusive social clubs—a place maintained by virtue of the slightly patronizing tolerance allotted to those who, in spite of gaucherie and ineptitude, still "belong" enough to escape ridicule and rejection. Later, finding friends among the artists and poets at the university, he managed to alienate them too. His manner seemed to disturb even sensitive souls like himself, perhaps because the completely passive way in which he accepted failure as inevitable showed from behind a bland facade.

Dr. P. Threatening to stir up in those others similar doubts about their own strength.

A.C. No doubt. He usually managed to attract women strongly at first, but when this romantic-looking, dark-eyed Adonis remained politely impervious to charms most blatantly flaunted, he was apt to end up on the receiving end of scorn, if not actual hatred, from those he would not seduce.

Dr. P. Was he homosexually inclined, do you think?

A.C. Not that anyone knew of, least of all himself. No, but I'll tell you more about that later. At the university he was exposed to a wealth of stimulating courses, given by the greatest of great men, and he couldn't help passively absorbing some content from each by a form of osmosis. The partly assimilated conglomeration of unrelated facts and ideas that did seep into his brain was sufficient to establish in his own mind, as well as in the minds of others, his reputation as a literary man of scholarly bent. However, it was not strong enough to replenish his ever-dwindling stores of mental energy.

By the middle of his second year, Eliot Jr. was about as amorphous intellectually as a young man could possibly be. Although he realized that all was not quite as it should be with his development, recognition of how truly amorphous he actually was came about in a rather peculiar way.

From the time he was fifteen, thoughts about a girl named Molly so completely dominated the mind of Eliot Jr. that every other thought or idea had effectively been kept at bay. At the time, Molly was the undisputed

belle of New York subdeb society and progressed
rapidly within the next few years to the position of
number one debutante of her season. She was the kind
of girl with whom every man who had even heard of her
was in love, and who at parties danced no longer than
ten seconds with any one of the congregation forming
her own private stag line along a whole wall of the Ritz
ballroom. Eliot had stood in that stag line—in fact, had
devoted himself exclusively to it at every dance he
attended—and had received for his devotion the same
gracious smiles that Molly bestowed upon everyone in
pants along the entire Eastern Seaboard. Molly had
smiled at Eliot and had been friendly at a number of
smaller parties; in so doing, she had installed herself as
an almost ineradicable subject for his fantasy. In fact,
she had inspired innumerable feats of heroism, myriads
of noble deeds, and enough acts of love to keep Eliot
absolutely preoccupied for at least five years of his life.

While sauntering through the streets of his university
town one afternoon in late autumn, Eliot was idly
dreaming of Molly as he was wont to do. There was a
smokiness in the on-coming twilight, and brown leaves
whisked along the sidewalk. As he walked, sunk deep
within his own thoughts, the daylight darkened, street
lights came on, and house windows winked orange
through their drawn shades. The old, intimate quality so
characteristic of New England pervaded the damp cold
and touched Eliot to a point where he actually
perceived the world around him. Suddenly he stopped
short. It was a paralyzing moment. In that instant, Eliot
realized that the fantasy about Molly had ended a few
minutes earlier, and suddenly he knew there would be
no new episodes and no revisions of episodes past,
because everything there was to be said had been said,
and there was nothing more there. As he stood there in
the semidarkness, Eliot realized there was not a thought

of any kind present in his mind. Molly was gone, and once his revery about a virtually nonexistent love affair had ended, he was as empty and hollow as a drum. In that moment, Eliot became aware that five years of his life had gone down the drain. He had learned nothing, and from all the advantages handed to him on a silver platter he had taken none at all.

It was in the wake of this humiliating observation that he decided to accept his father's offer of a junior year of travel to "broaden his mind." Perhaps he could recover his losses in Europe and make something of the intellectual opportunities he had so far lavishly wasted.

Daddy had not seen El for seven years, and although there had been some communication between them, largely mediated by Mother, he had not the slightest idea of what his son was really like. However, he had a very clear picture of what his son *should* be like and planned accordingly. A man of refined, cultured background should obviously have the advantages of *Wanderjahre*, so he proposed the idea to El and El compliantly began to wander.

Once again he was alone with his thoughts for months, although by that time he had been exposed to words of philosophers and poets, visions of artists and architects, and was himself "clothed in the mantle of a budding poet." He still had no real idea of how thin was the veneer covering his uncertainties and, strolling among the relics of past cultures, felt he might hear through the ears of great men, see through the eyes of genius, something to convey meaning to his own life. There was no doubt in his mind that men of vision from other times and places could point the way to his own soul. With all his heart, Eliot hoped to make their way his own.

Dr. P. By that time in his career, he had obviously acquired a profound distrust of his own way.

A.C. From childhood on Daddy had drummed into him a concept of thinking for himself, of learning to make decisions and forming his own opinions. The only trouble was that every time he made a decision or formed an opinion, his father reversed it or told him it didn't indicate the "finest development." Daddy couldn't even imagine El's viewpoint, let alone understand it, so his invariable conclusion was that his son had made a great mistake. El had learned thoroughly to despise his own opinions because they were not worthy of a Man, and having no ability to think for himself, he would obviously have to accept guidance from those who knew.

Dr. P. That is a fine example of what I call "masked authoritariansim"—"make your own decisions so long as you decide to do what I want you to do."

A.C. That's exactly what he was exposed to all through his youth. Nobody could have tried harder to do it than he did, either. Steeping himself in the moods of bygone centuries, he brooded upon the spirit of the Middle Ages, trying to find his soul as men of those times found God—through Gothic spires and stained glass windows. He "searched for sublime and mystical messages crying out from wood and canvas" and often did thrill to the glorious forms and colors of Old Masters. Even then, however, something was missing. Standing before one marvel after another, looking for his soul therein, he confronted attitudes so utterly alien that he only sank lower and lower in the increasing knowledge that their spirit could never enter him. It became more and more clear with each passing day that he was destined forever to remain a nothing.

Then one day, wandering aimlessly through a gallery in a state of apathy and near despair, he had for a second time in his life an experience that took on the character of a revelation. Eliot found himself quite by chance standing before the "Sunflowers" of Van Gogh, and in that moment something cataclysmic happened to strike a deep chord within him. He had wandered through great cities and beautiful small towns without lighting a single spark. He had stood in cathedrals, castles, plazas, and parks seeking something that could never be found. In that instant, standing before the picture of a simple flower, Eliot knew his search had ended. In that moment, and in that place, he felt that he had found Himself.

Later, Eliot felt that he had been pretty naïve, flying into an ecstasy of discovery over something already familiar to many of his peers. At the time, however, the sight of those swirling yellow petals opened up a whole world in an instant. "Sunflowers! They bloomed wild and bewildering from a pot without depth against a blue so clear that at sight of it, shadows in [his] mind felt a broom sweep through, dismantling cobwebs to reveal the brightness of a spacious room." As "tongues of fire leapt out from the gold, [he] felt a melting inside, dissolving [his] past and brewing it into a pattern of new loveliness." That's the way he described it later. For him the Gothic no longer existed, and the Renaissance faded away. He had been touched by a strange force, and that force plummeted him into the modern world at last.

This episode was the precursor of other intense emotional reactions with far-reaching consequences. Stunned with awe at the brilliance with which a simple flower, loved since his childhood, had been conceived by a genius, Eliot reexperienced what he first felt when gazing at lilies in a woodland pool and reopened for a while the area of aesthetic feeling dormant within him since the age of five.

After that experience in Munich, El for the first time in many years felt strong enough to "do battle against the wall of iron" clamped on his intelligence in the past. Having woefully neglected his regular studies in Europe, he decided to spend the summer in Briarpatch catching up on required reading, and on the way, he stopped to see his father who had become quite a stranger.

Eliot had always been very fond of Daddy. There had been moments when he "nearly foundered upon the shoals of [his] father's positive impact," but those moments had been brief, accompanied simultaneously by sincere affection. In his autobiography he describes dreams in which his father appeared as a tyrant—Hitler or von Hindenburg in a spear-topped helmet of steel. When his father appeared as himself, just innocently walking along, it caused in El a "virtual spasm of constriction and frustration," enough to turn the dream into a nightmare.

Dr. P. The deeper layers of his mind contained profound hurts caused by that dominating man.

A.C. Opposed to this, however, was the waking mind, the self of the morning. That self, less all-knowing and less concerned with the basic, was quite capable of seeing his father as a man who meant well, who would never have hurt his son if he had had any idea what he was doing, and who had, according to his own vision, done everything possible to make his son happy. That self cared for his father and was very glad to be seeing him again after so many years of separation.

El only barely mentioned what occurred between them, but I'm sure I can describe it to you just as it must have been. Knowing both him and my father, knowing how we all reacted when we were with him, I can see it as clearly as if I had been there myself.

Eliot Sr. was at the station, eager and excited as a child, pacing the platform with impatient strides, frustrated that the train would not submit more quickly to his will. Beaming with pleasure, he grasped his son's hand, and the intensity of his desire to please was almost pathetic to see.

"Well, Mac! Well, well, well! How good to see you! You have become a fine man, Mac! Fine! Splendid! We will go to Fritz's for lunch where we can talk. The finest Wiener schnitzel in the world! The very finest! You will see! I'll give you such a meal as you never had in Paris or Rome!"

Charming and gallant as always, that was his father. They literally blew into a restaurant, where Eliot Sr. greeted the waiter as an old friend.

"Here is the son I've been promising you, Fritz! Just back from Europe. Look at him, Fritz! Isn't he a fine fellow? Eh? You bet, Fritz!"

All in his booming voice, and the pride on his face brought smiles to the faces of other patrons who at first had looked up startled and rather annoyed.

"We will have your best Wiener schnitzel, Fritz! Nothing but the best for my son! Nobody makes it like you do. I told him—nothing better anywhere in the world, that's for sure!"

He wanted to hear about his son's travels, of course, and as Eliot Jr. was clearing his throat to begin, his father was off, telling him about the skulduggery of politicians who were making it hard for him to wind up his affairs in the Middle West. Louder and louder he ranted, and the more the volume increased, the lower his son sank in the chair. Nothing had changed since his childhood so far as his father's behavior was concerned, and nothing had changed about the way Eliot Jr. reacted. It was all he could do to get through lunch without strangling on his delicious Wiener schnitzel.

Finally it came time for the train and blessed release from his agonized conflict of feelings. Eliot Sr. jumped up apologetically, clapping him on the back and telling him again how good it had been to have a chat. He was glad to see what a fine son he had and would try to get away for an occasional weekend in the country. They would go for a swim, and when it was over, he would hear more about Eliot's travels. They parted in a state of mutual affection, he to go his way, his son to go the other.

Of course he never came to the country, any more than he had when we were children, but when he said it, he was absolutely sure he would. It was all very clear in his mind's eye—how they would take a swim and walk together through the woods to the cabin, a father and his son close as only a father and son can be. He saw them sitting by the fire in the cool of the evening, talking man to man of things that concerned them, and sharing views on life and the state of the world. That picture was no doubt crystal clear in his mind, shadowed by no awareness at all that it had never been like that or ever would be. By the time he left the restaurant, the picture had surely faded, and he was already thinking about the latest brief he had to file. I'm sure he never knew for a second that there had been no conversation, because before he left the restaurant, he had ceased to think about the meeting with his son entirely. By the time he caught a taxi, his mind was already completely occupied with something entirely different.

El spent the summer in Briarpatch, seeing its beauty again through eyes of his own, without the intrusion of borrowed imagery from poets and painters. Under the inspiration of one who could say, "I have painted sunflowers as I saw them," he too suddenly felt confident of senses trustworthy enough to perceive the world around him and returned for his senior year at the university fired with confidence and alive with a degree of energy he had almost never known. Not long afterward, however, he had another strange experience, one again tapping unknown areas of emotion and seeming to bring warning as well as promise.

One Indian summer day, Eliot was struck by a weird mood of heightened tension which, to the best of his knowledge, bore no relationship to anything at all in his life at the moment. A kind of spell had been cast upon him, a peculiar state of restless disquiet that defied description and could not be dispelled by willpower or distracting activity. Finally, since nothing else seemed possible, he lay down upon his bed, folded his arms, and thought about nothing at all.

Suddenly it happened. Eliot felt almost possessed by another self as words began to pour through his brain in a bubbling flood. Without effort or warning, without idea, plan, or intention the words became a poem, not a wild tumult of emotion at all, but a rather simple little verse that had only to be written as it appeared full-fledged. It was not even a very good verse by Eliot's standards, but it was as sincere a work of letters as had ever jumped from the depths of his mind and was undoubtedly the first really creative experience of his life.

The poem that came out was in the form of a dirge, a lament for the north woods and beauty rediscovered after a period of blindness. It was a love poem with a sigh of sadness, addressed to experiences in which "awakening also carried a promise that self-revelation might not be an unmitigated blessing." A warning was in the poem that creativity might exact a price—a price of recognizing dark places within himself—and that his search for awareness might lead far from anything he had previously known. From somewhere in the center of Eliot's being had come an autumn wistfulness, and with it came the knowledge that once free from the protection of ivy-covered walls, good times might again recede.

Jingo and Sid

A.C. Jingo was the one I knew best during that period. She lived on Long Island where I frequently spent weekends, and even though I was just the "little sister" for a long time, she talked to me quite a lot. Mostly she talked about her rages at Daddy and her worries about what would happen to Mother, but later she talked some about her own marriage, although not about her sex life until much later. Anyway, I always had a fair idea of what was going on in her life up to a certain point in history. Beyond that point, I had no idea what was going to happen until it actually did.

When I think about it now, Jingo and Sid's whole life together seems absolutely fantastic to me. If you were to try with all your might to think of the most unlikely marital partners in the world, you could hardly come up with a pair that filled the bill better than they did. To the same degree that Jingo and Alex were alike, Jingo and Sid were different. There wasn't a single thought, attitude, or point of taste on which they agreed, nor a single aspect of experience that they had shared in any way before they met, except for the fact that neither one had ever known or imagined what it might be like to be financially insecure.

Sid was a playboy who had rollicked through a small college playing expert golf or bridge and cracking a book only in extremis. Now a banker living on Long Island, his life consisted of horses, setters, and sailboats, bathtub gin and orange juice, bread with every meal, and sporty blond women in tweeds with hearty laughs and very few brains. Jingo was dark, dainty, and given to wearing extremely feminine, European-styled clothing. She was completely unathletic, loathed games of any sort, and was, as I have noted, a voracious reader and conversationalist who had hitherto cared only for slightly effete, intellectual men. The only time she had ever ridden a horse he took a bite out of her shoulder which had taken a long time healing, and every time she had been in a small boat, she had been seasick. Much of her interest in Paris had been focused on learning to prepare exotic French recipes, matching them with appropriate fine wines, and she was irresistibly drawn to Pekingese dogs. What these two could ever have seen in each other would be hard to imagine, and it is only the unaccountable fact that they had been drawn together immediately that could possibly explain why they got along very well for quite a long time.

Dr. P. It wasn't just Jingo's desperate need for a man to replace Alex?

A.C. No. There is no doubt in my mind that they loved each other, no matter what Jingo said later. He was crazy about her from the moment they met, and I'm virtually certain that she responded in the beginning. He was a very attractive young man, and they both wanted very much to make a go of their marriage.

For his wife's sake, Sid abandoned a dream of Cape Cod decor in his rather large modern house and became reconciled to Italian Renaissance antique furnishings. He could still enjoy hunting prints in his own den and found it very cozy to be surrounded there by the leather-bound works of various classical authors (with uncut pages), which had been removed from the living room. He was glad to buy a grand piano, learned to eat soufflé and chicken Marengo, acquired a more discerning bootlegger, and went sailing mostly with his men friends while their wives eagerly supported Jingo's efforts to form a Junior League book discussion group.

For her part Jingo became reasonably interested in watching polo, bought Brooks sweaters and suits from Fortnum and Mason, added the "Charleston" and "Chloe" to her more classical musical repertoire, and learned to play a passably good game of both golf and bridge. What is more, she learned to play a passably good game of sex.

Dr. P. That in itself was no mean feat, considering her background and the era in which all this took place.

A.C. Especially so since despite all her reading, all her talk, her flirting at parties, and her encounters with pinching Parisians, Virginia at the onset of her marriage was about as naïve concerning the real facts of life as a girl could be, even at that period of history when most girls of her class and condition were all pretty naïve, despite their great verbal sophistication. Jingo had been brought up by a mother who had very mixed feelings about discussing sex with her children. Our mother had been as honest as she knew how to be and cannot be blamed for the fact that the words she spoke did not always convey the same message as the tone of voice with which she spoke them. She had always encouraged her daughters to come to her with their questions, and when her daughters did, she gave them the best answers she could. However, the intensity of her uneasy blush while demonstrating the act she could not mention—by inserting her sewing needle through the hole of a spool—clearly conveyed the concept that conversation about such matters would best be avoided so far as possible.

I'm sure that Jingo had been taught the anatomical differences between men and women at an early age, although I doubt very much that she ever saw her baby brother without his diaper, except by accident. Later she learned that men and women "did things together" which eventuated in the conception of "dear little babies that a mother carries under her heart." Jingo even knew *what* they did, and that it was a "beautiful act of love" if carried out "within the bonds of holy matrimony," although unthinkable under any other circumstances. Any man who tried to do it outside of marriage was "taking advantage in a most ungentlemanly way" and must be resisted at all costs.

On the other hand, in spite of all the douche bags and bottles of antiseptic on view in the bathroom, I'm sure she had never been taught that anyone did this thing for any other purpose than to produce the "dear little babies," or that anyone might wish to prevent having such a one to "carry under her heart." She was certainly never taught that this "act of love" could be done purely for pleasure. Quite the contrary, in fact. The tone of voice, if not the words, clearly conveyed a concept that the "bodily appetites of men" are not shared by "good women," and that although a "good wife" allows a husband to "use her body for his pleasure" whenever he so desires, a "good woman" does not enjoy it, and a "good man" does not really respect a woman who does enjoy it.

Dr. P. After all, Jingo was the first child of a late Victorian mother, who was still closely attached to her own mid-Victorian upbringing.

A.C. Of course. Jingo's friends had all led equally sheltered lives and had been taught much the same things. When she talked these things over with them, they all laughed at their mothers' Victorianism. They all necked with their beaux, and some of them had even petted. In fact, they had all enjoyed this. However, everyone knew "just how far a good girl goes," and none of them would have considered letting anyone "take liberties" beyond the prescribed limits, any more than their mothers would have. They knew that "necking is supposed to stop at the neck" (even though it occasionally progresses a little farther down) and that when one begins to get excited, "it is time to stop lest one get carried away." The idea that there might be anything desirable about getting excited fell totally outside the realm of their mental experience.

All those rules were very clearly defined by the peer group, and although it was not the kind of thing one discussed in "mixed company," even with a very intimate male friend, their beaux knew the rules too and made only a token show of trying "to go too far." The boys of Jingo's circle had all been brought up in the same kinds of families as the girls, and while their fathers had let them in for a few strictly masculine angles, the lines between a "gentleman" and a "cad" were very distinctly drawn. A "gentleman" simply did not suggest certain things to a "nice girl," and the prohibitions against hitting below the belt did not apply only to prizefighting. I'm sure young people today will find it hard to believe that people of that time really talked like that—it has become such a joke in times since.

Dr. P. They might find it hard to realize that many things never were discussed at all, even between intimate girl friends. Masturbation, for instance, or the phenomenon of orgasm.

A.C. Heaven forbid! Even if the girls in Jingo's group had heard the word *orgasm*, I'm sure most of them would not have known what it meant. What's more, it's highly probable that when most of those girls finally did find out about that phenomenon, either in the privacy of their own bedrooms or on the marital bed, they were just as overwhelmed by guilt feelings as Jingo was the first time it happened to her.

It happened fairly early in her marriage, but she managed to keep it well concealed from Sid until one day when he caught her secretly crying in the bathroom and pried a confession from her. Jingo half expected to be sent packing the next day and was distinctly disconcerted when, instead of showing horror, he emitted a shout of raucous laughter. However, on that day she learned a few things that relieved her life of considerable anxiety. It may be said parenthetically that she also passed on to her mother some information that enabled me to have a rather broader type of education. Anyway, from then on, things were not too bad at all in the sex department for quite a while.

What destroyed their marriage was not their diversity of interests, sex, money, or in-laws. Jingo liked most of Sid's relatives, and they liked her. Sid thought Mother a cute, adorable, remarkably unintrusive mother-in-law and was hospitable to all of us. Nor was there a problem of children. Sid, being an overgrown adolescent himself, did not really want a family, and after one traumatic miscarriage, Jingo was not at all sorry to forego having one. Of course, she was fearful of criticism about this and made good copy of her tragic experience, implying, if not stating directly, that she was unable to have any more pregnancies. However, in her secret heart, she did not want children either and had by now learned that there were ways to prevent them from appearing.

The train of events which finally brought their marriage down after ten years arose from a problem that neither of them had foreseen or had the capacity to deal with once it became evident, so deeply was it embedded in the fabric of Virginia's personality. That problem was her ever-growing hatred for her father, a bitterness of such corrosive quality that it gradually consumed both her mind and her body.

As I may have mentioned, Sid's father was a very prominent man, one whose banking interests brought him into contact with many political figures. Our father did not hesitate to call upon him in his frantic search for financial backers of the fight against "evil" and would have been quite ready to solicit support from anyone of power whom his daughter even vaguely knew, so righteous was he in his cause, and so convinced that justice must triumph. As one noisy crisis followed another in his career, and as Jingo felt increasingly frightened that scandal would wreck the world of her escape, her hatred mounted to a point where it could no longer be drained off by ordinary means. As it mounted, her physical disabilities gained momentum, until finally she was swept into a maelstrom of almost constant illnesses, rashes, infections, operations, and accidents. Finally Sid got tired of her ill health and, in turning to others for fun and companionship, inevitably turned to other women for sex as well.

Dr. P. Bringing upon himself all the wrath of an innocent wife betrayed, humiliated, and abandoned just when most in need of protection.

A.C. Yes. I won't belabor the point, for anyone can fill in the details of such an ending to a once reasonably successful marriage. Before it was all over, Sid had become in Jingo's mind the devil incarnate, second only to her father in villainy. Ten years after her wedding, at the age of 29, Jingo was again a single woman who moved back in with her mother, bag and baggage.

6

Four Seasons at Glen Alden

A.C. The years at Glen Alden were, I think, the apex of our lives. We lived there for only a short time, but for all of us it was a crucial period—one filled with frustration, yet in some ways one of the happiest that any of us had ever lived through. For me it was a moratorium, for Jingo the beginning of an end, and for Eliot, in a certain sense, the end of a beginning.

There, after ten years, we again came together as a family. Only our father was missing, and by that time none of us considered it a loss except Mother, who never really accepted the fact that he wasn't there. His presence was palpable to her at all times, and there was no doubt in her mind that at any moment he would appear in the flesh.

We were again in the country, country that meant as much to us as the Briarpatch of our childhood. Jingo had less emotion invested in the land, but to El, in spite of his preoccupation with other matters, and certainly to me, it awakened all the nostalgias of early life, almost promising to fulfill the yearnings that had never quite been satisfied. There, for the first time, I felt I really *belonged* to the family, and although I only actually lived there during college vacations, I was part of a togetherness that I suspect none of us had ever experienced in quite the same way.

There we had the Christmases when we gathered around the tree to laugh at Mother's traditional little jingles about the activities of each child; the jokes when I filled every receptacle in the house with wild grape jelly that never jelled; the triumphant shouts of pleasure when Mother successfully outwitted an army of marauding rabbits by planting pink celluloid pinwheels among her vegetables, and the excitement when, snowed in for five days without furnace oil, we all gleefully banded together to drag abandoned hunks of broken telephone poles from a heap by the roadside into our big fireplace for warmth. Many of my happiest memories are tied to the land itself and to the seasons of the year. Just as the magic of the midwestern north woods colored our childhood, so the beauty of New England touched all our hearts, tying the family together with a bond no human differences could sever. Whenever I think about it now, the thoughts and moods are somehow connected with the climate and scenery—lonely white winter, hazy yellow-green spring, exuberant red and gold autumn. Perhaps that's relevant—the fact that those elements are so important in determining our emotional states.

I'll describe a couple of days that somehow seem outstanding in my mind, because they were among the few times when El and I ever approached talking about ourselves, or when anything really important ever happened.

In the dark blue of a late winter afternoon, Glen Alden lay under a deep layer of snow. An ancient maple tree stood out sharply against the old Colonial house, and across a wide expanse of pasture, the leafless black trunks of trees made patterns on the rocky gray hillsides. It was cold and lonely on this New England countryside in January, but it was also peaceful. No roar of traffic crept in, because there was no traffic. Nothing was there at all except scattered old houses and silent fields surrounded by a bowl of wooded hills.

Inside the house, however, a fire crackled in the huge stone fireplace and smells of roasting lamb wafted in from the kitchen. Amy, wrapped in an eiderdown quilt against drafts, was curled up on a circular love seat by the fire. Beside her, the remains of an early tea rested on the marble coffee table, and in her hand was a toddy of water and hot lemon juice laced with whiskey. Whiskey, no longer against the law, had recently been allowed into the household on the insistence of three grown children over the protests of a disapproving parent, and now the invalid by the fire sipped with pleasure a potion which she was still allowed to have for medicinal purposes only. Her face was flushed, but her eyes had lost the anxious, hectic glaze they had had a few hours earlier when she arrived home from college feverish and wracked by a debilitating cough. In an easy chair alongside, her handsome, ascetic-looking brother lounged with his feet on the coffee table. One hand was busy manipulating a clinking glass, while the other carried a cigarette to and from his lips with rhythmical regularity. These two young people had been chatting for the past hour in trivialities about the recent snowfall and were just beginning to embark on a more personal discussion.

"Well, kiddo, you really must have blown up a storm in that infirmary of yours. The doctor was spluttering so loud over the phone that Mother had to hold the receiver away from her ear."

The tone of voice was neutral and slightly amused, expressing the same mild, detached interest that Eliot Jr. usually directed toward any human affairs not strictly involving himself. Amy giggled.

"I gave her a bad time. She was terribly mad, and I guess I don't blame her. What did Mother say?"

"She said, 'Well, I don't know what's the matter with

*her either, but I know my child. If she says she wants to
come home, she has a good reason, so you'd better
release her.' Then there was more sputtering, and I
suppose the doctor must have said you were too sick to
travel, because Mother just said you knew what you
were doing, and if you wanted to come home, she'd take
the responsibility for whatever happened."*

*"Good old Mother. She always comes through in a
pinch, doesn't she? It's really great to know that she has
confidence in my decisions, dumb though they may be.
In spite of all her nagging about small things, she is
remarkably good about letting me be free in big things."*

*"This time it might just be that you've been given the
freedom to catch pneumonia if you don't watch out."*

"At least it will be my *pneumonia, and I'll be
responsible for it. Mother knows I won't blame her, and
I'm glad I can run my own life without having her
question my good sense."*

*Eliot looked up quickly, not sure for a moment
whether this last remark was intended as some kind of
veiled dig at him. This sister of his tended to alternate
between being very supportive and very critical. The
criticism often came out in sharp, unintentional cracks
that she then tried rather unsuccessfully to take back,
leaving him both wounded by her attack and touched
by the obvious attempt to protect him from her own
disapproval. At that time, he was particularly sensitive
about being financially dependent on his mother and
knew that even his best ally in the family found this
position incomprehensible. He immediately realized,
however, that she was not thinking about him just then
but was wrapped up in her own problems.*

*"Why did you make such a big thing of it, Amie?
(Ah-me, or the French word for friend—who knows
what this pronounciation meant? With a name like
Amy, one doesn't get many nicknames, but this one had
been used exclusively by her brother since its long-*

forgotten origin in childhood and always gave Amy a sense of the intimacy between them.)

"Well, I'd run out of the number of infirmary days you can stay free under the overall student fee and was going to have to start paying ten dollars a day. I guess I just got sort of panicky."

"Ye Gods, woman! We aren't that hard up! You aren't required to kill yourself for a few dollars. Anyway, you could have stayed several days for the price of the train ticket. You must be nuts."

"I know. I'm really ashamed about making a fuss. The doctor and nurse were both disgusted with me, and I know I was stupid. Sometimes I can't seem to help it, though. I just get this feeling that I can't stand something for one more minute. If I don't do something, I feel I'll just blow up. I don't know what's the matter with me any more than the doctor does. When I heard they weren't going to let me out of there, I felt I just couldn't stand it. I had to get out, silly as it was. The only way to do it was to come home."

"That's too bad. I know how you felt. I feel that way around here sometimes."

"Now and then I get these crying spells, right out of the blue for no reason at all. Sometimes I think I'm going off my rocker. Everyone at college thinks I'm feeling on top of the world, and the funny thing is that I really am most of the time, but then all of a sudden, whammy, it comes over me. I feel like shooting myself afterward, because it's so degrading to lose control for absolutely no reason. Somebody says something perfectly innocuous, and all of a sudden I'm in hysterics and I don't know what triggered it off any more than they do."

By now Amy was beginning to get teary and became convulsed by a coughing fit. Eliot cleared his own throat several times and fidgeted around uncomfortably for a moment.

"You aren't in any trouble—I mean, well, you aren't in trouble are you?"

"Sometimes I almost think I am—oh, you mean am I pregnant or something? For Pete's sake! No! What a crazy idea."

It tickled Amy that El was afraid to say the word straight out, and her giggles brought on another cough to sober her up.

"No, I'm not pregnant. Sometimes I almost wish I were, though. Maybe that's part of what's the matter with me. I can't seem to get really close to boys. It's really ironical, because I'm supposed to be one of the sophisticated set, and I'm sure lots of people are critical because they assume I'm 'fast.' They see me at dances, and boys ask me out often enough, but I get all sort of shy and frozen up when I get alone with any of them. I just don't feel like myself at all. Anyway, there must be something peculiar about me, because everyone treats me like a God damned pal. I guess I just don't have sex appeal."

At that moment Jingo literally blew into the room, along with a blast of icy outdoor air, arriving for dinner from her own apartment in the rebuilt section of a massive old barn out back. All she heard was Amy's last statement.

"Don't be ridiculous. My friends never stop telling me how attractive you are." *Her words were supportive, and at that stage of her existence, Amy did not catch the slight edge to her voice. She thought her sister the most attractive woman alive, and any idea that Jingo could feel jealousy toward her would have seemed as fantastic to Amy as it would have seemed to Jingo herself.*

"All you need is to meet the right man, although heaven only knows how anyone would expect you to do that, packed away in a women's college where all anyone thinks about is field hockey and ancient Greek.

The trouble with you is you're too smart for the callow American college boy. You probably scare them to death because you want to talk about something besides horses. What you need is an older man who will appreciate you—a European, I think. American men aren't sensitive enough for a woman with brains."

Amy, who was involved with neither field hockey nor ancient Greek, ignored the overstatement.

"And how shall I go about meeting all these glamorous Europeans who will fall at my feet?"

Even though she knew this was just Jingo, Amy couldn't help feeling encouraged by that kind of talk and halfway believed it was true.

"Well, we'll have to work on that."

Jingo got herself a drink and settled into the other easy chair, prepared to take over a situation that was obviously being poorly handled without a mastermind in control.

"That young Englishman who stayed with Liz and Jack last month—he was most attractive, and his family are very prominent in London even if they are in trade. Maybe his mother knows someone that would take you for the season and get you presented at court. There are English ladies who do that, you know. I used to meet girls in Paris who had done that. I'll call Liz tomorrow."

She would do it too, Amy mused. The next day Jingo and Liz would talk it all over on the phone, and by the end of about an hour and a half's conversation, they would have figured a way to dispose of Mrs. Wallis Warfield and marry Amy off to the Prince of Wales. What's more, sometimes in the Carpenter family it was not hard to get pulled into thinking that such a plan might actually materialize.

"What will I do for money during this gay London social season? I don't suppose the English ladies do this just for love of us sweet, young American girls."

At that point Eliot piped up. Poor El! He hadn't learned yet.

"Maybe Dad's settlement will come through soon. Mother says—"

Jingo was already turning purple, and even he could see that his foot had fallen into quicksand. One could have cut with a knife the moment of silence that ensued before Jingo exploded.

"My God! She has infected you too!"

By the time the tirade was well launched, Amy had sunk back into a semicomatose state of befuddlement, aided by fever, hot whiskey, and a strong impulse to escape. By that time, she had developed an ability to tune herself out at the onset of any verbal barrage threatening to produce unpleasant emotions, and she was already anesthetized against the angry torrent about to flow over her. Eliot, flustered and defensive, tried once to twice to break in but soon gave up. Fortunately, before too long the rattle of dishes presaged Mother's entrance with a dinner tray for Amy, and silence fell upon the group by the fire.

"Here you are, dear. Eat as much as you can, and as soon as we finish dinner I'll tuck you into bed for a good night's sleep. A few days' rest will put you on your feet again, as right as rain. You work so hard; it's no wonder you are a little overtired. Come on in, children."

Her eye fell disapprovingly on the pile of cigarette butts.

"Eliot, why do you smoke so much? Remember what happened to your Uncle Charley. What's the use of ruining your health like that? Go and wash up now, instead of waiting until the food is on the table. And don't forget to turn out the lights. Amy only needs this one lamp, and we can't afford to burn our money, you know. After we eat I want to show you all a sample of the lovely chintz I'm considering for the bedroom curtains. It seems just right for a house of this period and fits very well with the furniture we have. I'm

anxious to get everything finished so it will look nice
when your Daddy comes.''

Amy's amused glance caught Eliot's eye, interrupting
an irritable comment forming on his lips. With a gesture
of mock despair, he got up silently and started turning
off lamps. Jingo too had been struck dumb and, for
once in her life, trailed off speechless on her mother's
heels.

On a fine day in late April, Glen Alden was almost
too beautiful to describe. Through a pale green haze of
new leaves, black branches still stood out against the
rocky rim of gray hills, but fields in the foreground were
beginning to turn green, and the house stood very white
upon dark, shiny flagstones, accented by beds of
flowering forsythia and lilac. In the bright blue sky of
noontime, fat white clouds bobbed around in the
breeze. Occasional days were already warm enough for
sitting outdoors in the sun, and wooden porch furniture
had emerged from inside the house to stand on the
flagstone terrace beneath the tree.

Amy, home for Easter vacation, was filled with joy.
Just being alive on such a day was so exhilarating that
nothing else mattered. There was no room for sadness or
anxiety. All distress had been suspended, all dissatisfac-
tion and disharmony held in abeyance, while every pore
of her body was wide open to let in the sensuous impact
of spring. Her saddle shoes were muddy, there was a
bramble pull in the Brooks sweater she had finished
knitting only the day before, and her arms were full of
pussy willows. Everything was beautiful, pure, and
refreshing. As she came in, letting the kitchen door bang
behind her, Amy had nothing on her mind but the
necessity of finding a vase deep enough for the branches
she carried.

The sound of a typewriter stopped with a final ping
of the bell and the click, click of the last few words in a

paragraph. Eliot had heard her come in and was winding up the morning's work on his manuscript. In the morning, when north light filtered into a studio over his half of the barn, he usually seized the opportunity to paint. For the past few months, however, he had been giving full time to his writing, through which financial freedom had to be won. He was completing the final stages of a light novel about love and intrigue in a New York society setting, and with the part of his mind dedicated to wishful thinking, he felt sure it would be the best seller that could set him at liberty. On the other hand, the more rational part recognized that he knew no more about the kind of characters he had chosen for his subject matter than he knew about men from Mars. He had visited in their homes and danced with them at the Knickerbocker, but their ways of thinking were totally alien to his own. Both of his own abortive love affairs with girls from this background had ended in misunderstandings arising from tactless blunders on his part, and the sensible half of his brain realized how deeply he was locked up in his own emotions, isolated from comprehending those of other human beings. Since both parts of his mind were in full operation simultaneously, he had been working feverishly, night and day, frantic, hopeful, and in utter despair.

Amy's presence at home for the past week had been a distraction about which he had mixed feelings, but on that day, unable to get involved with his story, he was glad to relax for a while in her company. Jingo had gone off to New York on some errand connected with her new interior decorating business, with Mother along to visit Kate, and Amy had suggested picnic lunch outside for the two stay-at-homes. Eliot, grateful for an excuse to interrupt his work, ran down to join her. While he took over arranging pussy willows on the piano, Amy crushed mint into the iced tea and carried a tray to the terrace.

"On a day like this it's hard to remember anyone has a care in the world. Just smell that grass, El! Isn't it wonderful?"

"Yeah. It's a beautiful day all right. I just wish I could enjoy it. I'm so damned anxious to get through my first draft that I can't think about anything else."

"How did you manage that part where Daphne and Fulton were trying to find something they had in common besides sex?"

Eliot helped himself to potato salad and started trying to explain the intricacies of his plot but soon gave up.

"God, Amie! I'm so bored with it. At this point, I couldn't care less what they do."

That, of course, was what was the matter with his whole novel. It was so obvious that he couldn't care less. Amy, who thought she had read everything of consequence written since 1900 in connection with an honors thesis on "The Contemporary Novel in America," fancied herself a pretty sensitive literary critic. She shuddered with apprehension whenever it was forced on her attention that El was staking his whole future on a novel she didn't consider any good. His writing was so poetic and lyrical in spots, but so empty of any real feeling about people. It was tragic to think there was no money in poetry or painting, both of which he was really good at. She nodded sympathetically.

"If I don't get some money soon and get out of here, I'll go crazy! You can't imagine what it's like, between Jingo nagging at me to "be a man and go get a job," and Mother constantly moralizing and picking at little things."

"She's getting worse, isn't she? Poor Mother! She's so frustrated and lonely. The more worried she gets about the future, the more she picks. If only she could just give up and realize Daddy is never coming back, maybe she could make some kind of life for herself instead of

living from day to day in a state of suspended animation. She never will, though. I realize that now. I don't see where it will all end, and I don't see how you do stand it. I couldn't."

"I have to, until I get this done. If I get a nest egg, I can paint, which is what I really want to do. If this doesn't get it for me, I don't know what I'll do. I can't let myself think about it. Mother has really been very understanding, yet when she picks and picks like that, I want to kill her. It's a mess. I thought for a while things might get better once Dad got out of—"

Eliot fumbled and tried to recover, but Amy had caught the confusion.

"Got out of what, El?"

"Out of his most recent set of troubles—I don't know."

"El! Got out of what? What were you going to say?"

Eliot sighed deeply and lighted a cigarette.

"Nobody was supposed to tell you, but I guess you might as well know. Don't tell Mother I told you. He's been in jail. Contempt of court. Mother was frantic for a while and wanted to go out there, but he wouldn't let her. Said it would only make him feel worse to have any of his family come to a place like that."

"What in the world happened?"

Amy suddenly felt sick to her stomach and wondered what else she wasn't supposed to know.

"They put off his case again, and he just blew up and told the judge what he thought of him, and the rotten lawyers, and the whole legal system. Got six months. After about two days, the lawyer from the paper came and said if he would drop the suit they would get him out, but he just said he would see them in hell first. You can't help admiring his guts. Even if he can't win, he's right. Damn it, that's what makes it so awful."

"He's both right and wrong. That's what makes it so awful. If he were all right, you could really admire him, and if he were all wrong, you could hate him, but this

way you're caught in the middle. Even if the business was legal, his whole setup was morally wrong. The paper was wrong to persecute him, but really they were right to assume he was a crook."

"A man isn't a crook if he operates within the law."

"It isn't enough to follow the letter of the law. It's the spirit of the law that counts," Amy quoted in her mother's most sanctimonious tone.

"Maybe so, but practically every big business in the country is set up on the basis of practices that are legally right and morally wrong."

" 'Just because other people's children think it's right to do something like that, I'm not going to have my children thinking that way.' How many times have you heard that, El? Do you think for a single minute that Mother would think what he did was right if anyone but Daddy had done it? You're quibbling. God knows I realize how much you want to defend him, because I do, too. Sometimes I feel as though I'm being ripped apart by all the contradictions. In a way I'm glad I didn't know last semester that he was in jail, because I probably wouldn't have been able to keep my mind on my work, but it makes me mad to be treated as though I'm too young to be told anything. Mother's sweetness and light in the middle of all this is just as maddening as all the turmoil, too. I wonder what will happen next?"

"One thing has already happened. A few weeks ago, a lawyer came around, threatening to attach the house because Mother had signed a blank note for lawyers' fees! He said she owed him three thousand dollars, but when we convinced him Grandfather owned the house and car and everything else except a few sticks of furniture, he settled for five hundred that she had to borrow from Jingo. He could have put her in jail! It seems Dad has been trying to get money for his defense from everyone he knows, but he's running out, out of friends as well as money, I imagine.

"*And now another step is in progress. He has somehow managed to uncover the fact that the paper has been evading several million dollars in taxes by some shenanigans that are definitely not legal, and he is threatening them with a taxpayer's suit if they don't come up with his settlement pretty quick. It apparently worried them, because they sent someone around with another tentative offer to settle under the table, but it wasn't enough. He's determined to get what he thinks of as just retribution.*"

"*Doesn't that sound like blackmail to you?*"

"*Maybe it is, but by God, Amie, I don't blame him. They've got the biggest, most corrupt political machine in the country working for them, and if he can find a way to beat it, more power to him.*"

"*All the same, he'll never win. They're too strong for him. He's got guts, but he's a fool.*

"*The trouble is, if he gave up as he should and came back as Mother hopes, the whole situation here would be even more unbearable than it is right now. Can you imagine that bull in this china shop? Her wanting him is just a habit by now. I don't think she could actually stand having him around again. How does one know what to wish in a bind like that? Either way you wish, you're a heel to wish it.*"

Amy shivered and began to pile dishes back onto the tray.

"*It's getting chilly out here. The sun isn't really warm enough yet to sit out for very long. I think I'll go up and take a nap until teatime. I'm a little tired, and I don't feel very well.*"

In the heat of summer at Glen Alden, lawns were limp and dusty, while peonies drooped on their stems, scattering white petals messily onto the driveways which they bordered. Although leaves on the maple tree beside

the house formed a heavy cover of shade over the
flagstone terrace, even there the atmosphere was op-
pressive, sultry, and full of mosquitoes. Human in-
genuity, however, had devised a partial solution to the
problem of utilizing whatever air might stir in the
vicinity. Doors had been removed from the front and
back of the massive old barn, forming a breezeway in
the central section between Jingo's apartment and
Eliot's studio. There the porch furniture now stood,
shaded in the daytime, and in the evening offering box
seats for a firefly ballet over the lower pasture.

It was the middle of a July afternoon, and Amy
lounged listlessly on a chaise longue in this breezeway,
drained of even the energy to lift a half-read book lying
face downward beside her. The book was Buddenbrooks
in the original German, part of her campaign to avoid
"going native" now that college was over. To reinforce
this resolution, she was also studying shorthand and
typing every morning and had refused all invitations to
spend time visiting her numerous friends and auxiliary
mothers. Resisting temptation, however, took a lot of
energy, and a day like this had taken away every ounce
of the low supply she could usually muster.

Amy was fighting a very hard battle. Her "mother" at
the camp where she had spent so many happy summers
had wanted to hire her as a counselor, and she had also
been urged to spend a month in Maine visiting with her
erstwhile New York "mother," now more familiarly
addressed as Marty. She felt an almost irresistible pull
toward those places and those people, with whom she
felt relaxed and welcome, to pour into loving and
listening ears the contents of her heart and mind.
However, she recognized this as a pull backward into
childhood and knew it was time for her to start learning
how to live in the world as an adult. Amy struggled
against powerful impulses and was doing fairly well. On
that particular day, however, the whole campaign to

maintain morale had broken down. Only a fraction of her brain cells were working, and these were busy going over a conversation with Kate that had taken place the night before.

Kate was spending the summer at Glen Alden. Her aged spouse had finally died, leaving not the large fortune she had anticipated, but an income adequate for comfortable living if frugality had been compatible with her nature. Since it was not, she was at work trying to snare a wealthy, elderly Russian bachelor known as "the doctor," but was enjoying time off from the job while he was on a trip. Life was never dull with Kate around, and the Carpenter household was considerably brightened by her presence. She had a number of parlor tricks to keep them entertained, among them palmistry; and the previous night, just for fun, she had given everyone in the family a character reading. Amy, being a rational creature, did not really believe in quackery of that kind except as a game, but nevertheless she had read Cheiro's book on palmistry, along with books on astrology, spiritualism, and one on the interpretation of dreams by that Viennese doctor everyone was talking so much about. There was something very intriguing about trying to discover things about people that they didn't even know about themselves, and it was often surprising how someone with native intuition like Kate could hit the nail on the head. Last night she had said Amy was a "deep soul, sunk so far into herself that she had cut off her modes of expression and was doomed to introspection if she didn't snap out of it." Amy, having spent considerable energy in attempts at self-analysis, had known this for a long time, but it seemed rather uncanny that anyone else should be able to perceive her so accurately. She wondered if Kate wasn't a little bit psychic. Thought transmission and extrasensory perception had not been dismissed as pure quackery, and it was to some such power that Amy attributed whatever

*success occurred in hand reading and other forms of
fortune telling.*

*As she lay there in the breezeway, half-dazed by the
heat and her own inertia, she was wondering how to go
about reversing these dangerous tendencies to sink
within herself. Plans for positive action had been
underway for a long time, with summer concentration
on business skills preparatory to seeking a secretarial job
in New York until enough money could be saved for a
return to graduate school. She would never have
dreamed of asking her grandfather to finance any
further education, even if she had thought he might be
willing (which she did not), and it had never occurred to
her to ask for "charity" in the form of a scholarship.
Although Amy had never questioned her sister's right to
live on alimony, or an artist's right to be cared for in
some way, preferably by some government agency
rather than by private individuals, she would have
considered herself a deadbeat if, after so much expensive preparation, she were not ready to assume her own
support. Secretarial work seemed the only way to get
her where she wanted to be, but would getting there be
enough? Amy would not have admitted this to anyone
else, but her real motivation for an academic career was
the hope that opportunities to be with the kind of man
she liked, in a natural working relationship, would help
overcome her shyness and automatically solve most of
her problems. At that moment, however, confidence in
a simplistic solution wavered, and she was not completely sure that all her inner conflicts could be cured by
merely changing the circumstances under which she
lived. While unhappily brooding in this vein, she heard
the door beside her open and saw Jingo emerge with a
bathing suit over her arm.*

*"Liz has invited some people for cocktails by the
pool and said if you'd like to come, they'd be delighted
to have you. Someone is bringing a glamorous man from*

*New York whom she thinks sounds just right for me. A
writer—English, I think, who's down on his luck but
supposedly very attractive. All we need around here is
another writer who's down on his luck!"*

*Jingo laughed but she was obviously anxious to go,
and Amy too sprang up with alacrity. She hadn't been
home long enough to make many friends of her own
yet, but she was often included in parties to which Jingo
was invited and found them great fun. Maybe if Jingo
didn't hit it off with this man, he might be interested in
someone who had just graduated with honors as a
literature major. The idea of competing with her sister
for a man would have been the last thought ever to
enter Amy's mind, but Jingo often encouraged her to
consider those whom she herself had rejected as
possibilities, and even though it had never worked out,
Amy was grateful. You never could tell what might
happen, and in any case a swim and a party were just
what she needed to break up her self-centered mood.
Amy did not believe in self-pity and loathed herself
when she indulged in it, but she often found it necessary
for someone or something else to pull her out of it.
Jingo's friend Liz lived on a beautiful estate across the
valley, complete with swimming pool and stables. It was
a pleasure just to be in such a lovely setting, regardless
of what was going on, and anticipation almost immediately started transforming Amy into the amusing,
attractive young woman who, although included in such
gatherings as an adjunct to her sister, was nevertheless
well liked and in need of no outside support once she
got into a group.*

*As Amy and Jingo, eager to join the party, crossed
the lawn from a cabana where they had donned bathing
suits, Liz jumped up and came toward them, holding by
the hand a tall, dark man with a mustache. Even at a
distance he looked vaguely familiar to Amy, who turned
with a question on her lips. However, one look at her*

sister's face was enough to answer her question. The man who came forward to be introduced, the down-on-his-luck writer from England, the glamorous man from New York and hopeful prospect for one of the two Carpenter sisters, was none other than their old friend Alex. Alex, the promising young author. Alex, the faithless lover. Alex, the reluctant husband of another woman. Alex, the man who had never been out of Jingo's mind or far from her heart. Alex was coming toward them and was about to reenter their lives.

In autumn, New England reaches its peak of beauty, and that particular October, the coloring in the woods was unusually fine. The maple tree beside the house was vivid yellow, and although the zinnias had dried up in the garden, a riot of spicy chrysanthemums had taken their place. Fences along a country lane beside the house were loaded with wild grapes, trees in the orchard were heavy with apples, and all nature exerted a drag upon the emotions which only accentuated the pull from all directions taking place within the house itself. Too much was happening too fast, and no member of the family really had surplus energy to counteract the momentum propelling them forward into the unknown with ever-increasing speed.

Jingo had been caught up in a whirlwind of reunion with Alex. When they remet after so many years, he was just as charming, lovable, and interesting as ever, and within a week they had returned to the same footing as of old, talking with the same speed, the same intensity, and the same unanimity of opinion as if they had never been separated a day in their lives. Both had begun thinking almost immediately of a future together, and all misunderstandings from the past were ironed out rapidly. Each had admitted his or her part in the muddle of events that had caused their original parting.

Jingo should never have gone away and left him for

so long, and Alex should never have let his father keep him trapped in an impossible situation. In fact, it became quite clear that his father had actually been the villain of the piece. In any case, Alex, having more than paid for his wild weekend of youthful folly, was in the process of getting a divorce. He had had no trouble convincing Jingo that his wife's secret Lesbian tendencies were responsible for destroying the marriage, in spite of his best efforts to make it work, and that this, plus the burden of five noisy children, had prevented him from concentrating on writing. It had so completely undermined his morale that a serial story contracted for by one of the slick magazines could not be completed, which accounted for the fact that at present he was temporarily blackballed by them all. His wife, who had turned out to be totally unstable, was in and out of mental hospitals, and the best interests of his children were being served by parceling them out among her various relatives. Of course, Alex would assume a fair share of their support when he was on his financial feet again, because he loved them all very much, but right now he had to be free from the turmoil of family life. The successful play he once wrote for a famous actress would give him an entree to Hollywood writing circles, where he already had contacts, and if he could regain the ability to concentrate, big money was just around the corner. All he needed was inspiration and encouragement from the woman he had always loved, and who understood both him and his work so well. All this had been reviewed at length and accepted by both Alex and Jingo in perfect unity.

Within a month of their reunion, over the horrified protests of her mother, Jingo and Alex had started sleeping together in the barn apartment every weekend. Now they planned to set off for Hollywood any day and marry when his divorce became final. Jingo had moments of sadness about leaving the family, but soon she would be the wife of a man she had always wanted, a brilliant man with the promise of a fine career before him, and she looked forward eagerly to the future.

At that point in time her mother's future was not quite so clearly defined. Grandfather had died a month before, making it necessary for someone to live with eighty-five-year-old Grandmother, and Laura, being temporarily without the responsibility of caring for a husband, was the logical candidate. Her feelings were very torn indeed, because she badly wanted to keep the Glen Alden house to live in when her Eliot came, but after all, she was needed at the moment by the "dear little grandmother who has been so good and generous to us all," and the grown children who had found refuge there at a time of need no longer had use for that particular nest. She was happy to devote a few years of her life to caring for someone she loved and glad she was able to brighten her mother's last days, which could not possibly be many. She felt needed and wanted, even though she did not know that Grandmother, who had already had her hair cut and had bought a new wardrobe in anticipation of all the ladies' tea parties and club events she would now be able to attend with her Laura, was certainly in no mood to join her husband very soon. After sixty-odd years married to a godly man who had spent the last thirty-five devoting himself almost exclusively to Bible reading and atonement for sin, she was eager for some fun and had made it clear how impatiently she awaited her daughter's arrival. Laura looked forward to joining her with a sense of purpose, if not wild anticipation. She had already rented the house furnished and found a permanent tenant to take over the barn apartment as soon as Jingo moved out.

Amy also had everything set up, her new life in New York awaiting only her own readiness to brave the depression-torn city. A friend's father had guaranteed some form of work in his company to start off with, until she could work into the kind of job she wanted, and another friend had located ideal living arrangements for her in a brownstone rooming house run as a hobby by the wife of a wealthy banker to accommodate working sons and daughters of friends ruined by the stock market crash. Lovingly known to its inmates as the "House of Decayed Gentility," it was filled with people just like herself and sounded like great fun. Being completely on her own three thousand miles from the family was a somewhat frightening prospect, but Amy was more excited than fearful, looking forward to her future almost as eagerly as Virginia looked forward to her own.

Only to Eliot Jr. was this a moment of real crisis. In spite of all his frantic efforts, no publisher had shown the slightest interest in his novel or given any encouragement to his hopes of making it more acceptable by reworking it. The side of his mind given to wishful thinking now had no goal, and the realistic side was confirmed in the knowledge that he should never have undertaken that kind of book anyway. Since fantasies of instant success and deep-seated feelings of inadequacy were totally incompatible in the first place, his only recourse was to cast his self-hatred outward in a burst of fury at the banal, materialistic attitudes in society which reject true creativity and even deny a meager living to those artists who stoop to meet degraded tastes. After a futile trip to the fifth publisher about a week previously, he had abandoned the novel in a desk drawer and spent his time walking alone through the autumn countryside, cursing unappreciative critics and brooding on the futility of existence.

Everyone else in the family, wracked by pity and guilt for their own relatively good fortune, had been driven to offering advice in an attempt to avoid sharing his despair. Jingo and Alex held forth fervently on the subject of how few authors achieve success with a first novel and suggested that working for a while at something besides writing would give Eliot the kind of first hand life experience essential to every author. Amy suggested that maybe novel writing wasn't his meat, and why didn't he aim for a teaching job that would offer opportunities to paint and write poetry, which was what he really wanted to do? Mother suggested that he "think positively" and not allow "error" to take over his mind. While expressing firm confidence in his ability to solve his problems, she was nevertheless worried to death about the increase in his smoking and drinking and, remembering her brothers Paul and Charley, was frightened about what might happen to him if everyone left him alone. The worry and fear were all too obvious, particularly since she had begun hinting about her own need for company on the trip west and suggesting that maybe a little vacation visiting Grandmother might be good for him until the next "positive step" became clearer in his mind. All these suggestions—so well-intentioned and expressing concern, so rational and sensible, so well-designed to protect his self-esteem— when woven together, had fashioned not a shield but a shroud in which to bury his sense of being considered a man capable of recovering from disappointment and taking over the management of his own destiny. Eliot, wrapping it around himself and sinking into a state of apathy, had given up the ghost. After only a faint struggle, he agreed to help his mother start feathering a new nest for them both.

So they were all on the eve of departure from Glen Alden, each one affected in a different way by events of the last month, and all carried along together in sadness toward dissolution of their life together. Each one both wished and feared the next step, and each felt considerable pain as their roots were slowly torn up from the much-loved earth on which they stood. Even Jingo had responded emotionally to the New England countryside.

No matter what the sorrows and frustrations had been, affection, fun, and togetherness had existed in that house during the past few years, and everyone suffered at the knowledge that at least one stage of their life as a family would soon be over.

They did not leave Glen Alden in a burst of mutual farewell. They dribbled away two at a time, first Mother and Eliot, then Jingo and Alex, with Amy going last, aching for the true closeness that was almost, but never quite, achieved.

Amy did not cling this time to the bole of a beloved maple tree. Life had already taught her that when one phase has irretrievably ended, the time has come for letting go and passing on. A piece of her heart remained there, however, and for no other place did she ever again feel so much nostalgia. Much joy and love were shared with her family in that beautiful place. There had been bad things too—anger, frustration, and personal insecurity. However, after ten years apart, they had reunited there for a while before going their separate ways. Earlier uprootings had occurred, and there would be more later, but to every member of the Carpenter clan leaving Glen Alden was the uprooting that hurt most of all. For Amy, the hurt was particularly deep because, after leaving Glen Alden, she never again really "belonged" to her family.

Interlude

At a halfway point in this account of the Carpenter family let me pause for a moment to comment on what we have seen. In the foregoing chapters three children grew up, and we participated in significant episodes from their early years, experiencing something of what it was like to live in the home of Laura and Eliot Carpenter Sr. Let us look now at what happened to each one and try to assess the impact of particular events on developing personalities. How did the experiences these children had and the emotional climate in which they lived contribute to forming the three very different kinds of young people now standing on the brink of adult life?

Although they were born ten years apart, into very different family circumstances, Jingo and Amy had certain of the same important basic experiences before age five. Both were born at a time of great anxiety and insecurity for their mother—Virginia early in the marriage when an immature, homesick young bride struggled with adjustment to a quixotic husband and a whole new way of life far from the parents to whom she had always been close, and Amy coming when her mother was already a matron over thirty whose settled way of life was in danger of being disrupted by an unwanted third pregnancy. In response to Laura's anxiety, both infants refused to nurse until physically tended by someone else. We are not told how long Jingo's feeding disturbance persisted, although we do know that she remained largely in the care of a mother subjected to many anxiety-provoking situations during the first five years of her daughter's life. Amy's feeding problem lasted only six weeks, after which she thrived on a bottle in the care of a mature, tender, and experienced nurse. However, both girls showed symptoms of emotional upset in later childhood and onward, which psychiatrists generally attribute to reaction patterns established at that earliest period—Jingo, a tendency to express anxiety as infants do, through disturbed function of bodily organs, particularly the skin, and Amy, a tendency to develop depression, the groundwork for which is laid at a period when the child's earliest sense of basic security depends so much on attitudes transmitted by the mother through care-taking procedures.

Throughout the toddler period the girls also had certain similar experiences. Neither, so far as we know, showed any evidence of difficulty in acquiring bowel or bladder control, and although their position within the family circle was very different, both had a similar relationship to important parental figures.

Between infancy and age five, Jingo was very much a focal point of family interaction, stimulated, encouraged to show off, and admired constantly by numerous adults, while Amy spent the same years virtually isolated in a nursery, relating primarily to her nurse and the other servants, and seeing her family for the most part only under rather formal circumstances when she was dressed up and brought down to join them for little more than an hour in the evenings. However, both girls felt extremely valuable to their father at the start of a phase of development where such feelings are crucial to acquiring a strong sense of feminine identity, Jingo as the only child, and Amy as the youngest and acknowledged favorite. Both also had the almost undivided attention of a mother figure, Jingo as the confidante and constant companion of her own mother, and Amy of the nurse who had achieved a position as "psychological mother" by consistently carrying out the child's daily care. Whatever tendencies to feel insecure had been built into their personalities earlier, both these girls went through a period in which they had considerable reason to feel that they "owned" a mother and were very important to her.

When each girl reached age five, she lost an important love object and reacted by developing symptoms of emotional disturbance. From that time on, however, the emotional development of the two girls veered in different directions. The outcome of their reactions to loss was different in each case, and different kinds of experiences during the period from five until adolescence set them on an entirely different course.

When Amy's nurse was discharged, the security of a relationship to her closest mother figure ended abruptly, leaving her for a time a stranger in her own family, alienated from them even by her tendency to think in German. Her reaction was to push out of consciousness by repression all feelings about being deserted, while at the same time refusing to eat and withdrawing emotionally from everyone in a state of recognizable childhood depression. During the period immediately following this reaction, however, a number of factors combined to mitigate her pain. Her own mother offered a much-longed-for increase of closeness, later Alma came back, and eventually Amy regained sufficient security to make possible a form of spontaneous self-conducted play therapy in which she used the tigers to work through feelings which eventually were dispelled.

At the same age, Jingo retained a close relationship with her mother in spite of her brother's birth, but in effect suffered the loss of her father. Although he did not leave the family scene, continuing to have a strong impact upon it, his relative neglect of Jingo after the birth of a "son and heir" was a severe blow to her self-esteem which she never worked through, and from which she apparently never fully recovered. At an important moment in her development, she was thus catapulted from a fantasied position of being "all-important" to him into one where she felt of no worth at all—a situation particularly hard for a little girl whose sense of self-importance had been built up to such a marked extent by earlier experience. At the point of his desertion, her father died as a love object for Virginia as surely as if he had been permanently removed from the family, leaving her with a damaged self-image which could only be restored by again feeling "all-important" to some substitute for him. She reacted with her first attack of a skin eruption, while also directing toward her father a persistent sense of anger and outrage.

In spite of this, during subsequent preadolescent years, Jingo remained in the family and social environment she had always known, one in which her life with peers flowed along rather smoothly. Although her father remained a focus for hostility, she was apparently not impeded in forming appropriate relationships with boys her own age, and she arrived at adolescence in a normal condition so far as anyone could tell from her surface behavior.

Amy, during that same school-age period, had a completely different set of experiences. Although her ability to relate warmly to mother figures had been regained, and she still felt loved by her father, a groundwork was gradually being laid for fear of masculine aggression through the rather sadistic teasing by her brother, which continued until his accident when she was seven, and afterward through the erotically stimulating interest in medieval tortures into which he initiated her. At some time during this period, either in reality or in a highly realistic fantasy, she was sexually molested by an older man. During most of that same

period, anxiety had run high in all members of her
family because of her father's increasing business difficulties, a situation which culminated in a complete
disruption of the family and another period of emotional disturbance for Amy in which she again had eating
problems. When permanently separated from her father
just before the age of twelve, she reacted by again
repressing all feelings about being deserted but this time
turned away emotionally only from males, avoiding the
early relationships with boys normal to her peer group,
and throwing herself instead into intellectual and
athletic activities. She arrived at adolescence in a state
of regression to intense dependence on mother figures
and, from then on through her college years, made
contact with boys only on a purely friendly, rather
superficial basis.

Jingo, on the other hand, found at the age of fifteen
one man with whom her originally fantasied position as
"all-important" could be reestablished, and her self-
esteem with it. Although "going steady" was not common during her era, she formed an intense attachment
and sustained her exclusive position with him in her
unconscious mind even after he too had deserted her. In
spite of the terrible blow that she had suffered, Jingo
was apparently able to focus all angry feelings on her
father and temporarily find a new love object.

The early experiences of Eliot Jr. were quite different
from those of his sisters. He was Laura's only child to
enjoy an undisturbed infancy, born as he was at the
time of her greatest spiritual calm, delivered without
hard labor or anesthetic in a condition free of anoxia,
and breast-fed with ease and satisfaction to both mother
and child. We have, of course, no way of checking the
exact nature of that mother-child relationship or of
knowing Laura's unconscious reactions to the birth of a
son, but a son had been much desired by both parents
and was welcomed with great joy. To the best of
anyone's knowledge, he was a physically robust, normal-

ly aggressive, and happy child throughout the toddler years, with no recognizable difficulties at that stage.

By age five, however, he had already begun to show evidence of reaction to pressure from his father to "be a man," becoming a rather dreamy, introspective boy subject to fears and phobias which, although not uncommon at that age, nevertheless indicate some emotional conflict. He was still a happy child who was not particularly coddled and was permitted considerable freedom to play around his neighborhood without supervision and in summer to roam the countryside with only a pony for his companion. However, he remained untutored in the practical skills common to boys of that age. Both in physical appearance and temperament he was felt to resemble a beloved artist-brother of his mother, who tended to encourage him in activities conducive to developing imagination and sensitivity to beauty rather than the more "masculine" pursuits his father might have encouraged had he been able to give the boy much of his time.

During the early school-age years Eliot still gave the outward appearance of being reasonably well-adjusted child—top of his class academically, interested in baseball and football, and well accepted by the boys and girls of his class. However, the sharp reversal of attitudes toward himself, precipitated by an accident at the age of twelve, introduced an adolescent period in which he almost totally withdrew again into a world of dreams and fantasies as he had done when the pressure of anxiety first threatened his ability to cope with the world.

Three young adults are now ready to face the prospect of mature living, each hopeful of finding his or her rightful place in the world at an early date. What are they like as they leave Glen Alden? Where do they fall on the scale of sexual maturity and capacity for personal intimacy which are such important indicators of emotional health in adult life? Where do they fall on the scale of ability to cope realistically with the everyday problems of existence? In other words, what assets and liabilities of character and personality have they developed from earlier experiences to meet the emotional stresses and strains of participation in the major tasks of maturity—loving and working?

Virginia at thirty-one is the only Carpenter child who has shown herself capable of normal sexuality. Her sense of feminine identity has been clear since early adolescence; she was able to establish intimacy with two different men, achieved orgasm soon after beginning to have intercourse on a regular basis, and although temporarily single after a divorce, adapted reasonably well to living with a husband for ten years and never seriously contemplated not remarrying. She has now reestablished an intimate relationship with a man, and the possibility of genital as well as emotional response to her prospective husband has already been demonstrated.

In other areas of functioning she also gives evidence of a capacity for leading a normal life, although she clings to a rather particular life-style. Jingo is the Scott Fitzgerald heroine—the rather eccentric but nevertheless typical representative of social groups like that in which she spent her married years. She has become one of the intelligent but nonintellectual, conventional but nevertheless gay and fast-living women found throughout groups called "society" as defined by the society pages of metropolitan newspapers and the Social Register of her era. With many other members of such groups she shares conservative political views, formed largely in response to those of bridge-table companions who lack both solid information and interest in public affairs, does not concern herself with matters requiring abstract thinking, and is only now, under the renewed influence of Alex, on the verge of reawakening literary interests which had gradually been obliterated during her life with Sid. She adheres with almost no question to a value system held by people who differ little from those in

the "society" where she grew up, and although fondly
regarded by her many friends as a somewhat zany
spinner of wild exaggerations and tall tales bordering on
the fantastic, she is seen by those who know her as an
outstandingly attractive, interesting, and popular "gay
divorcée" destined to shine in a world remarkably
similar to one she has always known.

Virginia now faces a new phase of her life with
important assets to help her succeed—intelligence, an
artistic flair, and the capacity for making good social
relationships with both men and women while also
maintaining intimacy with the one man whom she loves
and admires. She has proven herself capable of taking
direct, although rather impulsive and opportunistic,
action to escape an intolerable home situation, of
making considerable successful compromises in adapting
to a new kind of situation in her marriage, and later
again taking action to establish a successful decorating
business after her divorce. One can say that on the
surface her behavior has been realistic and her flexibility
good.

In spite of her propensity for severe outbreaks of
"psychosomatic" disease, only those concerned with
deeper levels of psychological functioning would see any
liabilities to prevent future success. However, it is
obvious from the story that she makes use of what a
psychiatrist sees as unhealthy psychological mechanisms
for dealing with anxiety and internal conflict—displacement, denial, and rationalization which are all based on
the conscious and unconscious inability to face reality
as transmitted by rational knowledge and perception. It
appears somewhat questionable whether Jingo can
tolerate any real threat to an idealized image of her alter
ego Alex, upon which her own self-esteem depends. For
that reason, it seems ominous that her original concept
of him, buried at a deep level of her unconscious mind
more than ten years ago, has so readily reemerged and

been reinstated without being altered in any way by more mature judgment based on experience.

In the area of sexual development, Eliot Jr. presents a far less mature picture than his older sister. His inner sense of masculinity is shaky to say the least; at age twenty-six he is still a bachelor who has never been seriously involved with a girl except in fantasy, and his capacity for genital potency is as yet unproven. He shows, in fact, a marked incapacity for intimacy with a companion of either sex outside of his immediate family, and he is still enmeshed in both emotional and practical dependence upon his mother.

In other areas his adjustment to the realities of living is also marginal. Social relationships with members of both sexes are tenuous and restricted by rigidly conventional patterns of behavior, participation in peer group activities is minimal, and he is without interest in or knowledge of any matters beyond the sphere of his immediate experience. He seems to live largely in a state of preoccupation with his own dreams of future success without having developed any skills of a practical nature to prepare him for making a living, and he simply refuses to think about anything which might suggest that his dream is unrealistic. All of these tendencies are serious liabilities.

Nevertheless, he has a record of some significant accomplishment. At the high school level, he won school prizes in poetry and sculpture; in college he contributed to the literary magazine and won the highest award offered by his university for lyric poetry. More recently, he has acquired considerable technical facility for oil painting without formal instruction, showing acknowledged talent for design, and although at the moment his first efforts at fiction writing have met with bitter disappointment, Eliot has demonstrated a great potential for becoming an artist in some field.

A psychiatrist sees in him dangerous passivity and an

unhealthy tendency to counteract unpleasant aspects of reality by substituting a world of his own imagination for the real facts of life that he faces. He is clearly a vulnerable, withdrawn man who, at periods of anxiety and heightened sensitivity, tends to have intense aesthetic experiences of a quality bordering on mystical religious ecstasy. Nevertheless, he has managed to channel much instinctual conflict into artistic creativity and has the talent eventually to produce on a high level of competence if he sticks to his work. This creativity is a great asset, not only for changing his uncomfortable position in the outer world but for dealing with pressing internal problems.

When viewed from the standpoint of her surface behavior, Amy at the age of twenty-one seems on an equal level of sexual maturity with a majority of young women who also attended an eastern women's college. Living in an era when most such girls do not marry before graduation, and when unmarried girls from her kind of background are certainly not expected to have experience with sexual intercourse, her status is similar to that of nearly all her peers. By now Amy has developed extremely effective social techniques for getting along with men and women in groups as well as in individual relationships with people she likes, and although not much of a "joiner," she has established a firm coterie of friends who admire and are fond of her. She enjoys dances and mixed parties, has a reasonable number of dates with different people according to the customs of a day when limiting one's dating to one man at a time was frowned upon, and indulges in necking and petting which at times gets pretty "heavy." All this looks very normal.

In the story, however, we are permitted brief glimpses at a deeper level of her psychic functioning and made aware of internal conflicts which belie what appears on the surface. Here we note confusion in her sexual identity and see indications of a fantasy life in which eroticized submission to force and cruelty plays a prominent part. It also becomes obvious that although there are a number of contemporaries among her confidantes, the relationships in which Amy displays the greatest degree of intimacy are all with older women. Although at this point she hardly knows what the word *homosexuality* means and would be utterly horrified at the idea of indulging in overtly erotic behavior with women, she has not yet been able to extricate herself from the basically homosexual orientation which is normal at a somewhat earlier developmental stage and, although not consciously aware of it, fears a degree of intimacy with any man which could lead to sexual involvement.

Amy still adheres pretty much to a conventional way of life but began early to evaluate and challenge the attitudes and mores of the group in which she grew up, and by now she has discarded many of the ideas and values espoused by others in her family. More than any other Carpenter child, she has had intimate contact with thoughtful parent-surrogates from a less restricted segment of society, people whose interests are broader and whose lives less governed by rather rigidly proper upper-middle-class conventionality. She tends to identify herself with these intellectual women who, although themselves happily married to men who treat them as equals, do not see marriage as the only goal for an intelligent college graduate interested in and capable of real involvement with people and issues in a wider world than that of the polo field and bridge table. Amy wants to be a "doer" and at every stage has developed the skills necessary for active participation in peer group activities. Now, even at a difficult period in the country's economic history, she has equipped herself to make a living at a job she can actually get, even though her aspirations are eventually to acquire more education leading to professional training.

A psychiatrist looking at the ways in which she regulates anxiety sees repression as a major mechanism, one by which conflict-producing ideas and feelings are pushed out of awareness, although under favorable conditions they may be fairly readily restored to consciousness. Amy clearly has unconscious conflicts of formidable intensity which periodically announce their presence through unmotivated bursts of weeping from a nameless cause, and she is the only Carpenter child with such clear-cut symptoms of psychoneurosis. She also has one other characteristic conspicuously absent in her siblings—a conscious and unconscious tendency actively to reject wishful fantasy in herself or others and to check constantly on the reality of her own perceptions. This is a great asset, one which supplements her other abilities and fits her well for the kind of life she wants to lead.

So we have three vulnerable, sensitive, and to some extent handicapped young people, each with characteristics carrying a possible danger to their future mental health, and each with considerable strengths to help them combat the danger. All have made it without serious difficulty through the period of adolescence where so many breakdowns occur in those who are predisposed. None has as yet shown clear evidence of psychotic thinking or behavior, and all have had areas of success and proven capability during a developmental period where encouraging or discouraging experiences may be so crucial in determining what happens in the future. We will leave until later a discussion of how the characteristics we have seen relate to the potential any or all of them have for developing schizophrenia later in life.

PART IV: ADULTS

7

The Golden West

A.C. During the next seven years, I was almost totally cut off from news of the family and really had no idea at all what their lives were like. I corresponded regularly with Mother, but the letters were brief on both sides, designed only to convey assurance of a wish for continued loving contact. Knowing by then pretty much how she was, I tended to comment on how I currently liked my job, told of opportunities that came up, mentioned a current event, or sent regards from someone Mother knew. Mother, in turn, spoke of what was coming up in the garden at any particular moment, the state of Grandmother's health, or an event they had attended at the women's club. Occasionally she would comment that "Jingo is better now" or "El got back last night," but since the incident would be long past before I could ask, "Better from what?" or "Back from where?" I seldom bothered and only wondered now and then what my siblings might be up to. In spite of our mutual affection, it would never have occurred to any of us to write each other directly. I lived in one world, they in another, and it seemed perfectly natural to all of us that news should be mediated through Mother. Any remarks she made periodically about the imminent return of our father were by then a joke that only occasionally still irritated me. It was only much later that I began piecing together a coherent picture of what they were going through while I was busy establishing my own career in the East.

Eliot Jr.

When Eliot Jr. first arrived on the West Coast, his cup of frustration was full to overflowing, and the thought of living even for a short time in the old Victorian house with his mother and grandmother was nearly suffocating. He told himself that the condition was very temporary. With his unsuccessful novel as an example of what not to do, he would surely now be able to create salable material, probably even scripts with Hollywood potential, and get on his feet in a big way. From his small realistic core within, however, came a message loud and clear that he didn't have it in him to be a commercial success in that field and that, in fact, it was highly unlikely that he could make a living at all, except through unskilled labor totally incompatible with the pride of a man raised to sit among America's leaders. By the time he had settled himself and his typewriter in the chauffeur's old apartment over the garage, his self-confidence was zero and his self-esteem way down in the minus column.

It was not long, however, before Eliot discovered opportunities of quite a different nature. The street on which his grandmother's house stood was part of a still-respectable neighborhood, inhabited largely by old people remaining in their own homes or in the nursing homes now entering the area. Surrounding about four blocks of this district, however, were main arteries lined with cheap bistros, dance halls, and houses of prostitution which were creeping in along with the nursing homes behind the well-tended facades of houses on the dignified residential streets. Living outside the main house, where he was free to come and go with no questions asked, Eliot had only to walk a few blocks from his door after a dreary day of writing junk and find himself in a brightly lighted world of fifteen-cent martinis and two-dollar whores—a world actually compatible with the meager allowance on which he was surviving his presumably temporary lack of earning power.

Up until this time, Eliot's sexual experience had been incredibly limited. For a man to have arrived at the age of twenty-six with an amatory record of no more than a little adolescent petting and one tentative bordello encounter in Paris is hard to believe, but such was actually the case. He had been an extremely inhibited young man, a fact that he attributed almost entirely to the nature of his education among the Eastern Seaboard aristocracy. In his mind, cultural conflicts were responsible for the fact that purely physical relationships had always been distasteful to him, while, for some strange reason, sexual desire was absent in relationships with girls of a caste and character considered worthy of love and respect. Here, where he was isolated from the gaze of anyone who might recognize him, there was an opportunity to change these unrealistic reactions and release the pent-up lust with which his mind had been almost exclusively occupied since the age of twelve. He therefore lost no time plunging into an orgy of pure sex, night after night, and pretty soon he knew almost every whore, every call girl, and every barfly in every tawdry bar in the vicinity.

Unfortunately, relief from sexual starvation did nothing to improve Eliot's self-esteem. This son of a mother whose fundamental Methodism had been little altered by her diversion into a sect that degrades all

sensuous experience tumbled from the frying pan of
physical frustration into the fire of severe conflict
between bodily enjoyment and outraged morality.
Unaware of his deep underlying feeling that all sexual
desire was a sin, Eliot was also unable to recognize
himself as one of the countless men able to desire a
woman only if, in his unconscious mind, her caste or
color put her in a "degraded" category, regardless of
what she was like as an individual. He had been taught
as a child to like and respect lower-class girls who played
in his own backyard and was overwhelmed with shame
and degradation at the realization that pure lust,
unaccompanied by any finer feelings, pervaded his
present promiscuous relationships. The more he enjoyed
his life of sin, the more despairing he became, and on
one particular night he was saved from suicide only by a
strange circumstance.

Returning late from what he considered a sordid and
defiling experience, Eliot felt at the end of his rope. In
fierce battles with the devil, he had been routed every
time, and now he determined to end once and for all the
futility of his existence. With rat poison from the garden
shed, and a bottle of whiskey to brace his courage, he
decided to end his life. Nobody ever disturbed him in
his hideaway, and by the time anyone missed him, the
disgrace of his entire family would be at an end. The
decision was made, and he had every intention of
sticking by it. However, as he thought over his life
before ending it, the senselessness of its outcome
overwhelmed him, for in his soul he recognized what a
capacity for happiness had been wasted. He remembered
his relish for the countryside on a windy day, his
pleasure in voluptuous, fat sunflowers and beautiful
women. He remembered his feeling for moonlight, the
lilt of words, and the brightness of colors. He was
suddenly all too aware of what would be left behind,

and he did not want to go. Eliot was no crybaby but, at this moment of his extremity, he found himself wracked with sobs.

It was exactly at this moment, in the middle of the night, that his mother climbed the steps to his garage apartment and heard his sobs. This may be hard to believe, and those who do believe it could be accused of leaning toward the occult, but that is exactly what happened. She, who had never before invaded his privacy, invaded it at just that moment, for no reason other than a vague feeling of uneasiness that came upon her as she lay in the big house across the yard. Some intuition was aroused in his mother, perhaps some subconscious perception of his mental state acquired earlier in the evening, and she rose from her bed to visit him at just the moment that he had decided to take his life. She arrived at his bedside at the moment of overflow, managing to hear at its maximum intensity her son's outpouring of guilt, degradation, utter hope-lessness, and sorrow, and she responded as this mother was wont to do at certain moments of crisis. She recognized that one of her children was in the grips of a situation, which, although past her own comprehension, needed respect and support. For once she forgot to mention "truth," "error," or "mortal mind," and responded directly from that core within herself which knew very well the meaning of frustration and despair.

As she sat there by his bedside, waiting for his sobs to abate, Eliot's mother told him that she understood and did not blame him. She knew that men had these appetites that had to be satisfied, and although she felt sure some day he would find "just the right nice girl to marry," she realized that right now he had to do what he was doing. She also said that she knew an artist had to be an artist because God made him that way and, from now on, Eliot must give up money-making as a

major goal of his work. He must paint, if that was what
God meant him to do, and in whatever way she could
she would help him find his true self. Then she kissed
him tenderly on the forehead and tucked him into bed
like a little boy. She said he mustn't think about it any
more tonight, took away the rat poison, and went away
as silently as she had come, leaving him to sleep his first
truly restful night in a very long time.

Eliot awoke next morning considerably purged of his
guilt and anxiety, threw away his Horatio Alger scripts,
and got out the paints and canvas abandoned since early
Glen Alden days. Able now to express morbid fantasies
about women in strange, surrealistic pictures, his actual
ability to see them as people improved quite a bit.
Evening routines were not altered along with the change
in his daily work life, but hopes for many changes in the
future rose by leaps and bounds.

On a particular night several months later, Eliot stood
leaning on the bar of a newly discovered dive somewhere down the avenue, watching couples whirl around
a tiny dance floor with dizzying speed. So it seemed to
him, anyway, whether the dizziness was a product of
their pace or generated in his own head. He was in a
place offering maximal stimulation to all the senses—a
low-ceilinged room heavy with cheap perfume and
sweat, rattling with staccato music from a jukebox and
the tap of women's high heels to the beat of clapping
castanets. His eyes were slightly glazed, and to a man
almost saturated with atmosphere as well as with
alcohol, the sight of hips undulating rhythmically in the
soft rosy light did induce a certain giddiness.

Further down the bar sat a black-haired Mexican girl,
dressed in flowered chiffon cut to show a good deal of
flesh, and by her side a Mexican youth was paying her
most rapt and devoted attention. In her eyes was a very
particular kind of responding look, a look to which
Eliot had always been very susceptible, and when it

caught his eye, he too began paying her close attention, although still from a safe, respectful distance. Through the mists in his unsettled brain, that girl suddenly became the answer to a vague prayer, assuming at the moment a monumental significance in his emotional life.

There she was at last, the girl of his dreams, the wish come true. Fortunately, Eliot was not quite drunk enough to forget that the young man at her side might very well be carrying a knife, and he confined his activity to looking intently from where he stood. His admiration was not lost on the young lady in question, however, and with a subtle, barely perceptible movement, she conveyed an invitation perceived both by the watcher and the escort at her side. As the eyes of the two men met, the moment became distinctly uncomfortable for Eliot.

After all these years, he had at last found the one perfect girl in the world, just at a moment when he was clearly not in command of himself or of the situation as a whole. Knowing full well that to gaze any longer would court trouble with the Mexican youth, he shook himself loose from the spell he was under and steered an unsteady course between the tables toward the hall. Just as he made it and was about to try navigating the stairs, there, wonder of wonders, stood the girl herself.

She looked even prettier up close than she had from a distance. It was not merely her face and figure that affected Eliot, however, but her voice, her manner, and the way she held herself. To his eyes at that moment, she radiated a quintessence of femininity and represented everything he had ever longed for. What was even more astonishing, however, was that Eliot found himself in the throes of a condition which he had never known before. He was confronting in himself a phenomenon that he could hardly have imagined, let alone believed when it happened, but Eliot suddenly realized that he wanted all of her—wanted not only her body, as she doubtless had surmised from the way he had been looking at her, but her whole self. Physical desire and sincere personal liking were suddenly focused on the same human being—a wanting to be with her and to know her as a person as well as to enjoy her physical charms. At the same moment that he realized all this he also knew that the whole thing was absurd. He was irresponsibly tight and very nearly out of control, but it made no difference in his plans for the future. What seemed important to him was the determination made right then and there to see the thing through, to meet her on another night when, more in possession of himself, he would come to know all about her and establish a real relationship. In this resolution, the feeling of shuttling back and forth between two worlds was completely absent. He understood quite well in what kind of place he had met this girl and could imagine her background very well indeed, but it still made no difference. His motives were utterly sincere, and in his mind lay no conflict of any kind. This was true for the first time that he could remember.

When Eliot returned home to sleep off his besotted condition, there burst into his dreaming mind a wild roar of flame. The whole world was on fire, and as he stood on a hillside, seeing a swirl of flames light the sky, he heard the drone of a dirge for the son of President Roosevelt who had just died. Aware that his relations with the President's family had not been cordial in recent years, he nevertheless wanted to go and offer condolences to the President's wife, because he knew she would feel badly about losing her son. Then the flames leaped higher, consuming the whole world with purifying fire, and always in the background could be heard the drone of lament for a son who had descended at last to a place of darkness, leaving in his wake a conflagration that consumed the world.

Waking with a colossal hangover, Eliot was not in the

best condition to do much thinking, but nevertheless he
did think long and seriously about the events of the past
evening. It took only a slight decrease in the brain's
alcoholic content to make him realize that last night's
dream girl was a figment of his own imagination rather
than a girl whose actual qualities were apt to appeal to
his rational mind. At the same time, however, he felt that
the whole experience, including the dream, represented a
distinct shift in the balance of forces hitherto controlling his sexual inclinations. Eliot had great faith in
dreams as an expression of unconscious knowledge and
had given considerable attention to examining his own.
The President's son, a product of Groton and Harvard
who bore his own name, had appeared in his dreams
before, symbolizing a hated part of himself, the part
induced by contact with the Europe-oriented, elite
educational establishment which he felt had crushed his
native responses and brought about all his snobbish,
inhibited reactions. For the first time, a dream had tied
up this part of himself with his relationship to his
mother and indicated that in its death lay the possibility
of knowing and liking a woman for whom he also felt
lust. Taking the whole experience as evidence of a
turning point in his unconscious attitudes, Eliot was
encouraged and felt good in spite of his pounding head.

Dr. P. There were messages in that dream that
he did not interpret, but just the same, Eliot had
obviously come quite a long way in a short time. It
sounds as though he was not prepared to go any farther
with insight, and on the whole it is just as well he didn't
try. Total awareness would certainly have evoked
considerable agony at the time.

A.C. The agony came later, but before then he made
a lot of progress as an artist.

Dr. P. That dream gave promise that his tangled
sexual attitudes might eventually straighten out. Did he
ever have a good relationship with a woman?

A.C. Yes, but that was a long way off. Even after he

began to paint in earnest, the constriction of his emotional life remained much as before, and his release still awaited a lot of strange developments.

Eliot's life as a painter seemed at first fairly auspicious. Starting with landscapes done from nature in a somewhat stylized manner, he progressed toward what he considered "imaginative memories leaning in the direction of surrealism" and threw himself eagerly into attempts at immortalizing moonlight over cedar crests and bluebirds circling before the red barn at Glen Alden. Slapping great blobs of color onto canvas with a knife, he also found exhilarating enjoyment in the painting process for the first time. In retrospect it seemed nonsensical, really, but perhaps it gave the first indication that he could be an artist—someone at least daring enough to paint an inner vision with strong feeling and use a wild technique with carefree abandon.

Now and then a picture would raise hopes of pleasing the tyrant chosen for his art dealer, and off he would dash, canvas under arm and head filled with dreams of imminent fame. Now surely that stubborn man would agree to handle his work and make him some money at last. Poor dealer! Every amateur in town had the same idea, of course. However, his patience was infinite in explaining again and again that this was not yet quite the picture he had in mind. Over and over and over again he would encouragingly proclaim there was real promise in this work, but it takes time to become professional, so home Eliot would trudge, sickened by disappointment and ravished in his manhood. He was, after all, still his father's son, and who could claim any worth if nobody would buy his work?

Eventually abandoning these early strivings for his own way of painting, Eliot decided to study with a famous teacher and found a job as assistant in a small art gallery to help pay for the lessons. And he did very well, becoming professional enough to win first prize in a museum exhibition of unknown artists from throughout the nation. There was no money yet, of course, but a promise of real recognition now loomed before his eyes, a promise that filled everyone he knew with joy and hope. Even Eliot himself felt a momentary surge of hope, and a sense of manly vigor arose from his success. However, this surge was only the precursor of despair, for as he hoped, he began to realize what he was hoping for, and that realization became the straw to break his morale completely. Eliot became aware that, in spite of all his efforts to shake false values from the past, in spite of all his dreams of changing attitudes and hopes of development as an individual, in spite of all his visions of emancipation from the "cultural establishment" and of freedom to paint according to his own nature, all he really hoped for was acclaim from the companions of his youth and reinstatement in the world to which he must belong to call himself a Man. When he realized that, he also realized that the supreme discomfort he had been feeling at work in the art gallery was nothing more or less than a fear of being seen in that menial position by someone who had known him in the past. With that insight, the success of his current life turned to ashes in his mouth. His momentary hope of manhood received a deathblow, and the sickness of his soul finally burst out in forms he could no longer avoid recognizing. Eliot at last knew he was in real trouble.

One day he suddenly became aware of a strong urge to reach out and kiss every man he passed, an urge so compelling he could barely manage to resist. Upon returning home in a state of inexpressible horror, he again felt an irresistible compulsion, this time to pick up his brush and paint almost automatically a series of weird visions. First came a forest of dead trees hung with strangled female figures, then an inferno of

tortured wraiths, and finally a strange portrait, produced without volition, as though his hand were guided
by an unknown force. A cross-legged nude of andro-
gynous character emerged on the canvas before him,
elevated in a place of semigloom, where only one small
window showed the world outside through a dull and
misty film. The face of this creature was small in
proportion to the masculine body and breasts, wasted in
form and expression, while his-her hand held a stone
cup without a handle into which he-she poured a liquid.
Reminiscing later about his state of mind at the time,
Eliot remembered that, while painting, he thought of
that liquid as tea. Tea! Alone and crepuscular, a being
utterly bereft was impersonating a good British-Ameri-
can with a nice cup of tea. That is what he painted, and
that is obviously what he felt himself to be—a bisexual
wraith on a shadowy pedestal, pouring away his life
substance at a tea party.

Looking down at what he had painted, Eliot suddenly
knew what he was facing and realized that unless he did
something without delay no mother climbing the attic
steps could save him again. In despair, he reached for
the only kind of help he knew how to ask for. At a
museum party he had met the head of a clinic for
Mental Therapy Through Hand Analysis, where supposedly the scientific study of lines in the hand was
extended into therapeutic discussions of personality
characteristics depicted therein. It was there that he
now turned.

Nobody raised a voice against Eliot's decision to seek
therapy in such a place, because nobody other than
himself had any idea what he was suffering or what he
planned to do about it. He understood that most people
would find it impossible to comprehend, let alone
tolerate, the idea that any decent person could have
such a problem, and that it would be specifically
impossible for anyone in the Carpenter family to

recognize his emotional state without disintegrating. Even his sister Amy, who could be counted on for understanding in many areas, could not be counted on to tolerate this, and in any case, it would have been unthinkable for a gentleman to discuss homosexual impulses with his mother or sister, no matter how intimate they might be in other ways. Since there was nobody who could bear to hear of such things, he mentioned them to nobody and found his only hope of salvation in Mental Therapy Through Hand Analysis.

Eliot had never shared his mother's reluctance to seek medical help for physical illness, and he did not reject it now. It simply never occurred to him that a doctor could help anyone with this kind of problem, and he did not question the validity of palmistry as an instrument for psychological evaluation. After all, he had been intrigued since early youth with shrewd analyses of family members by his Aunt Hattie and his mother's friend Kate and saw nothing at all unreasonable in a concept that destiny writes in the palm as well as on convolutions of the brain. He therefore entered treatment with confidence and enthusiasm, never doubting it could lead him to the source of his troubles. Even in retrospect he never regretted the decision and felt his experience to be more valuable than anything else that had ever happened to him.

To facilitate recalling his past, Eliot started an autobiography that also described his feelings about important current events and in it expressed the emotion with which he began uncovering the secrets of his unconscious mind so long imprisoned by an over-powering mass of inhibitions. As he and the therapist studied his hands, seeing the potential with which he had started life and the ways in which his natural inclinations had been tortured and twisted into alien forms, the forces that had been stifled throughout the years seemed to flow through his body in a torrent of joy and excitement, replacing the weak tea of his life with a revitalizing current of great intensity. It shattered the chains that had bound him since childhood and "burst through the gloom of [his] painting as a glorious dawn bursts through the gloom of darkest night." His senses were freed, and with it all came a capacity for mystical understanding with which to conquer the mysteries of his own soul. Other people might not understand, but that no longer mattered. At last the smothering, strangling world of the "finest development" no longer cast its shadow over his heart and mind.

From the black finale that took him into treatment, he awoke at last into a feeling of new existence which opened as the breaking of daylight on canvas. Out of the blue dawn, a glittering crown of jewels rose above the horizon to the singing of strange birds.

Throughout his life, Eliot had felt there was a "paint motif" buried within him and had sometimes even seen it. Once during his college years, while arguing with a friend, there had drifted across his inward vision the weird branch of a tree hung with strange fruits and objects, colored in a way that made it distinct from any branch he had ever seen in art or nature. In retrospect, he felt it an image emerging straight from his artist-self, and although it did not appear again for another ten years, now it came out at last. Even if others did not know it for what it was, he knew, and that was all that mattered. The truth was emerging, and emerging in a way that he saw as merely a final step in the natural development of his progress toward enlightenment.

One night in a dream he saw a strange flower, a flower like a Canterbury bell, with a series of cubes leading up to terminal blossoms on the stalk. Feeling impelled to paint this image, Eliot selected from the old canvases stored to be reused one which happened to have a bright area where a sunset had been sandpapered out. In the new painting, flowers at the stalk's end fell upon this area, with cubes running into a dark part, and the brightest part of the sunset came just at the juncture of cubes and flowers. By brightening the place still further, he suddenly achieved an explosive effect. Then the stem of the flower began to disintegrate as paint slopped over it, and the cubes began to look like a rock blown to bits by a blast. Out of this blast, "flowers were shot up into the abstract air of [Eliot's] life." He felt this as the moment that his own personal pseudomorphosis was giving way to the explosive forces of pent-up libido. A rock-crust covering was breaking, flowers were shooting up, and there was not an end, but a beginning.

Thereafter, bit by bit, the covered paint motif in his life began to come out. Gradually he began to see glimmerings not only of pictures reborn but of a world reborn. Once the form was elucidated, the scope of what he discovered was endless. He realized too that he was coming upon this paint world not with astonishment but with a wonderful feeling of recognition. At last he had really found himself, and although far into the years of maturity, he had now come together and knew himself for what he was.

The autobiography, started as an adjunct to therapy, was never to be finished in the spirit of its onset. The more Eliot scrutinized the conditions and development of his life, the less he was able to accept the singularity of his situation. As he viewed himself and his story, it seemed that he gazed upon a panorama not of one man's misfortune but of a collective condition. He began to realize he had been put on earth for a purpose, and that it was his destiny to lead American culture away from the morass into which it had fallen.

During the many years of his youth, Eliot had been a student of sorts, a wastrel student to be sure but even so a student who, shortly after graduating from college, "suffered the tragedy of encountering a black book." This book, immersed in gloom, said that the world of our era is dead and creativity in any true sense impossible. Others had been fortunate enough to read Spengler's *The Decline of the West* and sneer at its message, but for Eliot this happy course was impossible, because he knew Spengler to be right. His whole life had proved it, and he himself was a living example of the American tragedy, suffering from "infantile paralysis" common to the whole land. Not until after the onset of his therapy, however, did he recognize his suffering as ordained in order that he might save his countrymen from destruction.

Spengler had coined a term to describe this disease on a historical level—*historic pseudomorphosis*, a term derived from mineralogy meaning "false form." Eliot saw Americans as a young people trapped within alien European forms and selling their birthright for a mess of pottage. He felt his destiny was to use newfound understanding for changing the direction in which his countrymen were going.

It has been said that the American problem is "paralysis of the feeling function." Certainly Eliot was a personification of this problem, a tortured sufferer of the terrible, voiceless nightmare he had had some time earlier.

Along the ocean shore in early evening, sand was being washed by gentle waves, and the whole mood was one of peace. In the distance a group of men appeared, walking in a deep hush on the stillness of dream footsteps. In their midst, they led a man stripped to the waist, and at a certain point they stopped, tying his hands to a stake in the sand. While they savagely began to whip him, he made no outcry at all. All remained still, peaceful, and lovely under the twilight sky. The only sound was of beating, to the lapping of noiseless waves.

For years it had been going on. This man, with no reality and no power of resistance, had been created by the "finest development" of an alien culture—this cultivated pseudo-European gentleman who could not cry out but only felt his failure and humiliation as the whips fell. The true self had been hiding, but now it was found. Eliot finally realized the agony had had a purpose—the purpose of teaching him how to return Americans to their own spiritual form, away from historic pseudomorphosis into a new state of consciousness and a new space continuum. Under his direction, this country would eventually play a role of "earth-navel to the liberation and ultimate Paradise of the whole planet." From now on, he had no time to waste.

With the dawn of his enlightenment, Eliot Jr.'s work expanded and veered sharply away from its previous direction. The autobiography, begun as a purely personal document, now became the foundation for a historico-philosophical treatise of considerable magnitude. Having discovered that his mission in life was to refute Spenglerian prophecies of doom, Eliot proceeded in an attempt to become the messiah who would lead Americans away from false forms crushing and distorting their lives and bring them into a new spiritual dimension. His painting, directed to the same end, shook off the restrictions of technical perfection and loosed upon the canvas luminous visions of a free world in metamorphosis. Dawn broke in a flow of oil and gouache, flames shot from the brush to destroy gloomy decadence, and throughout strange, shining landscapes, totally new forms sprang from the ashes. The coming world bloomed with ingeniously designed stylized spikes and steles placed upon rounded objects, and alongside such complexes, over and over again appeared variations of jewel-encrusted cups, crowns, and unearthly flowers growing out of imaginatively constructed objects, all similar in shape.

It would have been difficult to persuade Eliot that

these forms and structures bore any relationship to recognizable objects in the world around him, so firmly convinced was he that emanations from his unconscious mind were visual representations of entirely new concepts. However, it would have been equally difficult to persuade anyone who did not know him that he had never to anyone's knowledge seen anatomical drawings or diagrams, so much did many of these forms resemble representations familiar to any student of biology. Nevertheless, both these statements were true. Eliot's education had been totally lacking in exposure to any kind of biological science, and it is rather doubtful that he even knew the names of internal bodily organs. There could be no question, however, that in every painting he had somewhere portrayed a perfectly recognizable Prussian helmet, over which floated the anatomical uterus with fallopian tubes, whose bell-like fimbriated infundibula sometimes appear so distinctly floral. Totally unbeknownst to himself, he was filling his new world with a wealth of skillfully executed, beautifully designed, imaginatively painted, and hardly at all disguised symbols of bisexuality. This was his happy and inspired occupation at the time that a piece of good fortune befell him.

Jingo

A.C. While all this was happening to Eliot, Jingo and Alex hit Hollywood like a high wind that sets dry leaves whirling and flying on an autumn day. You never saw two people so full of energy and high spirits with which to enter the full life before them, or with more enthusiasm with which to tackle anything that might come their way. The world was their oyster, and they were about to open it with the fullest enjoyment.

In no time at all, Jingo had invested her last lump sum of cash in a lovely house, not expensive or in a really fashionable neighborhood, but a solid house with character and potential. After all, scriptwriters and other literati with whom they would soon be associated appreciate charm and originality so much more than pretentiousness. Some remodeling, painting, and planting would turn it into a little gem, and the resale value would probably double before Alex was high enough in the hierarchy to think in terms of Beverly Hills. If things were a little slow at first, they could always grow mushrooms commercially in the basement. Alex knew somebody who had made a fortune that way by studying some brochures from the Department of Agriculture, and that person hadn't known any more about mushrooms to start with than he and Jingo. Jingo might even set up a little business, combining mushroom sales with promotion of a cookbook she would write. She had always been very practical and ingenious about thinking up original ways to make money, and although her imagination had so far been wasted in trying to help friends and relatives organize their lives, she could now capitalize on her own talents. There were so many possibilities, they hardly knew where to start.

By the time the house was bought, Alex's divorce became final, and they were quietly married. Jingo's alimony stopped at that point, of course, but Alex had a little money left over after all the divorce expenses, and this, along with a small loan from his brother against the share he would get from their eventual inheritance, would tide the couple over nicely until earnings started rolling in. Mortgage payments would be no problem for a while, and two people don't eat much. Nothing foreseeable could put a hitch into these perfect plans.

Unfortunately, they had overlooked one small detail. The whole plan was predicated on the idea that earnings would roll in rather soon, but as a matter of fact, earnings did not roll in at all. Friends who had all but guaranteed a fine job for Alex by furnishing the "in" to proper writing circles didn't fulfill their promises. They did introduce him to a number of producers and gave several parties to acquaint him with all their colleagues, but the producers turned out to be unexpectedly evasive, and although the writers were fascinated and charmed by Alex and Jingo, they simply didn't come up with anything concrete to get Alex established. Some people have no sense of responsibility. They make fine promises but don't feel called upon to follow through. Alex was very disappointed in all his friends, and finding himself with offers of only a few hackwriting jobs far below his potential, he decided it was not worthwhile wasting his talents in potboiling when he could use them to write the novel he had always had in mind. Jingo, also quite indignant with the turn of events, agreed completely. While Alex settled down to write, she worked on the house. Being unusually clever and creative about the use of colors and interesting combinations of texture and materials, she created an exciting background for her lovely antique furnishings. They had some wonderful parties and made a great variety of friends in a very short time, but it turned out that two really could not eat quite as cheaply as she had hoped.

Both Jingo and Alex appreciated good food and felt it very important to make a good impression on their discerning friends. California wines are all very well, but you can hardly serve anything but a good little French wine to someone with an educated palate. Even if you have only a few people to dinner now and then, the cocktails, the wine, and the highballs, not to speak of the brandy, come to more than you would expect.

Dr. P. Hadn't Jingo run the household when she was married to Sid?

A.C. She had, for ten years. However, she had never been in charge of the liquor and had never paid the grocery bills. Although she knew how to transform bargain meat cuts into gourmet dishes, her sauces included a good deal of sour cream and fine condiments that can be found only in rather esoteric food stores. She had always prided herself on doing so much with cheap cuts of meat and had never realized the cost of the little extra ingredients that always just seemed to be in the house. It was really astonishing how the bills had mounted before they even got started.

After a few months, Jingo began to panic a little and talked the situation over with Alex at great length. Both agreed that household expenses must be reduced until he got on his feet and vowed to eat with utmost simplicity. However, it was not quite as easy to cut down as they had hoped. Alex, out shopping for breakfast eggs and a loaf of bread, would happen upon an exciting new brand of potted pâté, and before arriving home, he had also picked up some anchovies, along with a few jars of artichoke hearts. Only the most incidental little snacks, really, and hardly worth counting. Jingo panicked some more, however, when no change returned from a ten-dollar bill, and she soon began to nag. There would be a terrible scene, but after an angry outburst she usually forgave him, because she didn't want to damage his morale, and financial insecurity was already beginning to interfere with his ability to concentrate. After each altercation, he soon stopped sulking and then, while talking with great animation about the progress of his novel, both he and Jingo settled down to a splendid array of hors d'oeuvres with their drinks. A battle whetted not only their appetites but their thirst as well, and the liquor bills went up rather than down.

As time passed with no diminution in the number of Alex's little irresponsible purchases, the battles were stepped up in frequency and fervor. Virginia became

more and more punishing, Alex more and more humble
and contrite after each spanking; this preceded a
restoration to good humor by food, drink, and a mighty
reconciliation in bed, but through it all, there was
hardly a break in the animated conversation that had
been going on between them, with only a ten-year
interval, since the age of fifteen.

Life might have continued like that until the last
dime was spent, but happily fortune at last smiled upon
them. Through friends came an opportunity to buy the
nearly defunct weekly newspaper of a beach town not
far away, and after extensive discussion pro and con,
both decided it was just what they needed. They had no
idea why the paper was failing but felt perfectly sure
that with talent and energy it could be restored to life.

Here was a real chance for Alex to show his true
capability. The novel could wait until they were
established and would only profit from the marvelous
experiences they would have while gathering news.

Jingo found the perfect tenant to rent their house
furnished—a doctor who actually preferred that part of
town to Beverly Hills and was glad to pay well for a
beautiful and tasteful setting. A second mortgage on the
house would bring enough for a down payment on
another house in Ocean Sands, and the rent would cover
all carrying charges. Alex's brother was sufficiently
enthusiastic about his buying a newspaper to risk
another loan, and for a remarkably low price they found
a highly atmospheric little house in a picturesque hollow
just outside the town. Before long, Alex and Jingo were
in the publishing business, living in a community
bursting with interesting characters and material for
zany anecdotes. But neither of them had much business
experience, of course.

Dr. P. I thought Alex had run a book store for many
years.

A.C. He had, in a sense. However, a business manager took care of all the tiresome details. All he really had to do was confer with publishers and keep up with the output of new writers.

He and Jingo learned fast, however, and were soon on their way to making the paper thrive. They ran their feet off getting advertising, talked to people, wrote columns and editorials, and did such a fine job that circulation jumped. In time there was promise that the revenue would not only cover the small salaries they paid themselves but produce a substantial profit as well. The townspeople, charmed by these two attractive, enterprising folk, cheered and applauded.

Jingo and Alex were nearly euphoric with excitement, undaunted even when they discovered that their house had been so cheap because water running down the hills on all four sides collected in the hollow and flooded the lower floor. They merely extracted hysterically funny stories from the whole situation, selling the house at a slight profit to in-coming Easterners during the next dry season. With the proceeds, they bought two more little houses, one to live in, the other to rent. Now their combined rents covered loan payments and carrying charges on all three houses. Jingo, who had always prided herself on her business acumen, gave here demonstrable proof that if you just use a little imagination, things pay off.

It might actually have worked out for them too, had their luck held a little longer. Unfortunately, the nice Hollywood doctor died rather suddenly, and it proved exceedingly difficult to replace him with another tenant willing to pay the same rent, because "nouveaux riches peasants" who were invading Hollywood in droves seemed to prefer a flashy address in the Hills to a house of solid worth and good decoration. Some were even crass enough to say they preferred early American or modern decor. Jingo did everything anyone could have done to get a tenant who would value and care for her beloved possessions, but in the end she had to put them in storage and rent the house unfurnished for slightly less than the cost of the payments on its two mortgages, to say nothing of the storage costs.

Meanwhile, she and Alex were encountering a different kind of crassness in the newspaper world. The success of their publication was beginning to cut into advertising revenues of the local daily, owned by a "vulgar rich boor" with large interests in most of the town's established businesses. After they had indignantly refused his offer to buy them out without loss of their original investment, he began to put pressure on advertisers. Pretty soon the weekly was just making it from one printing to the next, with no capital behind it, and nothing to fall back on. Alex and Jingo worked harder and harder, everyone in the little town sympathizing with the raw deal they were getting, but business is business, and if your major financial backer says to advertise only in the daily, what can you do? Eventually the weekly had to close down, just as it had to do under its previous owner, and what with all the mortgage payments, Jingo and Alex were about as broke as two people could possibly be. It was heartbreaking, really, and everyone was terribly sympathetic. All was not lost, however. Just about that time, along came another wonderful opportunity.

There arrived in town a retired naval lieutenant and his wife who were immediately captivated by Jingo and Alex. He had just finished drawing up engineering plans for the invention of a new model machine gun that would revolutionize the arms industry, and he had plenty of contacts in high Navy engineering circles to get it into production. All he needed at the moment was money to build the miniature replica required for demonstration, and where could he find two people with a more magnetic, imaginative approach to fund raising than our friends? He and his wife would share their own house, Alex's and Jingo's house could be rented to cover the cost of food for all four, and before long everyone would be rich.

Alex couldn't have been more enthusiastic. This time Jingo had a few qualms, but they were not great enough to counteract everyone else's confidence in the venture, so they all started working like beavers. They did manage to arouse quite a bit of interest in the gun among people who know about such things, and they even raised a little money. It wasn't enough, however, and after a long, painful time, the whole project fell through. The rents hadn't managed to cover their expenses either, try as they might to economize, and eventually all three houses were lost by mortgage foreclosures.

Financially Jingo and Alex were back to where they had been five years earlier, but in every other way things had deteriorated badly. As frustration had built up, so had Alex's need to bolster his morale with extravagant little items of self-indulgence, and with everyone drunk well before dinner time, violent battles occurred daily, with less satisfying reconciliations. Toward the end of that period, Jingo developed intractable pain in a knee unstable since childhood and began to suffer from acute, intermittent attacks of a weeping skin disease covering her entire body. As anxiety and pain built up, so did her anger. This was channeled more and more toward her mother for putting up with the runaround dished out by her father and toward Eliot Jr. for being such a bloodsucking deadbeat.

Dr. P. Her tendency to displace feelings about Alex hadn't changed much.

A.C. No, it hadn't. Finally the combination of pain and anger became such a total preoccupation that Jingo could no longer think about anything except her own problems. She gradually became a chronic invalid who, within a month of her grandmother's death, moved herself, her husband, and two cats into the garage apartment vacated when Eliot moved his studio to the top floor of the main house. While Alex resumed work on his novel, Jingo began breeding pedigreed Persian kittens to sell, taking up a life largely secluded with her husband, in which unremitting conversation about his novel, mutual recriminations, and a rehash of the injustices they both had suffered furnished almost their only form of diversion. Fortunately, the interest and animation with which they talked together did not abate one whit, regardless of what else might be going on, and they seemed to need little outside stimulation. Neither disappointment, alcohol, bitterness, or boredom could extinguish Jingo's eager delight in constant communication with Alex. Nor could anything stifle her faith in her husband's ultimate success.

Meanwhile, Laura, recognizing that the artistic gifts of her children periodically tended to create financial problems for them, decided to sell Glen Alden, the only real asset she had free from control of a trust company, and distributed the proceeds to each of her three children for living expenses "until they could get on their financial feet." Then, confident of her own ability to get along nicely on a small income derived from capital nobody could touch, she settled back to busy herself with a very interesting and creative doll collection while waiting for Eliot Sr.'s business in the Middle West to be concluded.

Amy

A.C. Mother sold the Glen Alden house shortly after I arrived in the West myself, but before going into the effects of that, I'll have to tell you what was happening to me during the time all those things were happening to El and Jingo. As you know, after leaving Glen Alden I set off for New York where the House of Decayed Gentility was waiting to welcome me with open arms. By that time, of course, my path had veered sharply from the one on which my former friends were serenely traveling, and I was a little hesitant to look up some of them because I felt so "different." On the other hand, I felt very much at home among the men and women with whom I was living, and on the whole things really went rather well for me in the business world right from the start.

Anyone making an objective evaluation of Amy's progress during her six years in New York would have to admit that she was an exceedingly favored young woman who had operated under a very lucky star. All her efforts were crowned by unmitigated success, and in that short time she established herself in a career that any girl might justifiably envy. Propelled by her own conscientious work, charm, and a little pure luck, Amy managed to put herself just where she wanted to be and, by the age of twenty-seven, had attained almost everything she could possibly want. Almost.

After only a few months in the secretarial pool of a large advertising company, she was considered promising enough to get a chance at writing radio commercials for an important steamship account. Before the end of her first year, Amy was hired by the head of that steamship line and given the kind of job many a young woman dreams about—a promotional job with good salary and intermittent travel throughout the world at company expense. For nearly two years she went everywhere, met people of all kinds, and made a few lasting friendships in every group. By the time she had learned that scholar-

ships were not "charity" and had decided to enter graduate school after all, enough money had been saved to carry her through a Ph.D. in one of America's leading universities, after which she received a much-coveted appointment to a fascinating and well-paid research project. Of course she remained unmarried, but with her personality and good looks, and with most of her life still ahead, who could worry about that?

During those years, Amy had put up a very good front, and only those with whom she was closely associated recognized that beneath the surface all was not quite as it should be. Those few all felt rumblings of concern for her happiness and shook their heads with worry about her future.

To a man, employers and professors thought Amy a fine girl who had a head on her shoulders and worked extremely hard for anyone to whom she gave her allegiance. All of them wanted her to continue working with them and felt a parental affection for her. This feeling was often shared by their wives, who inevitably clucked about Amy's rather hectic gaiety and tried to introduce nice, steady young men to make her settle down. Although rather stubborn and demanding of perfection in those she admired, Amy tended to get under the skin of those in authority over her and called up in them a feeling of protectiveness that often lay upon them as a heavy sense of responsibility for her welfare.

Boyfriends, too, were concerned about her. Many men found her attractive—a lively, amusing playmate and a stimulating conversationalist. One by one, however, they realized that, although she seemed responsive to preliminary sexual advances, it would be impossible to make a real connection with this elusive creature. She was such a mess of contradictions—one minute on top of the world, full of fun and ideas, the next minute heavy with a sadness that seemed to arise out of nowhere; able to talk intelligently on so many subjects, yet suddenly capable of going all gooey with clichés and vagueness. Sooner or later, in some strange unfathomable way, each one came to feel like a brute, walking on eggs to avoid hurting her, and eased away into a friendly relationship that persisted even after marriage to a girl who also liked Amy and who tried to marry her off to a friend or brother. Amy just naturally had a talent for making men worry about her, but she remained always behind an emotional barrier.

The same was true with her women friends, to some extent, and had been even during her college days. Everyone then had at least known who she was. Most contemporaries held her in some awe because of her athletic ability and the poise that inevitably got her elected to jobs like ushering VIPs around campus or introducing lecturers. However, many found her standoffish, resenting the polite, impersonal friendliness that made her seem "snooty." Her close friends had been mostly girls with whom she had gone all through school, and these alone had any idea what she was like. Many of them remained good friends throughout her working years—the ones, that is, who were persistent enough and aggressive enough to keep on asking her over and reassuring her that they still valued the friendship. Any one of these few would have commented on her situation somewhat like this:

"Until you've known Amy for a long time, you can't really believe that behind all that look of self-assurance she is shy and fearful of not being liked. People think it's a put-on because the whole idea is so incredible, but she just isn't sure of acceptance unless someone else makes the first move. She's a good friend, and when she feels relaxed she can be great fun, but you really have to worry about her too, because she's such a screwball—

always changing her major and acting like an intellectual when that's the last thing in the world she really wants to be. Amy adores little children, and little children respond immediately to her. Anyone who's that good with them ought to be having them, not studying them. You can't tell me she really wants a career, even if she is so successful. She just wants a man more capable than she is, and that's hard to find. If she ever finds anyone special enough to suit her, you can bet she will settle down and be quite content to let him have the career. If not, of course, she will without a doubt become our first woman president."

Although much of this was partly true, Amy's friends would have said it not because they really understood her, but because they assumed she was basically like themselves. Her close friends from college days were attractive, rather extroverted conformists from secure backgrounds, who probably did not recognize, and certainly could not have verbalized, what they dimly perceived about her and what Amy had known about herself for a long time—that her only real interest was to gain the love and respect of people she loved and respected, and that all her choices had been governed by a desire to reach that goal. Learning was simply a means of making relationships with people she cared for, as were her frequent changes of field, from the biology major inspired by Marty, her beloved high school science teacher, to the final English major urged by an English professor who almost adopted her into his family. Her friends correctly perceived what it was she valued, but they had no real insight into her motivations. Having themselves married professional men or business executives within a few years of graduation, the majority were happy in domestic lives brightened by interesting volunteer or creative activities and could not imagine anyone from their inner circle wanting anything different. Amy certainly wasn't the kind of screwball who would prefer academic life. That was for the "greasy grinds" of the world, and she was anything but that.

Only a few of Amy's closest post-college friends would have been able to report that Amy was deeply troubled—the very few who had been allowed behind her effective facade and had been given a glimpse of private anguish hidden from almost everyone else. Because they had shared with Amy the experience of feeling caught between two different worlds, they understood her better than others did and realized that, although she did want more than anything else to be a wife and mother, there were things within her that interfered with her ability to form intimate relationships with men. But even these understanding friends would have been inclined to say that Amy was only going through a phase they had all been through and would be OK as soon as she learned to make the compromises they had all been forced to make. For a long time, Amy thought the same thing herself.

Without voluntarily choosing to rebel against their background, this particular group of young women had been forced by circumstances to leave the world in which they grew up—a highly protected and special world—and to enter the competitive working world, where a majority of their associates had been reared with very different expectations from life. Until their families had become relatively impoverished by the depression, none of these young women had expected to have to make a living, nor had they had much opportunity to mingle with people from other segments of society. Nothing had prepared them for the clash of cultures that invariably takes place to some degree between people who, although congenial in all fundamental human ways, are accustomed to see things from a different angle. One could describe their point of view in these more general terms.

It is no harder to become part of a foreign culture than to move from one area in society to another. Attitudes, tastes, and speech patterns rooted in early environmental influences are often difficult to eradicate completely, even though the individual may consider them inappropriate to a new role in life. However, those who wish to escape poverty, ignorance, or a degraded position in the social scale find great motivation for change and the promise of great rewards in increased prestige and self-esteem. Those who move away from a place high on the economic totem pole into the everyday world where most people live have just as great an adjustment problem as those who aspire to a place higher in the scale of affluence; in fact, they may find their situation even more difficult to cope with. From birth on, they have been surrounded by those who regarded themselves as arbiters of good taste and setters of standards. They have enjoyed the benefits of luxury, deferential treatment, and the opportunities that come automatically without struggle or self-denial. Everything in their experience has instilled a sense of having rather special status, and although they might be glad to escape the rigidities and restrictions imposed by an exclusive ingroup, they often find it hard to relinquish feelings of specialness and to become merely human beings among other human beings. One of the most difficult adjustment problems is altering attitudes toward the values of those who come from less socially and economically "advantaged" groups.

Although American society is supposedly classless, every student of sociology knows there is a strict division of socioeconomic groups with quite different manners and mores. The values and attitudes of the so-called middle class often differ as greatly from those at the top of the ladder as they do from those at the bottom, and feelings about such differences often run as strong as feelings about differences in race, color, and creed. In fact, prejudices and snobberies attributed to the latter are often engendered primarily by class value distinctions, despite lip service to the contrary, and people raised with the same class value system feel akin regardless of how greatly they are separated by other cultural differences.

Those who identify themselves with the higher levels of society are accustomed to having what everyone else wants and to being both looked up to and resented because they have it. This feeling draws them as closely together as members of any minority group are drawn. Unlike members of other minority groups, however, their own sense of personal security and their position of prestige in the society as a whole are strengthened by the very fact of belonging. Outsiders, purely by virtue of their exclusion, may unconsciously be looked down upon by those who "belong," even though they themselves may not recognize their own attitudes and would hotly deny them.

Children from such a background have frequently accepted unusual privileges as if they were given by divine right, without even recognizing them as special privileges, and have had inextricably woven into their feeling of identity snobbish attitudes, stereotypes, and speech patterns considered by others to indicate affectation. On the other hand, they have also been imbued with a strong sense of the responsibility placed upon them by elevated status, and they have been taught that democratic attitudes are among the highest virtues. When such children are separated from their own kind and placed in a milieu that does not accept them as special, they may protect themselves against both real and imagined rejection by expressing intolerant atti-

tudes that they themselves are trying hard to shake, enduring agonies of self-hatred whenever they become aware of their own snobbishness. This cannot help but affect their relationships with individuals who do not understand the culture from which they come and who may ridicule identifiable signs of "belonging" to which they themselves aspire.

Such had been Amy's position, and that of the friends with whom she felt most identified—friends "born to the purple" who had also developed close relationships with people on all levels of society and who had been torn because they felt neither totally at home with anyone alien to their original caste nor completely satisfied with anyone still within its protective confines. These young women understood her tendency to find in every man she met qualities that either jarred her sensibilities or violated her more rational standards. The good, solid, loving men with whom she was really comfortable were seldom "smart" or sophisticated, often shocking her by a gauche expression or what she considered atrocious, vulgar taste in shoes or neckties. On the other hand, "smart" people lacked the pleasant earthiness of those from more homespun backgrounds and had appallingly narrow political views. Highly refined, intellectual men with urbanized tastes seemed too effete, but gentlemen farmers were too insensitive to human complexity and could be disgustingly pretentious about their English pipes or tailor-made tweeds. So it went, and she struggled against the irrationality of it in shame and self-condemnation. All her post-college women friends had been through the same thing and, sympathizing with the agonies of struggle, tended to attribute most of Amy's unhappiness to the fact that she had not yet resolved her guilts or outgrown the feelings with which she struggled.

Even her closest confidantes did not know that a split in cultural identity was only one of the many ways in which Amy was divided into different people who wanted completely contradictory things out of life. They could not have known because they were not sophisticated about psychological matters and because Amy could not confide what she was only beginning dimly to understand herself.

Amy had always been a somewhat introspective girl, aware of the multiple contradictions in her nature. As a matter of fact, she had secretly considered herself a fraud who would have no friends at all if anyone suspected the extent of her hypocrisies or knew how deplorably sloppy her thinking really was. The opinions she held were so often the opposite of what she really felt deep down, and the rational processes had to fight hard against a tendency to make emotionally based decisions. She was in a chronic state of fear lest good sense give way completely, leaving her at the mercy of impulse and absurdity. Her mother's example was ever before her eyes as a warning of what can happen if you yield to wishful thinking, and Amy so often felt just like her mother. It was torment to be aware of an inner war making it impossible to take a firm stand on anything. Even her emotional states were unpredictable. Moods slid up and down the scale from complete well-being to deep depression, and there seemed to be no sure base from which to operate. Often she felt nearly exhausted by all this sliding back and forth, suspecting that her energy would long ago have been consumed had it not been for the ability to regain strength like Antaeus, touching mother earth periodically in Vermont or Glen Alden. On the other hand, awareness of the need to return to adolescence whenever she couldn't cope filled Amy with shame and disgust. She did feel caught between two cultures but knew that this was just a convenient hook on which to hang her difficulties. Too many irreconcilable incompatibilities within her own soul were what she herself held responsible for her inability to fall in love.

A short time previously she had come to suspect the

presence of specific sexual problems, because only then had she realized that feelings aroused by nice, kind, suitable men did not approach in intensity the physical excitement aroused by men of an entirely different sort. What she had recognized filled her with horror and had driven her close to despair.

As she neared the quarter-century mark in her life, Amy, embarrassed by her virginity and hoping to conquer timidity through actual experience, made a purposeful decision to take as a lover the very next man who seemed attractive. And she did just that. Had she known a little more about herself at the time, she would have recognized that a big part of the attraction stemmed from her own cold-blooded intention to seduce, and that the man she chose was of a kind best suited to respond to such an attitude. However, recognizing only that here was someone exciting, she by-passed all the nice young men who really liked her and gravitated like a homing pigeon to a cold, egocentric man who cared nothing for her whatsoever, humiliated her subtly in many ways, and then, fortunately soon, cast her aside. A deep sense of loathing had already supplanted her fascination with this man, loathing for him and her own calculating, immoral plan that created such a mess.

Even after the affair ended, however, it was impossible to shake off his memory. So greatly was she stimulated by recapitulating his degrading attitudes in fantasy that the whole affair became a major preoccupation which threatened to drive out all other concerns. More and more, Amy retreated from people who related to her with tenderness and caring into a relationship based on submission to force and humiliation, a relationship that no longer existed except in her own head.

In this condition she finally left New York and

*headed for a new job in San Francisco. By the time of
her arrival in the West, Amy had been wondering for
some time whether she was on the verge of going crazy.
There was no doubt in her mind that she was in a very
bad way and that something had to be done about it,
but she had so far managed to stifle the thought every
time it came to the surface and had gone on with her
work as though nothing at all was the matter.*

   *On a cold day in August, not long after settling into
the first house she had ever owned, Amy looked out
into the fog and shuddered. A sharp wind off the ocean
blew fog into the hills, obscuring the view of all but a
few eucalyptus branches reaching up from the steep
slope beneath an over-cropping deck, and the house
seemed completely cut off from the rest of the world.
Hoping to counteract a chill in her heart by the
brightness of a fire, she closed the curtains and turned
back into a gay room paneled in redwood and bright
with books lining two walls. Reds and blues of canvas
sling-back chairs stood out against a fluffy white rug,
and the whole atmosphere was in sharp contrast to the
grey both outside her window and inside Amy herself.
Its cheeriness served only to point up her mood, and she
finally sank onto the sofa letting the tears flow.
Fortunately she was alone. Amy would have been
deeply ashamed to have anyone see such a disgusting
display of weakness, especially at a time when she
should have been happy, but couldn't help herself and
knew from experience that when a struggle for control
was obviously already lost, release of the storm might
actually be the fastest means of restoring her sense of
well-being. With a certain relief she set the sobs free, all
the while cursing herself for feeling like that when, in
fact, she was the luckiest girl in the world.*

   Why did she consider herself so lucky and yet at the

same time weep so bitterly? The answer to both questions lay in a letter on the table beside her, a typical one-page note from her mother which for once contained a significant and rather overwhelming message. The house at Glen Alden had been sold, and Mother was giving her children the proceeds to help them get on their feet. Of course, she had never had to worry about Amy, who had always been on her feet, but it "never hurts to have a little nest egg against a rainy day," and Amy more than deserved her share after all the hard work and achievement that made everyone so proud. Perhaps there would be a real bonanza later, if encouraging reports from the Middle West turned out as expected, but in the meantime this was a little something, and Mother herself could manage very well on the income "dear Father" was foresighted enough to provide for her protection. Nobody need feel the slightest compunction about accepting the money.

So Amy was indeed very lucky, lucky to have a mother so kind and generous and well-intentioned toward her children, so willing to sacrifice her only unencumbered asset in order that they might all be happier. It was for this very same reason that she wept, wept for the closeness so near and yet so far, for the good intentions so removed from real understanding, for the sweetness and light and eternal optimism that had wreaked so much havoc in the family. But she also wept for the house. Although by now she had friends in Glen Alden whose house was more of a home to her than that one had ever been, it had nevertheless been a symbol of something safe, beautiful, and beloved to fall back on if all else failed. It was gone, and with it the last tie to her childhood. Amy wept most of all because, although the world called her an adult, all she felt like was a little girl who wanted to go home and curl up in somebody's lap.

8

The Glen Alden Money

Amy's Share

A.C. The Glen Alden money was really my salvation.
I suppose if I hadn't had it I'd have muddled through
somehow, but I'm virtually certain I wouldn't be where
I am today. At the very least I would be leading a far
more limited, unrewarding kind of existence, and as a
matter of fact, I might very well be dead.

Dr. P. Do you really believe that?

A.C. I'm not sure. I do know that for a while I was
never free from the thought of suicide, and I know I was
near the end of my emotional rope. Under circumstances as they were then, I couldn't have continued
much longer to function adequately, even on the job,
and whether I could have carried that load of anxiety
without cracking mentally or killing myself, I really
don't know.

Dr. P. You were obviously very depressed and
obsessed with masochistic fantasies. Even so, I doubt
whether you would have done either one. You'd have
found some other way, even though it might have led
into a more restricted and inhibited life than you now
enjoy. I could be wrong, of course. When one feels like
that, so much depends upon an impulse of the moment.
Tell me how you feel the money saved you.

A.C. It took me off the hook of a decision I felt
totally incapable of making. They say the best things in

life are free, but don't you ever believe it. The best
things in life often cost a great deal of money, and at
the moment that check arrived, I was caught in a
tug-of-war between two of them. It almost tore me to
pieces, and I'll never forget how I felt when I suddenly
realized what Mother's gift meant to me.

*Her mother's offering changed the direction of Amy's
life from a downward spiral of despair upward toward a
whole new way of emotional being. It gave her the
capacity to meet an overwhelming inner need at a most
crucial moment of her existence and enabled her to
establish inner stability commensurate with the outwardly stable aspects of her life. At last Amy could
afford desperately needed help in overcoming her
emotional turmoil without having to sacrifice a seemingly
vital source of external support while going through the
process.*

*Amy was a woman of many facets, as I have said
before. She was a highly educated urban woman with a
strong need for intellectual stimulation. At the same
time, she was a country girl, one who could scarcely
breathe far from the smell of earth beneath her feet.
Contact with books, ideas, and sophisticated conversation nourished her spirit, but a direct relationship to
trees, grass, and sky kept that spirit alive. Without either
one, she was only half a person.*

*Since coming west, Amy had found a setting exactly
right to satisfy both sides of her nature. By chance she
had stumbled into a little-known area high in the hills of
the city, where there was for sale a unique, old redwood
house with an exhilarating panoramic view and a wild
garden of indescribable charm. This wonderful oasis,
hidden away in a eucalyptus grove, was ten minutes
from the heart of the great metropolis and was the
answer to an almost unfulfillable longing.*

As we have seen, Amy tended to make strong

emotional attachments to houses, houses to which she often reacted almost as though they were people. She fell in love with that house at first sight, at once recognizing it as a sanctuary in which to restore her soul. She took one look at it and needed it as others have needed to lie down in green pastures beside the still waters. Here she could sufficiently replenish her meager stores of tranquillity in order to keep going. That house had for her not only the soothing effect of a beautiful environment, but also the symbolic meaning of mother, family, and everything else human beings hold most dear. Amy felt an immediate, deep, uncontrollable need for that place and bought it the same day with all her savings as a down payment and a contract for two mortgages which took ninety percent of her salary to maintain.

Amy had never been one to care inordinately for property or possessions. Even with all her traveling, she had amassed few treasures, and although loving a home above almost everything, she had lived alone in dormitories, rooming houses, ships' cabins, and cramped city apartments without minding too much. She didn't want to do it again at this stage of her career and hated the idea of ever doing it again. However, before finding her present home she could and would have done so without feeling bitterness or outrage. Giving up this particular home was a different matter. It had instantaneously become a part of her, and the thought of losing it was almost unbearable. For many months now she had been wracked by indecision. In order to obtain relief from her emotional burdens she needed expensive medical treatment for an indeterminate period of time and would have to sell her sanctuary to pay for it. Maintaining both on the salary of a young university instructor was impossible. Amy knew very well that living in a beautiful place would not solve her problem. She knew that a major change in her ways of reacting

*was required and probably would eventually have given
up everything she owned to obtain help in bringing
about that change. However, the Glen Alden money
spared her the need for such a choice.*

*Everyone must find his or her own path to salvation.
Some find it in established religions and philosophies,
others in more offbeat creeds and -isms. Amy found
hers in classical psychoanalysis. She was a scientist by
profession, one trained in human psychology, and knew
exactly the possibilities and limitations of this form of
treatment. She knew her own diagnosis and also knew
that, for her form of neurosis, analysis was the
treatment of choice in contrast to other forms of
psychotherapy based on the same theoretical principles.
She also knew how to go about finding a reputable
psychoanalyst, and, without further delay, she carefully
chose one to whom she felt able to entrust her psyche.
When she finally made the decision, she gave her life
into his hands.*

*For fifty minutes of every weekday for over four
years, Amy lay on a couch, baring her soul to another
human being and trying to reorganize her mental and
emotional patterns. Sometimes, after a painful stab of
insight pierced her armor, she recoiled for days at a
time, bathing her wounds with a stream of trivialities.
Then, as she again became able, she forced open other
tiny chinks, tested the strength of what lay beneath, and
slowly discarded protective coverings that were no
longer needed. She worked, she sweated, and sometimes
she suffered agonies of guilt, sorrow, and despair. But
she kept at it. Little by little, the thinking Amy
connected with the feeling Amy, and gradually the split
in her personality healed. It wasn't cataclysmic, and it
wasn't one hundred percent perfect, but she came out
with what is considered to be a successful analysis.*

*While all this was going on, Amy's outward behavior
changed very little. Each day she rose from the couch,*

sometimes red-eyed and exhausted, and returned to her job. Her work remained satisfactory, her social life uninterrupted, and her daily routines unchanged. Except for a few close friends in whom she confided, nobody suspected that Amy was other than she had always been or that her whole life was undergoing a major upheaval.

When it was all over, most people found no striking difference either, although many did say she seemed more relaxed. They had not thought much was amiss when she began and saw nothing remarkable to indicate that her treatment had ended. Some who knew what she had been through told her there had been no need for change in the first place, as if denial of a need for change complimented one who had taken endless pains to bring change about. Sometimes it seemed that the only one who really appreciated the difference was Amy herself. Fortunately she was the only one who had to be satisfied.

Amy saw the difference, and what's more, she felt the difference. In fact, she was fully possessed of all her senses for the very first time since infancy.

Analysis gave Amy back her body, freed her from barriers to the experience of sensual pleasure unaccompanied by real or fantasied pain and degradation. It removed the torturers within who were responsible for sudden, outwardly unmotivated fits of weeping and let her save her tears for the inevitable realistic sorrows of human existence. It did not make her immune to worry or loneliness but helped her to tolerate strong feelings without becoming numb. Anger and love, sorrow and joy, concern for others without the prod of guilt—these she became free to accept as part of the human condition and to express without fearing loss of control. In other words, when her analysis was over, Amy at last was all in one piece, physically, mentally, and emotionally.

A.C. That's what the Glen Alden money did for me. It didn't furnish a solution to all my problems, but it gave me back to myself in a state of readiness to solve my own.

Dr. P. A pretty good result, I would say, and an excellent investment of your money in a potential for future happiness.

A.C. A whole area of my emotional life had been cramped and isolated from the rest of me—everything to do with instinctual pleasure. Analysis helped me break the shell that held it all in.

Of course, like most unmarried girls who are nearing their thirties, I suppose I hoped analysis would find me a husband in some magical way. It didn't, but it did give me back the capacity to love a man who could love a woman and be gentle.

Dr. P. Could anyone rationally ask for more? The most successful treatment couldn't be expected to accomplish the life tasks that people must do for themselves.

A.C. True. But I wasn't any more rational about things like that than anyone else. I was also well aware that even well-adjusted women of over thirty don't always have an easy time finding suitable mates. Magical expectations are so much easier than knowing you have to live by your own decisions. Finding the right man for me wasn't something I could be sure about at best, you see. I might have been even more worried than I was if I had foreseen the obstacles that still stood in the way of my getting married.

Dr. P. Was your mother pleased with the effect of her gift?

A.C. She never knew about it. Actually, she never let me tell her, although I desperately wanted to. Once I even tried, but it just wasn't possible.

Laura never asked any of her children to account for their share of the Glen Alden money. To do so would have been totally out of character, for a gift is a gift, and one does not ask where it goes or dictate its use. That had been her philosophy always and was completely unalterable. Money given to the children, even when they were quite young, was theirs to spend as they wished, even if they chose to waste it. Everyone understood that there were no strings on anything given as a gift rather than for a particular purpose. In this respect at least, the "official version" corresponded absolutely with the true state of affairs. Neither parent had ever tried to persuade the children to spend, save, or otherwise "voluntarily" dispose of their money according to parental wish.

Of course, Laura invariably knew where Jingo spent every dime she had—in childhood, because Jingo was her boon companion, and later, because Jingo regularly discussed her financial affairs with anyone who would listen. Despite the fact that Eliot had lived his whole life on allowances, gifts, or handouts by any other name, he spent them as he saw fit, without being questioned, even when he spent them in ways his mother disapproved. Nevertheless, it was not difficult to figure out where his money went. Empty paint tubes and wine bottles comprised most of the refuse from his quarters during all the time he lived at home. With Amy, the situation was different. Laura did not have the slightest knowledge of her daughter's financial affairs from the time she left home for boarding school at the age of fifteen. Nobody ever asked Amy what she did with her allowance while she received one, nor did it ever occur to her to tell anyone. She had been in complete charge of her own destiny since that time, separated even geographically from the rest of the family except during vacations at Glen Alden. What she did was so complete-

ly her own business that most of the time nobody in the family had any idea what her life was like.

Her mother could not possibly have imagined that Amy was in financial need. Her daughter would surely know she could count on her mother to take care of her in any emergency, and since she had asked for nothing, she obviously needed nothing. The idea that one of her children might hesitate to burden her with financial problems would have been both upsetting and incomprehensible to Laura, for keeping one's need to oneself was not part of the Carpenter pattern at all. Mother wanted to help if her children were in trouble, and everybody knew it.

Little did Laura know how much her daughter longed to talk to her—to tell her how much she had needed the money, and how important had been the opportunity to effect a capacity for change in a desperate life situation. Still less did her mother realize that at least once Amy had tried to confide some measure of her need, because Amy herself had been the one to help her wipe out the memory as quickly as possible.

Laura had accepted Eliot's psychotherapy with a certain equanimity. After all, an artist's mind runs in channels that not even a mother can understand completely, and if he enjoyed talking with someone about his dreams, certainly no harm could come of it. Her son had been deeply unhappy about his dissolute life at one time, but she knew he was now in the process of finding himself, and anything that helped was in a good cause. However, the one time her mother came close to hearing that Amy wanted help it nearly broke her up, until Amy managed to put the pieces together again. The idea of such a possibility had never occurred to Laura, and the fact that her attractive daughter was still unmarried furnished no clue. Throughout that daughter's youth, she herself had practically begged her never to be in the position of needing a man for financial security. Amy had just been busy getting firmly on her own feet so that she might eventually find love without financial dependency, and that certainly was no problem. What other problems could there possibly be for a girl so charming and successful?

Amy tried to tell her that she had considered talking to a psychiatrist—started to try, that is, until she saw the look on her mother's face and heard the anguished cry, "Oh Amy darling! Not you too? My God! What has become of my lovely little family?" And Amy, panicked at having poked a hole in the dam that held back her mother's heartbroken tears, wept with her not to ease her own frustration, but in sympathy and guilt for the pain she had unwittingly caused. Hurrying to minimize her own unhappiness and to point out what truly admirable things all her mother's children had accomplished in their lives despite their moments of vulnerability, she soothed her mother who, hearing what she wanted to hear, was quickly comforted and restored to blissful oblivion.

So Laura never heard what Amy did with the Glen Alden money, for to tell her how much better things were because of it would have given some intimation that things had not been perfectly fine all along. This her mother could not take, and Amy let her go on thinking happily that her dear, industrious, self-sufficient child now had in the bank a nice little nest egg against a rainy day.

A.C. Once in the middle of my analysis, I had a dream that I'll tell you because it seems to describe the feelings I'm talking about. I used to dream of Mother often, but I remember this one particularly because of the way I discussed it and the way my analyst responded. He didn't very often state his own opinions about anything, but he did that time. Somehow what he said seemed to break forever the terrible ambivalence that kept me in bondage to her so long.

———*I had another Mother-dream last night. A wild rush of wind blows open the kitchen door, driving in a malignant force that can't be defined. I run through the house crying for her, "Mother! Mother!" I'm crying in terror for her and for myself too, hoping to find and shield her and, at the same time, pleading for her to shield me. In the end I'm holding her in my arms, tenderly protecting her from something neither of us understand.*

What do you suppose started my seeking protection by becoming the protector? Was fear and sadness easier to bear if I assumed she shared it too? Already at the age of seven I can remember closing my eyes against scary parts of a movie. Then I would turn to pat her hand and say, "Don't worry, Mother. It's only a story."

Or was it that the fury of my disappointment seemed able to destroy her? When my troubles did force their way into her awareness, she was so genuinely incapacitated that I couldn't bear it because of the love I had for her alongside the fury. I could read her face from an early age, and nobody who cared for this loving, distracted, armored woman could bear to hurt her with their own pain. We all spent most of our lives trying to protect her from the knowledge that things frightened us.

———*The childlike Mother and the motherly child are still one. You will become separate from her only when you stop hoping for a closeness she simply cannot give. Don't underestimate what she did give you, though. To you more than to the others she gave respect, trust, and ungrudging freedom to obtain from surrogates what she herself could not furnish. Those were very great gifts, and to them you owe a great part of your strength.*

A.C. You know, I think it's true, too. I'm quite sure if I hadn't felt Mother's confidence in me, I couldn't have functioned. Never in my whole life did I really feel her disapproval, and that meant a lot. If I had, I don't know what I would have done.

Dr. P. Do you think one reason you put off marriage for so long was because you felt she didn't really want you to marry?

A.C. No. I'm sure she did want me to, and not just for the sake of appearances like so many mothers. Regardless of her loyalty to my father, she didn't want me to have a marriage like hers. I'm sure she felt that if I couldn't find the "right man," I was better off single. My career puzzled her, but I don't think it ever occurred to her I wasn't perfectly content as a "bachelor girl." As I see it now, Mother envied my freedom, but never by word, deed, or inflection did she ever make me feel guilty.

In a way, you see, I was the only hope for her, the only hope for her success as a mother. Somebody in the family had to make it, and by the time she gave all of us the Glen Alden money, I don't think she really expected the others to be able to pull themselves together, no matter how confident and optimistic she tried to appear.

Jingo's Share

A.C. Jingo and Alex went through the Glen Alden money in a little over a year. In that year, however, there blossomed a whole garden of renewed hope and promise. Amazing how much difference a little financial security makes in adding juice to the pulp of life, particularly after a long, tight squeeze. Almost overnight, the cares and anxieties of the past six years faded away in memory. Now the not-so-young but still vivacious couple took up where they had left off, before bad luck started to pursue them.

The first order of business was ridding the premises of cats and, after a while, of the cat aroma which permeated the very walls. Jingo, who had a passion for small, soft animals, was truly sad to dispose of so many charming kittens, but the breeding business had not been very successful. The blooded Persian female, upon whom so many hopes had rested, stubbornly refused to mate with an aristocratic spouse hired for her pleasure at considerable price, and repeatedly evaded supervision in favor of a boy friend with a rather eclectic background. Offspring of such a union do not bring a price regardless of their mother's superior lineage, and Jingo found it difficult even to give them away unless she knew all about the homes to which they would go. An accumulation of unsalable kittens who were rapidly becoming cats, in a one-room upstairs apartment without easy access to the ground below, had produced an atmosphere that often discouraged even the most devoted friends from visiting more than once. It was now time for the human occupants to rejoin the human scene, so Jingo gritted her teeth and took them all to the S.P.C.A. After the walls had been repainted and the carpets replaced, it made a funny story.

With freedom from immediate financial pressure, Virginia's skin began to clear, and a fifty-dollar foundation garment restored a satisfying body image. New electric equipment for the kitchenette and a stunning new set of Swedish ironware pots stimulated renewed interest in cooking. Before long, the apartment rang again with laughter and sprightly conversation at dinner parties for those bohemian friends who enjoyed sitting cross-legged on the floor and eating gourmet food from their laps. Enthusiasm ran high, spirits regenerated, and Jingo had a new lease on life.

Alex was also restored to a sense of well-being. With

opportunity to take up work on the half-finished novel, he again assumed identity as an author who could hold his own among creative people, and with hard labor he actually finished the book within about six months. Before the following year's end, quite a respectable number of copies had been sold, and he received some recognition in writing circles, but unfortunately, there were also some difficulties. His agent failed to insist on a more adequate percentage of the royalties, the publisher's advertising efforts had been inadequate, and the printer slipped up on sending a sufficient number of copies for autographing at a bookseller's promotional party. The financial returns were not what he had expected a successful author to receive, and Alex's novel did not sweep the country as a best seller, good as it was. Disappointment and indignation really spoiled the triumph he deserved to feel, and it was accompanied by some rather demoralizing thoughts.

With the discovery that successful completion of over a year's hard work would probably augment their dwindling resources just enough to get them through another year or so without improving their standard of living, Jingo and Alex for the first time saw the possibility that their dreams of sudden affluence might be ephemeral. They began to realize that maybe even a modest income through writing would require unremitting, mundane, sometimes tedious day-to-day labor over the years. Although both soon shrugged off such fears in view of Alex's clearly demonstrable talent, the very thought that he might work hard, sell his work, and still never hit a jackpot large enough to ensure immediate and permanent financial security came as a distinct shock to this idealistic couple.

Alex and Jingo weren't afraid of hard work. They often worked very hard indeed to do a good job on whatever they had undertaken, but the idea that they might not be among the very few individuals in the world talented enough and lucky enough to make a large fortune without submitting to the ordinary grind of daily routine was something neither of them had really ever considered.

Dr. P. Nothing in the early life of either one had discouraged the idea that they were somehow rather special. Everything that pointed to the contrary was always somebody else's fault.

A.C. They were not cowards, though. Those two had faced other disappointments and were determined to face this one. However, although Alex planned to start work at once on another novel, inspiration did not return on schedule, and the inability to call forth his muse at will dealt another deathblow to his morale.

I have already pointed out that Alex's morale was a tender flower which, once bruised, required rather special forms of nurturing for restoration to health. Due to all these blows from bad luck, it was now in a fragile and bruised condition, but Jingo plunged in with might and main to offer the necessary nurturance. Visits with friends ceased, and every evening again became devoted to avid discussions of Alex's work—discussions dedicated to developing every aspect of his plot, every setting, character, dialogue, and idea.

While Alex paced, gesticulated, and threw out thoughts for inspection, Jingo analyzed, criticized, and supplemented. Cocktail time was again the time for animated, excited, absorbing talk between husband and wife—talk so intense, so passionately eager, so totally involving that everything else was completely eliminated from the center of their awareness. Time was a-wasting, and with so much to be done, Jingo was completely preoccupied with encouraging Alex and transmitting to him her complete faith in his ability to create a masterpiece. Soon.

Under these conditions, dinner was frequently a piecemeal affair, sometimes overlooked altogether in favor of a few more drinks before Jingo stumbled off to bed and Alex descended uncertainly to his tiny work space in the garage storeroom. Virginia usually slept too heavily to wake when he finally did come up in the early morning, and Alex then slept until almost time for the next evening's round of discussions to begin. A familiar routine had been established automatically, and Jingo took it so much as a matter of course that she was not quick in discovering that Alex was doing little work on his novel at all. In fact, it was quite a long time before he felt it necessary to let her know the true state of affairs.

Shortly after receiving his first royalty check, Alex had started having an affair with one of Jingo's friends. Miriam was a rather silly woman who knew nothing about literature and cared less, a woman who enjoyed extramarital intrigue, thought him an attractive man, and made no demands on him whatsoever. She didn't care if he developed his creativity or turned out a masterpiece. She found Alex good in bed, and that's all she wanted from him. That's the comfort Alex sought for failing to set the world on fire, and that's the comfort he continued to seek night after night as he courted his muse in vain.

Dr. P. Forbidden fruit now substituted for potted caviar and hearts of palm to bolster Alex's sagging morale.

A.C. Yes, and he was satisfied for a while without adding the gratification of ensuring that Jingo would suffer from his self-indulgence and punish him for his pleasure. It was therefore several months before he confessed to his wife that every evening, after all their intimacy and interaction, after all their sharing of ideas and plans for the future, after all their mutual work and interest and joy in creating, he had been leaving her side to head straight for the arms of another woman.

To Alex a day without Virginia was a day without his

own life's blood. He lived through her as she did through him, sharing with her a network of flowing communication to feed them both as Siamese twins may share a single vascular system. Shared thoughts, experiences, and reactions were to them the mutual bloodstream through which flowed creativity, emotional vitality, and the very motivation for existence.

Dr. P. At moments when all these ebbed in Alex, an intensity of need for an increased flow from his alter ego obviously impaired in him the sense of manhood which only thrives in one who can claim a self of his own. Denying to himself his need for fusion was as vital to Alex as indulging it was, and punishing Jingo for being needed was as important as punishing himself for having the need. In his need to derive strength from Jingo, Alex had to stave off awareness of his need for her by spending nights with another woman. To give his sense of freedom substance, knowledge of the transgression had to be shared with his mate.

A.C. Well, it turned out that one thing was new anyway. Nothing in his many years of experience with Jingo's response to his behavior had ever warned Alex that, no matter how much punishment she might accept in order to purge her own guilt for a lifetime of seething anger, her capacity for enduring betrayal might eventually run out. This time was different.

Eliot's Share

A.C. El's share of the Glen Alden money lasted quite a while. Coming when it did, the bonanza heralded a life as changed as the spirit within him. The most radical change visible to others was that, although retaining his quarters in the attic for a studio, he rented a small apartment in another section of town and started living with a woman.

Dr. P. That was a momentous step for him.

A.C. Yes, and a very successful one too. Anne was also a painter—a divorcée somewhat older than he, and mother of a teen-age son in the navy. However, she was blessed with the appearance of someone much younger and showed a capacity for spontaneous openness able to penetrate even Eliot's shell of anxious reserve. She had encountered him frequently in an art supply store and for a long time had been enjoying an occasional cup of coffee with him when they met—exchanging friendly, impersonal talk about her work and his before they parted to go about their separate business. El had always enjoyed these meetings, had even looked forward to them, and felt some disappointment when they did not occur. Until recently, however, he hadn't given more than a passing thought between encounters to the frail girl who shared so many of his own ideas about art.

Concomitant with his enlightenment, a surge of manly protectiveness toward Anne swept over Eliot, a capacity for aggressiveness unsuspected throughout the periods dominated by a sense of utter helplessness and inadequacy. He saw her suddenly as a woman not unlike himself in temperament, one who could enjoy with him the beauties of a full and mutual emotional life free of inhibitions and the restrictions of convention. He felt, in fact, that here was a kindred soul with whom he might eventually share the secret knowledge of his destiny, and who could possibly comprehend the sources of his new power. Friendship blossomed quickly into passion, and El was at last able to feel sexual attraction toward someone he liked and respected.

Dr. P. Until that time he really hadn't had any kind of sustained relationship with a woman?

A.C. Only in fantasy. He hadn't even had many friendships. Throughout his life he had presented himself to everyone as a gentle, amiable, inhibited, and completely ineffectual young man who sooner or later managed to say exactly the wrong thing to everyone he knew. Men and women alike felt only his detachment and were never touched by the tenderness of which he was capable. Mostly he showed warmth only to animals and children.

Dr. P. Those are the ones who are not fooled by facades or threatened by strong feelings in disguise.

A.C. It was really interesting. Wherever he went, to paint in fields or meditate in city parks, children suddenly appeared out of nowhere as if drawn by the Pied Piper. They responded to his empathy as dogs respond to the sound of a whistle inaudible to human ears.

Dr. P. That can present some dangers to a young man in a city park.

A.C. Yes. He knew full well the kinds of suspicions that fall on adult male loners who encourage the attentions of children and had no wish to bring such suspicions on himself. He didn't really need the admiration of children to bolster his ego, nor did he seek them out in attempts to lighten his isolation, but when they approached him, he talked to them as if they were people. I suppose that's why they sought him out. Fortunately, it never got him into any trouble.

As far as adults were concerned, there were really only two to whom he had ever been able to offer moments of affection and compassion—Mother and myself. Only with us could he forget his own misery long enough to think how we might feel.

Dr. P. He wasn't close to Jingo?

A.C. No, they tolerated each other, but just barely, during the period when they were all there together in the House of Usher. Earlier in life they had little to do with one another, but somehow he was able to be aware of me. I don't know just why.

Dr. P. From the time of his accident at the age of twelve, he seems to have buried the jealousy felt for a baby who displaced him as his father's favorite.

A.C. We apparently established the kind of totally unverbalized understanding that arises between two people who share feelings unrecognized or underestimated by others. Of course, he also had no trouble seeing through the phony optimism that Mother used to contain her abject loneliness.

Dr. P. Perhaps because you two also attempted to contain potentially explosive emotions with armors of uncertain strength, he felt as safe with you as he could with anyone and was able to give you a little of the warmth he had available.

A.C. Yes, but not until Anne entered his life did he feel free to express tenderness and solicitude toward someone for whom he felt sexual attraction.

Anne was a truly nice woman, one who understood El and was able to accept him for what he was, without either blinding herself to his problems or fearing his messianic tendencies. She was so likable and so obviously devoted to Eliot that even Mother came to accept her with equanimity. She wasn't exactly ecstatic at the idea of her son "living in sin," but neither was she one to "look a gift horse in the mouth." Having the capacity to see "rightness" in anything that was obviously inevitable, she gave thanks that her son had at last found himself and was grateful to the girl who helped him. However, she couldn't really let herself recognize how worried she was about his state of exaltation or how relieved she was that someone else had assumed some responsibility in caring for him. It only became apparent later how willing she was to have someone else assume that kind of responsibility.

9

Fall of the House of Usher

A.C. By now it was almost twenty years since we had been separated from our father. As the second decade of his trials and tribulations drew to a close, he was still tied up in the Middle West, unavoidably detained from rejoining his family. A great deal had happened, however, to keep his life anything but dull.

After a long fight, the charge of embezzlement, upheld in lower courts subject to the influence of local politicians, was set aside in a superior court with a rebuke to those who had filed it on such flimsy evidence. Daddy was thus set free to go ahead full steam on the libel suit, and, practically before the ink was dry on the court's decision, he went right to it.

The publisher of that mighty tabloid began to worry again, as well he should have. At that point, his adversary was about as angry as a man can get and still remain sane. There were even those who wondered whether he had remained sane, because the violence of his feelings was something outside the experience of many.

In any case, there he was in full armor, back to battle the archdemon, and the archdemon found himself in an uneasy position, because by now it was impossible to maneuver any further delays in scheduling the suit. To make things even more uncomfortable for that publisher, Daddy had discovered a tremendous weapon to hold over his head in case there were any more shenanigans to cause obstruction. That was what El was talking about at Glen Alden. Daddy had uncovered the fact that an obscure, obsolete law remained on the books, and that although few large corporations in the state paid any attention to it, several million dollars in back taxes due under this law were owed by the tabloid alone, to say nothing of what other big businesses owed. Since nobody in the financial community wanted a taxpayer's suit drawing attention to this oversight, even the publisher's own friends and colleagues were urging him to bring about a settlement as soon as possible. The publisher realized he was in for a lot of trouble if he didn't get rid of that Carpenter pest somehow. At any rate, that is what my father believed, and that is what a lot of other people came to believe after the next installment of the story unfolded.

A woman with whom Daddy had been involved in a minor traffic accident many years previously suddenly brought suit charging him with the responsibility for a chronic backache. Judgment for a monumental, crippling sum of money was brought against him in a local court, and while the case was pending appeal, he was clamped in jail for refusing to pay, even though such a procedure is totally illegal. Then, while vegetating in the county jail, he was presented with a cake presumably sent by his landlady. It is very fortunate that by then he had lost his appetite, because a couple of young boys to whom he gave the cake became violently ill in the night and might have died unattended if he had not raised a rumpus that aroused the whole building.

It was also most fortunate that the personal attorney of a man almost as powerful as the publisher happened to be in that place at just that particular time, covering another piece of business. When he heard my father's story and his outcry about attempts to poison him, he did not write the story off as the paranoid ravings of a crazy man, as the prison officials would have liked him to do. He believed the story and took it upon himself to do something about it. After that, things happened rather quickly. The following day Daddy was released from jail, a few weeks later the women dropped her suit against him, and within a short time things were back to "normal."

Finally the libel suit was tried, although there had been considerable doubt that it ever would be. This time there was a great deal of publicity about it, publicity which was for a change rather favorable to Daddy. Although not a single newspaper mentioned that a libel suit had ever been filed against the tabloid, a national periodical gave it quite a bit of sympathetic coverage. It even pointed out all the times that Eliot Carpenter had been cleared of trumped-up charges without ever having it mentioned by the press and implied that all was not entirely well with the local political situation in a very important city of our country. The article carried a strong implication that Eliot Carpenter had been given a very raw deal all around. To him this was cold comfort, however, because in spite of the fact that every lawyer in town admitted it should have been an open and shut case, the jury exonerated the publisher.

Many young lawyers interested in the case had told him that this would happen, that they had substantial reason to know that the jury had been intimidated. Daddy hadn't believed them, however. He had really believed that justice could eventually be obtained in the courts of the United States, but it hadn't worked out like that. Now he had to accept the court's verdict because all other resources had been exhausted. After all his years of hope and effort, all avenues of retribution were now closed.

Dr. P. I suppose even he could see at that point that carrying out his threat of filing a taxpayer's suit would only enlist the entire business community of the state in an all-out war to destroy him.

A.C. I'm not sure whether that alone would have stopped him. At that point, however, he was truly flat broke, with no more hope of help from anyone.

For once our father had to admit that he was licked, and to face that fact was a very bitter pill indeed. It was a pill so bitter that it temporarily threatened to choke him with rage and fury and murderous intent, and there were those who thought this had to be the last straw to drive him out of his mind. But being a very strong man, he finally swallowed it and, taking a new lease on life, girded up his loins for the start of a new career. Over a long period of time he had been developing some interesting ideas in his spare moments, and already he had in mind the basic plans for a most original and promising million-dollar venture. He could set it up in a very short time and then return to the bosom of his family.

During his long battling years alone in the Middle West, Daddy had found little time or inclination for amusement. Preoccupied as he was from the age of nine with a struggle for daily existence, he had never learned to play as other men do to relieve their minds from the incessant strain of work and worry. Occasionally, when we were quite young, he took us to movies or amusement parks as a chore of fatherhood, but such activities clearly bored him almost beyond endurance and created far more nervous tension than they ever relieved. He didn't drink, smoke, or gamble; he felt utterly alien at a ball game and would have been about as much at home on the golf course as on a flying trapeze. He had always been totally engrossed in working out his ideas and conducting his businesses, and he was completely unable to conceive of any interest divorced from his business.

Dr. P. Was there no reason to suspect that he had other women in all those years, at least occasionally?

A.C. I would suspect that of any other man in the world but not of my father. It was totally out of character. As far as women were concerned, he was ever gallant and charming, a "gentleman of the old school," with a tip of the hat, a joke, and a friendly greeting to anyone encountered in the course of his daily life—interactions totally devoid of sexual overtones or personal interest at any level. Anything else is inconceivable. He acknowledged the existence of women and graciously accepted their homage, but wife and two daughters notwithstanding, they had no place in his mind or in his life.

Dr. P. How do you think he managed to survive for twenty years without sexual companionship?

A.C. I'm sure he would have told you that the picture of his "dear little Laurie" remained ever bright before his inner eye, sustaining his moral fiber against the temptation to indulge in bodily appetites. I think he would have been quite mistaken, but that is undoubtedly how he would have seen the situation and truthfully told it to you. My personal opinion is that he was not greatly bothered by bodily appetites when engaged in his own pursuits, because his energies were discharged in other ways.

One thing he did need desperately was an audience, and he almost always was able to find one in a series of awestruck landladies. However, I'm sure he had no knowledge of and sustained no capacity for true companionship of any kind, sexual or otherwise. Daddy was a man sufficient unto himself, needing little stimulation from outside his own mind, and he always had been.

Dr. P. Even such a man must find some means to pass the time on an occasional evening when he isn't busy ferreting out obscure passages in the law or

planning strategy for his next technical maneuver. I
wonder what he did with himself at times like that?

A.C. At times like that he turned to the Scriptures
which had been so much a part of his early training.

Dr. P. I hadn't realized he was a religious man.

A.C. Far from it. From the moment of escape from
his mother's domination he had entered a church only
under protest and shown poor tolerance for any sermon
not delivered by himself. The Bible is, however, a very
dynamic document—full of blood and thunder and the
stories of men who, like himself, survived a multiplicity
of trials and tribulations by dint of their strong faith.
Daddy found in it all manner of inspirational messages,
as men have done throughout the ages.

Biblical messages filtered through the mind of a man
like my father came out with a rather unusual twist.
They came out in colorful terms of the common man's
vernacular, and as he brooded upon them, it occurred
to him that the Bible needed rewriting for the common
man. Over the years he began to jot down ideas for a
series of moral and ethical lessons, told in the ignorant
man's own language, and using examples from his own
kind of experience. Daddy knew all about how a poor
man lives and what he thinks about. He also knew all
about how to write "copy packing a wallop" that would
sell any product to anyone whatsoever. He used to say
that a good salesman can sell you the rug off your own
floor, and he knew what he was talking about.

His lessons were going to sell the good old American
way of life—a return to the homely virtues of *Mc-
Guffey's Reader*, illustrated in a dynamic rewording of
Bible stories known to everyone. He planned to put
them up in handy packets and sell them by mail to
anyone responding to skillful sample distribution according to the "sucker list" technique sacred to all
direct mail advertisers. Out of all this, he planned to
make a handy packet of money for himself, collecting

not only crisp, new dollar bills from banks in the big cities, but old, wrinkled, greasy dollar bills pulled out from under millions of mattresses throughout the Bible Belt. With them he planned to form the New American Church, with a fine building in a beautiful city, decorated with statues of Henry Ford, John D. Rockefeller, and Thomas Edison—real American inspirational figures rather than saints of plaster and gilt. With all this, he planned to do far greater good for the common man and make even more money than Mary Baker Eddy who, in his mind, was the greatest businesswoman of all time. He would become the most powerful leader of the most powerful church organization in western society. In fact, it would not have surprised him if his church eventually put every other church in the country out of business.

When the time came to direct his full energies toward carrying out these plans, all he had to do was search the laws on setting up a church, get himself ordained as a minister of the Gospel through one of the many organizations that furnish such credentials for a small fee, and set up a legal mail-order business for sale of the lessons. Daddy knew how to do that as no other man has ever known it, and when he finally recovered from the effects of his disappointment over the libel suit, he did it in a very short time. The Reverend Eliot Carpenter was then ready to start his evangelism.

At this point I must say emphatically that he did not see, and had no reason to see, anything unethical in such a procedure. To him, as it may be to anyone who lacks religious faith or awe for symbolic values, a church was a business organization like any other, devoted to meeting the demands of its investors. For him to see it any other way would have been quite out of character. He had great faith in his own ideas. His church was going to be a humdinger, giving a great many people exactly what they wanted, and giving it to them in a way they would find maximally comprehensible. What was wrong about that?

For the time being, he decided no better place could be found to start this undertaking than a big old mansion in southern California—situated in a city already known as the Mecca for all who are disenchanted with conservative, established religions.

Dr. P. Not the House of Usher?

A.C. The very same. What could be more convenient?

So it came about that almost twenty years after their parting, Odysseus came home from the wars to join his Penelope. What's more, he came on exactly the day he had stipulated two weeks before. For twenty years he had been saying, "I will arrive two weeks from Saturday," and two weeks from that particular Saturday, he arrived, just as his wife had known he would do every time he said it for the past twenty years.

But Daddy had made one miscalculation. Laura was not only a faithful wife but also a mother and a loyal daughter who was not about to see the home built by her parents fouled as her own had been twenty years before. After all the years of waiting and longing for this moment, after all the love and faith and willingness to see things his way, she heard what he proposed and said, "No! You may not found a church in this house. This house is sacred to the memory of my parents and the present life of my children. You may not make it the base for any more ventures that 'nice people' will consider questionable. My father's house has been the House of Refuge, and it is going to stay that way." For the first time in forty years of marriage, Laura spoke up and put her foot down.

When her husband shrugged this off in utter disbelief, she said, "If you insist on trying to do this, I will get a legal separation, because it is the one thing I will not tolerate. I will go with you wherever you want. I will help you in whatever way I can with what money is available to me, and you can found a church somewhere else. You may not come *here* with any such plan."

And her husband had to bow to her will. Fortunately, he had already learned how to recognize that he was up against something bigger than he was.

It was then that we children came to a full realization that it was actually our mother who had stayed away from our father, and not the other way around. It was the first time that anyone wondered whether Mother's generosity in distributing all her liquid assets to her children had been prompted by a desire to own nothing on which her husband could get his hands. It was also the first as well as the last time in anyone's memory that Mother gave any indication of feeling less than full approval for anything our father had done in the past, was doing in the present, or intended to do in the future.

Dr. P. In that moment, however, it became crystal clear that your mother felt it her first duty to protect her home.

A.C. And it became clear that in her secret heart she knew her mate would only despoil it. Nevertheless, she was willing to go with him and start again somewhere else. She had done her duty in shielding her children from scandal and humiliation. She would not condone exposing them to all that again, and to prevent it she was even willing to sacrifice the beloved mate for whom she had already sacrificed so much. However, as long as he was willing to go somewhere else, she would go with him. She had cared for her children long enough.

Dr. P. I can imagine Jingo's reaction to your father's return, but how about the rest of you? It must have been a terrible shock.

A.C. I have no words for it. However, during that period I corresponded fairly regularly with my friends Marty and Dan, and those letters give the flavor of the whole thing better than I could by recalling it now. You can see at least how it looked to me.

I was always a clown, you know, and tried hard to joke away my anxiety. Before it was all over, though, I was nearly undone myself, to say nothing of what happened to the others.

Dear Marty and Uncle Dan,

I'm truly sorry that my long silence worried you. However, I will have to acknowledge a little sneaky gratification from your expression of concern, for there really is nothing like knowing that people you care about reciprocate the feeling. Not that I didn't know anyway, but it's nice to get a little confirmation now and then. Thanks for worrying!

First to answer your questions. Yes, I am all right. I'm better than usual, as a matter of fact. I seem to have more energy than I have had in years, in spite of all the things I'll tell you about in a minute. And no, there are no problems on the job. I still love it, although I'll have to admit that the part I really enjoy is playing with the babies I'm supposed to be studying, and talking to the mothers. I wouldn't dare say this to anyone else for fear of losing my halo, but analyzing data and trying to conceptualize process is really not my cup of tea. I'm sure it comes as no surprise to my erstwhile teacher (who was forever fruitlessly admonishing me to "look for the evidence, Amy!") that I am neither a real intellectual nor a true scientist at heart. However, I'm still managing to fool people enough to get by. So far my results are a testimony to the value of your influence, for I have just been offered a permanent academic appointment and rather imagine I'll take it even though it seems ridiculous to regard myself as "college faculty." ("Stop fluttering, Amy! You are beginning to act like a pink feather powder puff!" How I need someone to stand at my side and tell me that now and then, because that's what I so often feel like.)

Well, what's really been keeping me preoccupied is my charming, lovable, exasperating family. Why didn't you insist that I either stay three thousand miles away or buy a house with no guest room? There was plenty of evidence to support such a procedure, but in accordance with my true nature I paid no attention to it and now find myself rapidly starting to run an annex to the House of Usher. I'll tell you about that after a while, but I guess I'd better start at the beginning. I don't suppose you could imagine in a million years, so I'll only preface it by saying that nothing, dear friends, but nothing, is impossible in the Carpenter family, and the impossible has happened.

About two months ago, Mother phoned, as she frequently has for the last umpteen years, to say "Please be sure to come down for the weekend of the 8th because Daddy is arriving on Saturday." I paid as much attention as I always have until Saturday the 8th, when I got another call saying, "Daddy has already arrived, and when is your plane due?"

There he was, after twenty years, delighted to see us all, and as casual as if he'd just been away for a couple of days. Sitting down to dinner must have set off some kind of reflex, because his first words were, "Virginia, don't slouch. It isn't becoming." Jingo turned purple, El got so pale I thought he was going to faint, and Mother got that helpless look. Obviously somebody had to do something, and I was the only one not completely paralyzed, so I tried to be calm and said just as quietly as I could, "Knock it off, Daddy, we are all grown up now." He just looked surprised, as though he hadn't realized. Somehow we all got through the meal, and fortunately I had to leave the next morning.

A week or so later I got a call from Jingo saying that she simply couldn't take the situation with Alex and Miriam any longer and wanted to come and stay with me until she could arrange for a divorce. Since then I've had first one, then the other, and then both together staying here and using me as a referee. Night after night I come home from work to find they have been at it all day, Alex pacing and expostulating, Jingo screaming and reviling, and before I've been home an hour, they are both furious with me for not thinking the other one should be shot at dawn. Alex insists that he desperately needs both Virginia and Miriam and can't understand why Jingo can't be reasonable about it. After all, man is not a monogamous creature, and it is completely irrational of his wife to expect him to be. Jingo alternates between telling him to get out and never darken her door again and threatening to have the police raid his love nest and drag him home by the hair. Meanwhile he is getting no writing done at all, and within a few months they will again be stone-broke. At last hearing, Alex had finally agreed to give up Miriam and start all over again with Jingo in a Mexican villa that I would "lend" them the money to rent for an indefinite period, and when I refused I became the villain responsible for keeping them apart. Mutual resentment of my selfishness will undoubtedly reunite them for a while, because that is what he is obviously ready for by now, and I really hope it will. However, I can't help feeling slightly bitter that the several thousand dollars I have already "loaned" them at various times over the past couple of years has already been forgotten. (Jingo thinks I owe it to her anyway because of "all [she] did for [me]" when I was fifteen and she was married to Sid.) They think I am a cold, heartless bitch, or at least they will until the next time they love me temporarily for giving them something they want. I'm so sorry for the crazy dopes and really so fond of them both that I'm sure to break down sooner or later.

Somewhere between their visits, El came for the weekend and nearly bent my ear double talking about the Collective Unconscious, Spengler, and some revelations of his own that he firmly believes are prophetic. He's so involved with the idea of a new world in which wonders of mysticism will be unfolded that I'm a little scared he is losing touch with this one. However, whenever I'm on the verge of really suspecting he is a little mad, he becomes so logical and convincing that he almost has me believing his theories. At the end of all this, he took off to see a friend of Anne's at Tahoe who might be interested in financing a one-man show for him, and since he didn't have any antifreeze in the old jalopy, he dumped my last quart of Gordon's gin into his radiator. (It worked fine, he says.)

Do you begin to get some idea why I haven't written for so long? Forgive me, and let's hope I can keep up a little better from now on.

Much love to you both,
Amy

Dear Marty and Uncle Dan,

What do you mean I should be writing a soap opera? What else do you think I have been doing in these letters to you? What else *can* one write about the Carpenter clan? Turn on your radio and get ready for the next episode. This one is about El, or maybe it is really just about me, but in any case I'm not sure whether it's a comedy or a tragedy.

The other night Anne called me at about two A.M.—woke me out of a sound sleep, and for a moment or two I didn't realize she was trying to ask for help. Apparently ever since Daddy's return, El has been talking more and more wildly about his imminent transport into a higher state of consciousness, and she has become more and more worried about the possibility that he will try to hurry up the glories to come by doing something to end this phase of his existence. That night he hadn't been feeling well and decided to sleep over in his studio. The more she thought about him, the more she got the feeling that he was planning to do something to himself, so she finally decided to call me since she didn't want to upset Mother. I, of course, began to "flutter" a bit myself, but I told her I'd phone home and tell Mother I had some sort of silly impulse to call and see if everyone was all right. She'd probably think it was perfectly normal, because children do get funny ideas, don't they, and mothers have to take them in stride, even at two A.M.

Anyway, I called the house and got no answer. The phone rang and rang, and it threw me into a panic because Mother hasn't been out of that house at night in all the years she has lived there, and at that point I was certain El not only had decided to enter his new world himself but had taken his mother along for company.

For a moment I got so hysterical I was almost paralyzed, but then I remembered I could call the police down there, and although it took some talking to persuade them there might be an emergency, they finally sent a couple of men over to investigate. What do you know? After beating on the door for nearly twenty minutes, they were just about to break it down when El came stumbling sleepily down from the attic. He had a bad cold and hadn't heard the phone or the pounding. Mother, with the phone in the hall right outside her bedroom door, slept through the whole thing. Someone in the house committing suicide? Ridiculous! Who could ever have conceived such a silly idea? Poor Amy! She must have had some kind of nightmare.

Do I need to say that *nobody* bothered to call me back? I had to call the police station again about three sleepless hours later to hear "Oh no, there was no trouble at that address. Everybody is just fine."

My analyst just says, "Your family are 'crisis prone.' You will have to learn to live with it." I'm working at it, but it ain't easy, let me tell you!

Love to you both,
Amy

Dear Marty and Dan,

I agree that "Uncle stuff" *is* a little Victorian for someone of my age, but you must remember how hard it is for me to think of myself as grown up. I'll try to get used to equal status if you will keep on giving me an avuncular shoulder to lean on occasionally. I have a feeling I'm really going to need one in the months to come, because things have rapidly gone from bad to worse at the House of Usher, and as the roof falls in I may need help in staying out from under. A first crack in the walls has already occurred, and it won't be long now before the whole shebang comes tumbling down.

As I told you before, Daddy went ahead and founded his church. The lessons are selling like hotcakes (particularly throughout the Bible Belt), one of the most famous architects in the country has drawn up plans for a magnificent building, and negotiations are underway for land adjacent to a park in the Cradle of Liberty. Here comes the clincher. Last week he wired Mother to join him in a "second honeymoon," and at this writing she has already left to live with her true love forever more!

What will become of us all, I wonder? Can Mother really survive life with Daddy again? Can El survive her desertion? Can Jingo survive her fury? Can I survive my apartness? Tune in next week and hear more exciting adventures of "One Girl's Family."

My analyst just says, "Your mother must live with her own burdens. You are not your mother." I wonder if I believe that.

> Best love,
> Amy

Dear Marty and Dan,

I'm sorry, but I really can't even try to be funny about the family situation any more. Right at the moment everything is just plain awful, and it's becoming increasingly difficult for me not to get pulled into a bloody mess myself.

I suppose we should have known it would be like this, but even after all these years it's still hard for me to believe in the enormity of folly my parents can perpetrate! Even Jingo is staggered! Why did we not take it for granted that in setting up his church my father would instate as trustees none other than his wife and his sister? It is perfectly legal, of course, and 90 percent of the little congregations in this country are set up in the same way, but it really is hard for me to believe that my mother would go along with something like that twice in a single lifetime. She has, and now The Case is about to be repeated too.

In order to raise money for the building, Daddy had an advertising company set up a puzzle contest, exactly like all the other perfectly legal puzzle contests for all sorts of causes, and just like the bingo games run by hundreds of churches to make money. Unfortunately some of the big established religious interests have become outraged by the fast growth of this upstart church, and somebody brought a charge that there really is no church, no intention of building anything, and the contest is a fraud.

Even though the head of the advertising company has testified that the contest is perfectly honest, with money on deposit in a bank to pay all winners, even though the architect has testified that the building plans have been drawn up for a long time, even though funds for buying the land are already in escrow, even though they have literally thousands of letters from enthusiastic readers of the "New Bible" saying they eagerly await a meeting place for opponents of un-American dogma and ritual—even in spite of all this, my parents are back in the criminal courts.

Dozens of reputable lawyers again cry "persecution" and offer their services, again every lawyer you talk to says, "they can't do" what they are doing and it must be some mistake, but the interests lined up against our parents are just as formidable as those who went before and, in my opinion, have just as good a chance of wiping everyone out.

Why must my father always have such *big* ideas? Why must he step on such *powerful* toes? Why, oh why, must he always get Mother dragged along through the mud with him?

When we heard there would be another criminal investigation, I persuaded Mother to come west for a visit. Virginia agreed she was too angry to see her, and Eliot obviously isn't hitting on all cylinders at this point, so I was elected to try talking some sense into her. She was a little scared, too, and I thought I'd made an impression. I even thought I'd persuaded her to admit she knew nothing about the church business and never had, but that shows how well I know my mother even after all the years we have spent together.

The investigator turned up while she was still with me, and my own hair turned grey overnight. Within five minutes I was reduced to a quivering, jibbering mass of protoplasm, but did anything faze my mother? I should say not! She showed him into the room like Queen Marie granting audience to an ambassador. Whenever he started to open his mouth, she graciously invited him to contemplate the beautiful view and offered him a cup of tea. When he asked her about the financial structure of the church, she told him of the joy it brought her heart to read the lovely letters of gratitude from thousands of poor souls made happier because of my father's vision. When he suggested there might be some question about the legality of certain church activities, she laughed in his face and told him he just didn't understand. Her Eliot knew more about the law than practically anybody else alive and wouldn't do anything illegal if his life depended on it. It was so clear that she believed every word of it that the poor man slunk out with his tail between his legs, having learned exactly nothing at all. I almost felt sorry for him, so gorgeously did she put him to rout.

That isn't the end, either. So gay was she afterward, so full of innocent pleasure in the victory of "right," and so obviously due for a celebration that I took her to dinner at Trader Vic. There she really startled me by wanting "one of those pretty drinks with gardenias floating in them," and even when I told her it was made largely of rum, this teetotaler drank it without turning a hair and pinned the flowers on her dress. I, old sot that I am, took two sips of mine and suddenly started diluting that pretty drink with big drops of sticky saltwater. Then it was her turn to be astonished.

"Amy darling! You weren't frightened by that foolish little man, were you? My goodness, you just don't trust your father at all, do you? Do you suppose for one minute he would let any of his family be in a position to get hurt? Why! His church is as pure and fine as any church in the land, and when the judge hears how those wicked people have attacked your father for no reason, he'll throw the whole case out of court in ten seconds, just you wait and see. Amy dear, I'm sorry you had to go through this worry, but your mother isn't in any danger at all, so don't you give it another thought. I think maybe that liquor went to your head a bit, so let's start eating some of that delicious-looking thing with mushrooms and water chestnuts I saw the waiter bringing those people over there."

It ended up with my feeling rather ashamed of having been scared.

Marty and Dan! Tell me I'm not the one who's

crazy! My analyst just says, "Your mother seems quite capable of taking care of herself. You do not have to carry her burdens."

Don't I really? Can she take care of herself? Is it possible to stop worrying about her? I wonder.

Best of love from
Amy

Dear Marty and Dan,

It was good to get your comforting letter. It is indeed hard to end an analysis, but in a way I'm relieved to know that I can continue to function in spite of "withdrawal symptoms." When a child is ready to walk alone, it doesn't reassure him to be kept on somebody's lap, does it, even though that lap felt mighty cozy for a long time.

It has been some months since I mentioned what has been going on in the family, probably because for a while it hasn't been in the center of focus. Things settled down in the East, where it now looks as though there will be no prosecution for lack of evidence. Although all the church funds seem to have been used up in defense against the accusation, Mother and Daddy live on her income in their little apartment as though they hadn't a care in the world. In a letter last week she said, "Everything is fine, dear. I'm busy with my clubs and Daddy with his lawsuits," as though that were the natural order of things. She has written a small book of children's stories that is really very nice and now belongs to a woman writers' group that gives lots of lovely luncheons and teas.

Now, however, there are rumblings again from the House of Usher, and all of them are ominous. Jingo

finally kicked Alex out after the fights got too
fierce to bear, but her health has deteriorated to
such a point that I fear for her future. She is
practically bedridden from a flare-up of her old
injury, and she looks so bloated and grey that I
think there must be something seriously wrong
with her insides. Poor Alex now dances back and
forth between his two women, doing all Jingo's
shopping and really waiting on her hand and foot,
while at the same time constantly tormenting her
with tales about his other love. Jingo is so
possessed by anger that it is literally eating away
her life, and I have an extremely creepy feeling
about the whole situation. For a long time it
seemed she was focusing all the anger she felt
toward Alex on Daddy, but now it seems to be
reversed, and while she is almost out of her mind
with fury at Alex, she has become rather dispas-
sionate about Daddy, even admitting the other day
that Mother seems to be happy with him at the
moment.

As for Eliot, there is no longer any doubt in my
mind that he is actually insane. Why I wasn't
certain a long time ago is hard to explain, but until
they have been through it, I don't think people can
appreciate how insidious is the process of recognizing mental illness in someone you love. I've so
very gradually become used to his peculiar logic
that by now it just seems to be his individual style
of thinking, and it always sounds so reasonable
that you are apt to go along with it until you
remember how crazy the premise is on which his
arguments are built. When he tells me he has sent
his manuscript to the Pentagon and expects when
they understand his theory they will call him to be
in charge of the war against Germany, I find myself

wondering whether he has an overcoat heavy enough for winter in Washington, until I suddenly snap back to reality and say to myself, "My God! What am I thinking? He isn't going anywhere!"

Several months ago he left Anne rather abruptly and moved up here—indeed, would have moved right in with me if I hadn't insisted that he get a place of his own and offered to pay for it. His money is almost gone, and he has set it as a test of his power that some miracle will bring him a fortune before he runs out. If not, he will know it is time for the Golden Wave to carry him to another plane. I can't get him to see a psychiatrist, and when I plead with him, he simply says, "Amie, either I'm right about my destiny or I'm mad. In either case, why would you want to keep me in a world like this?"

The psychiatrists I've talked to all say he could probably be committed but there's little chance he could really be cured, and in any case things might go along as they are now almost indefinitely. People with these ideas often are quite ingenious about finding excuses for staying alive. In any case, I couldn't possibly persuade Mother to commit him. The last time I tried to tell her how sick he is, she asked me if I couldn't take up dianetics and make him a "clear." Oddly enough, she hasn't mentioned Christian Science since that time a while back when I talked her into a thyroid operation to cure her weight loss when I'm sure she really thought that she had cancer.

At the moment I just go on talking with El quite casually about all the marvels that await him, and he assures me sincerely that as soon as he comes into his own, he'll see that I get repaid for all my kindness. He would do it too, and the thought of it all nearly breaks my heart.

It is so sad and tragic. Every time I see either my sister or brother I feel sick, but I just go along as if nothing was wrong and try to get through each day without collapsing. As Mother says, "What *has* become of our lovely little family?" We all started out with so much hope and promise. Why did it have to turn out like this?

In sadness and love,
Amy

Dear Marty and Dan,

It is all over.

Yesterday I got a letter mailed the evening before. In it were a front door key, a pawn ticket, and a folded piece of wrapping paper written all over and around the edge, which I enclose. Send it back to me sometime when you think I can bear to see it again. It is poems—nothing more. That's all there was.

I can't write any more just now. I am too sad!

Love from
Amy

A seed quakes and trembles,
A rift—a breaking.
Under the hard shell, the
Emerging of one long foretold.

Slipping into a deep sea
Is one molested of heart,
Obscure of vision.
But when the deeps enfold,
The obscure vision is clarified
*   with light.*

Cease fears and trust, for
Tonight is given thee
Mastery.

When dawn breaks
Then is gone forever the night.
The night is thyself as thou art
Whom thou hatest.
Born is Messiah, the Prince.

By the morrow, sunup
Lifts into eternal day
One whose name is written.

From a dream it comes, a
* dream and a waking.*
For the night ends, and
* returns never.*
It is not death but sleep
* in which thou comest*
* into thy horn.*

Infinitesimal is the bird
* in my heart*
The wings fledgling, the
* beak unknowing its*
* strength.*
A bird blue and bright
A quiet bird.
But when thunder comes,
Then in the early rumble
The wings spread, and in
* the flash of lightning*
* begins an ascension.*

A sunflower evinces
* a certain preoccupation.*
Gold the petals, the center
* is gold.*

In the sunflower there tends
*   into existence*
A golden life.
Let the flower of the sun
*   flower in my heart*
And its seed be my seed
And let its issue be I.

Dearest Marty,

It was such a comfort to hear your voice on the phone. I must have sounded really weird, but forgive me. I've been in a daze for the last few weeks and only now am able to think at all clearly about what has happened.

Of course, when I got that letter addressed in El's handwriting, I knew what I would find when I went over. It's odd, isn't it, how one reacts in such a moment! For a while I just stood there, thinking about nothing at all—and then I called Bob. I haven't told you much about him, because somehow he never came into focus before, but at that moment he seemed the perfectly logical person to call, and I did. He went over with me, and I really don't know what would have happened if I hadn't had him to help me.

For some strange reason I had never been to El's apartment and had no idea what a shock it would be to see it. I knew it was a basement in the Tenderloin District, but somehow I'd shut it all out of my mind, I guess. When we opened the door, there it was—reeking of gas and all dark except for a thin ray of sunlight coming through a crack in Mother's old velvet curtains drawn as tightly as ill-fitting curtains can be drawn. A single bright beam fell across the darkness of the almost bare studio room, spotlighting part of a large central table cluttered with piles of paper, overflowing ashtrays, and an old-fashioned office typewriter from Glen Alden days. Everything else was in shadow—an easel surrounded by scattered paint tubes and brushes, the couch-bed against a far wall, and the pile of empty wine bottles beside a gas burner in the corner.

On the easel stood a still-wet painting of a gleaming golden peacock, his feathers set with brilliant jewels and spread against a background of gold so nearly the same in color and texture that the bird and background were nearly indistinguishable one from the other. First my eye fell on it and took in every detail. Then it hit the bottles, and finally the couch where he was lying so still and peaceful.

Marty, in a way I'm glad it happened just like that. It was easier for me, anyway, because I saw such a look of joy on his face that I knew somehow it was better that way. No more frustration or disappointment or humiliation for him. I'm sure when he left the world, he knew his moment of glory had come, and who can ask for more?

There were many things to do, and we did them automatically. I don't think I felt very much at all. The reaction came later, but then—whammo!

Now I am recovering. The only good thing that came out of it was discovering how I feel about Bob.

Thanks again, for all these years!

Love,
Amy

Amy darling,

Your beautiful letter has been a source of

wonderful comfort, and I shall always cherish the memory of El's last message to his father and me. Perhaps some day the coroner's office will no longer need his note for the official record, but what is a piece of paper? Our dear boy will be with us in spirit as long as we both shall live.

Your Daddy was overwhelmed with emotion at receiving the gold watch my father left to his grandson. As I told you on the phone, he was devastated by the news and is just now recovering from a high fever. He could not have undergone the strain of a trip west, and of course I could not leave him at such a time. How grateful we are that you and your kind friends were able to handle everything so efficiently! Virginia wanted to help, but as you know she is not well herself right now. We had a nice talk with her on the phone, as I'm sure you did too.

Do not be too sad, Amy dear, for you know there is no death—only change. Your brother has attained a higher state of consciousness than any of us can know in our present limited state. Try to focus on the positive and realize he is at peace in a realm beyond our understanding. Whenever sorrow creeps into my own heart, I quickly start reciting all the poetry I know and soon drive that negative thinking away.

We will be all right, honey, so don't worry and carry on with your fine work like the strong, brave girl you have always been.

Dearest love from us both,
Mother

A.C. It wasn't too much later that I had another terrible blow.

"How long have you had this abdominal pain?"

"I don't know exactly, but I think it started not long after my brother's death four months ago. I thought it was just due to nervous tension from all the grief and upset, but about a week ago it suddenly got so acute I thought I'd better have you check as soon as I got home. I was away at a conference."

"Amy, my dear girl, that little fibroid of yours has increased five times in size since I last checked you, and from its consistency I have to tell you it may have become malignant. Why can't you be as sensible about your health as you are about everything else? You are always so God damned sure everything is psychosomatic! You know as well as I do that persistent abdominal pain should be checked immediately. What's the matter with you anyway? I'll operate tonight, and hope it isn't already too late!"

"Tonight? But Randy, I can't possibly! There's so much—"

"You can't possibly not. I'll put in the orders and expect you at the hospital within two hours."

A little while later, Amy sat in a hospital bed, calmly writing a few notes to her family and friends. Nothing to alarm anyone, of course, although she had already made a will and left complete instructions with a close friend about what to do in case anything happened during the operation. Obviously nothing would happen, but you never know, and you might as well be prepared.

Her mind was perfectly clear. She understood very well that, at the least, all possibility of childbearing was at an end, and, at the worst, she might be facing a death sentence. She had not shed a tear, however, because Amy had no emotional reaction at all. It was like the time of the fire in her house when, cool as a cucumber, she put out the flames with utmost efficiency before collapsing in total paralysis for ten minutes after the danger was over.

That night she quietly reaffirmed her affection for all who loved her and mentioned no word of anxiety because there was no anxiety. That night she felt absolutely nothing and went as calmly to the operating table as to her own bed.

The next day things were quite different—the next day and for quite a while afterward. The next day Amy wept over the end to her hopes for motherhood and the fears suppressed at the moment of emergency; she trembled for the danger averted just in time. For the first time in four months, she gave way completely and finally experienced a reaction of intense anguish to both her grievous recent losses. It was actually an outpouring augmented by the store of leftover grief from all the losses sustained throughout her life, for in her mind these losses were by then consolidated into a unit. Probably she would never again lose anyone important to her without feeling all over again, in a tremendous volume of sorrow, the griefs she couldn't quite express fully when they were first aroused.

A.C. Of course, I don't know whether the growth of those fibroids was connected in any way with my feelings about El's death, but I've been told emotional upset can produce that sort of effect. Do you think it did?

Dr. P. I really don't know. One can find in psychiatric literature articles by people who claim there is evidence for such a connection, and certainly the timing might tend to corroborate that. However, whether there is or not, you paid a high price for those years in lots of ways.

A.C. It's a wonder I didn't go crazy. I felt like it sometimes myself.

Dr. P. You've said things like that before, but I don't believe them. I can see that you might have committed

suicide at certain points, but I don't believe you ever
would have become schizophrenic. You didn't buy
illusory worlds as the others did, even though you kept
your rationality at a price. I think what saved you was
the availability of good parent-surrogates all along the
line and your own capacity to seek them out. Then too,
you weren't home for very long at a time. Your poor
brother was really exposed to an insidious corrosive
force of one kind or another for most of his life, wasn't
he?

A.C. All but when he was away at school and college.
Just about thirty years out of thirty-seven.

Dr. P. Tell me, Amy, at what point do you feel your
brother's fate became inevitable? It sounds from your
description that throughout most of his life he was
timid, impractical, and rather effete, but although he
was schizoid during his early life, he didn't seem to be
recognizably schizophrenic, and he did have considerable talent as an artist. It is a cliché, of course, to say
that there is often a thin line between artist and
madman, but a lot of people like Eliot don't cross that
line. Why do you think he did, at such a relatively late
age?

A.C. It's so hard to know. Of course, the groundwork for his vulnerability and his bisexuality was laid
down at an early age, but it does seem that things could
have been different if at certain points along the way he
had had a little better luck.

For instance, this sort of thing—I've often wondered
how much it had to do with his becoming ill. Do you
remember my telling you about the famous architect
who made Daddy's church model, Daddy's fraternity
brother at the university? One time he came out to see
Mother, and El showed him some of his pictures. He
really liked them and said he had a lot of contact with
well-known artists in New York. He volunteered to take

some of the pictures back with him to see if he could interest someone in a one-man show. You can imagine how exciting that was for El! He talked of nothing else for days. And then do you know what happened? Exactly nothing. There was absolutely not another word from that man. I could hardly believe it. After El died, I went to New York to collect the pictures, and I really let him have it! For once I didn't care about being polite, and I tore into him like a hellcat, but all he could say was that he hadn't been able to do anything and didn't know what to say to El. I said, "At least you could have told him the truth."

Another time one of his ex-roommates came to see him in the West. This guy had become very prominent, and when he saw what El was doing, he too volunteered to do something for him and then just faded out. It's true, of course, that it was very unrealistic of El to have this kind of expectation from people but he also did get quite a bit of a runaround. I think the rage and disappointment had something to do with his actual break, although it began to happen in the course of his therapy.

Dr. P. Yes. There was too much destruction of necessary defenses too suddenly by an inexperienced therapist.

How much do you think your own troubles were related to his? You seemed to be in very good shape after your analysis, but his suicide obviously threw you back into a depression for much longer than the ordinary period of mourning.

A.C. I didn't realize I *was* depressed after that.

Dr. P. It seems quite clear from your story that you were, whether you recognized it or not.

A.C. If that's true, I really don't know. In retrospect I can see very clearly that throughout most of my early life I was depressed, right alongside being Miss Merry

Sunshine and that little demon who hassled my teachers so much. I never connected it with my brother, though. I really was almost out of contact with him from the time he went away to school at the age of thirteen, except for holidays and vacations while I was still in school myself. We were close in a peculiar emotional way, but not really close in the sense of being able to talk freely to each other about our feelings. It wasn't until the last years of his life, after Mother went back to Daddy. At that point, of course, I saw him constantly, and he talked to me a great deal, but by then he was already pretty far gone. I wouldn't let him live with me, but he came almost every night for dinner and slept at my house frequently over weekends. I had become a substitute for Mother by then.

Dr. P. Did he talk much to her before she left? Could he tell her about his feelings?

A.C. Only at times of extreme stress. Of course, he did talk to her that night she prevented his first suicide attempt, but after all, a gentleman doesn't talk to his mother about fears of homosexuality, now does he! Anyway, one didn't exactly talk to Mother *about* anything. I could count on one hand the number of actual conversations I've had with her in my whole life. We might tell her about incidents that occurred, but as I told you before, talk in our household was purely anecdotal. Of course, if my father was home, he carried on a complete monologue, but Mother was almost as bad. She rattled on constantly but didn't actually say much.

Dr. P. What would happen if you tried to discuss something like politics?

A.C. Who ever heard of such a thing? We just never did. I have my doubts whether Mother even knew who was President most of the time, because it just didn't enter her orbit. We discussed no abstract issues, except

Christian Science in the old days, and that was all one-way—a continual day-to-day sermon. That's where we all learned to tune out, I think. I still do it some. Bob is always saying, "You don't *hear* me!" I tell him it's because he mumbles, but I think in truth it's a little of both.

Dr. P. It's not surprising Eliot had trouble focusing on anything. You were exposed to a barrage of chitchat and people's fantasies but never had a chance to discuss things seriously.

A.C. I've always thought that was important—that we were never able to get things *settled.* At the same time, there were those moments of real empathy between Mother and all of us. I still haven't explained to myself that night she went to El's apartment. Frankly, I haven't ruled out ESP, although I'm afraid to say so for fear of sounding as though I went along with the other kinds of nuttiness rife in our family.

Then too, in a lot of ways Mother was a tower of strength to us all—really terribly practical any time the chips were down and something had to be done. I can't think of a single time she ever let me down when I wanted help in doing something sensible; she either took the time to show me how or saw to it that I was taught the necessary skills by someone else. I'm sure she did the same for the others. With all her apparent vagueness, she had actual know-how in all sorts of areas—an infinite variety of little ingenious tricks to make housekeeping more efficient, and there was nothing she couldn't do with a hairpin, from making a doll to fixing the plumbing. None of the men in the family could do anything useful at all. I'm sure my father didn't even know how to change a washer in the sink.

Dr. P. That's another good example of how you couldn't have really clear-cut feelings about anyone.

A.C. Not even about each other. There was too much

exasperation mixed with the fondness, and too much love mixed with anger. Like with El—in those last years we talked a lot, about our feelings in regard to the family, and about all his weird ideas and fantasies. In fact, he told me a lot about the meaning of his paintings that I wish to heaven I could remember. The trouble was that at the time I didn't really want to hear—it made me mad, although I know that was a cover up for feeling so upset. I must have suspected he was crazy before I actually let myself know, and I guess I tuned out things that seemed too peculiar. I'd give anything now to recover some of those conversations.

Dr. P. When did you first recognize he was actually psychotic?

A.C. I think it was sometime late in my analysis. I was talking about my mother's siblings, and I remember saying El was supposed to be very much like Uncle Charley. Then I suddenly burst into tears and said, "I think my brother is losing his mind." I don't think it entered my conscious awareness until then.

Dr. P. And you still don't know what finally happened?

A.C. Well, all I can say is that the last straw was when Mother went back to my father. To all of us that was completely incredible. I was the only one who even tried to accept it. Jingo was so mad she practically never spoke to Mother again, although she was mad all the time anyway. Mother just picked up suddenly, you know. Within about a week of the time he suggested it, she was gone. After all those years of taking care of El, she just said, "Goodbye. You are on your own now." I was really furious about that myself. It wasn't fair to infantilize him and then suddenly abandon him like that.

Dr. P. He had made no effort to be on his own before?

A.C. A little abortive effort. He had that job in the art gallery for a short time, but nothing that amounted to anything. First he was going to make it with his writing, then with his painting. After a while, manna was going to fall from heaven. He considered it beneath him to take any kind of menial job, and there actually wasn't anything much he knew how to do except write and paint.

Dr. P. Eliot must have felt your mother really belonged to him.

A.C. In a way I suppose he did, although nothing could have been farther from his conscious thinking.

Dr. P. In his autobiography there seems to be some evidence of erotic interest in her; you can see it in some of the dreams he described.

A.C. Maybe all his whoring around was to get rid of those feelings as well as homosexual temptations. Mother was really very cute and cuddly, you know, and we were all quite physically affectionate with her during childhood. After El was grown though, I never saw him even kiss her. I don't know. There are so many angles it makes my head ache.

Dr. P. How did he react to Bob?

A.C. Well, he liked him a lot. Bob was terribly nice to him—invited him to go fishing, and things like that. El thought of him as a kind of Earth Father. Of course, I wasn't sleeping with Bob at the time and didn't really recognize my own interest in him until later. Looking back, however, I think El knew more about how I felt than I did. For all I know, he had an erotic interest in me too, although there certainly was never anything overt. It's funny—once my analyst asked if he had ever made a pass at me, and I was horrified. If one can be said to draw oneself up on a couch, I did just that. I drew myself up to my full height and said indignantly, "My brother is a gentleman! He wouldn't do that, even if he *is* crazy!" Then we both laughed uproariously. I don't think he ever acted on any perverse impulses, even though he admittedly had them.

Dr. P. Don't we all?

A.C. Well yes, I guess we do. We just don't all have to fight so hard to keep them under control.

Dr. P. But after your mother left, he came to you every night for dinner. That was real transference.

A.C. Yes, and I can also remember how pleased I was when he once said that I cooked something or other better than Mother did. I guess I was somewhat willing to assume the role.

Dr. P. What did your mother expect everyone to do after she left?

A.C. Well, she had given everyone the Glen Alden money and was giving Jingo rents from the big house as well as letting her stay in the garage. As a matter of fact, now that I think of it, she was giving El something every month even after she left. That whole period is so vague in my mind. Of course, she was perfectly sure he would soon find himself, but at one point a little later she wrote and asked me if I would "lend" her the money to give them all. Jingo and Alex were in some kind of a crisis, and she couldn't afford any more. Fortunately by then I was strong enough to say "No. I'll help El because he's sick and can't take care of himself, but if Jingo and Alex need more, he will simply have to go out and get a job." He did too, and neither of them ever forgave me for interrupting his writing.

Dr. P. Your mother ended up supporting your father too?

A.C. Yes, the money from the church got used up somehow. I've never really understood what happened about all that—never knew and never wanted to know. He was right about a lot of things he was fighting, in my opinion, but frankly I just didn't want to know about them. I couldn't have cared less what he did, so long as he did it three thousand miles away from me, and nobody connected me with his activities. He tried to tell me about them, but I just tuned out. I couldn't take it.

At that point I hardly knew what was real myself. I wanted to help everyone as much as I could, because I realized it had been an abandonment, and I had a nice house, where they all liked to come. On the other hand, I just didn't want the responsibility. For one thing, I was really afraid to have Jingo in the house for fear she'd burn it down. She was always laying her cigarette down and forgetting about it after she'd had a few drinks, and several times we actually did have small fires. There were times when I was actually scared of El too.

That was late in the game, but I'll never forget one night when he was staying there overnight. You know, my father always shaved with those ivory-handled straight razors; he used them right up to the time of his death, and so did El. They said they could shave closer, and both had heavy black beards that had to be shaved twice a day as it was. Anyway, one night I was sitting in the living room when he came up with one of those in his hand and, in the most casual voice you can imagine, said, "Amie, I'm thinking of altering my face. It doesn't look quite right to me." Well! At that moment I wasn't at all sure whose face was going to get altered before the night was over. However—and this is typical of a lot that went on between us—I just said equally calmly, "Why El, your face looks perfectly all right to me. That's a silly idea." A few minutes later, I asked him to give me the razor, and he handed it over, meek as a lamb. That was the only time anything like that ever happened, but I'll tell you I wasn't any too happy about being alone in the house with him after that.

The only reason I was able to stay so calm was that I just don't react very fast in moments of extreme crisis, but I get the shakes a little later. As a matter of fact, the day after that happened, we were sitting over our coffee after lunch when the phone rang; it was Jingo asking if she could come up for a month because she was having a "nervous breakdown" over some of Alex's high jinks. That really unnerved me. I said, "No!" and slammed down the phone, and then I turned and hit El with my shoe and said, "I'm sick of everyone's problems, including yours!" I think that was when he told me he'd make it all up to me when he came into his own. I'm pretty sure that toward the end he knew I thought he was insane, but he never forced me to say it directly, and he didn't hold it against me. I did try very hard to get him to a psychiatrist, but he was very happy with the therapy he'd had—felt it released him, which of course it did. It sent him completely off his rocker.

Dr. P. And when he suicided your Mother just let you take care of everything?

A.C. What else could she do? Daddy became ill, and she couldn't leave him. But you know, I don't think she wanted to either, and actually at that point I was so disoriented that it never occurred to me to wonder about it. In my mind it had become totally my problem.

I remember it wasn't until the next day I realized I hadn't told my parents! Then, of course, I called and talked to them both on the phone, but having them involved seemed quite unreal. I had told Mother a number of times that it might possibly happen, but she just didn't believe it. When they went to pieces on the phone, I'm sure I never even thought they might come. Jingo had known it might happen too, but when it did, neither she nor Alex suggested doing anything, and somehow I never even considered there was anything funny about that.

Dr. P. How did it become so much your problem?

A.C. Everyone else had just kind of dismissed him

from their area of thinking. Mother and Daddy were busy with their new life, and everything else was out of their focus. El was up here with me to take care of him, so everything was all right. As far as Mother was concerned, Jingo and Alex were fine too. She had already dismissed the whole western scene from her mind.

Right after El died, I was in a complete daze. It wasn't until a week later that I finally sat down and wrote Mother, trying to paint a lovely picture of what had gone before. He left no word to anyone, of course, but I wrote her all sorts of last messages—just made them up because I knew she wanted it. All I cared about at that point was to make her as happy as possible, and after all he was gone. Nobody was hurt in any way. She heard what she wanted to hear and was happy with it. In retrospect, I think I must have been extremely angry with her for needing all that, especially since I had to go through all the horrors of it.

Dr. P. Of course you were, and I'm sure it contributed to your own depression. You had to love and protect your mother, and all the time she was leaving you holding the bag. You should have been angry, but you couldn't let yourself.

A.C. I guess so. I really didn't realize I became depressed afterward, but it seems logical.

You see, by the time he suicided, he was convinced that a glorious future awaited him and made me feel I was really interfering with his destiny by encouraging him to stay on earth. I knew he must be very ambivalent, however, because he kept setting little conditions that would have to be met before a certain time or it would be an omen, but he kept changing the criteria. I had no way of knowing that he wouldn't put it off indefinitely. We used to talk so rationally about it. I'd say very calmly that of course I could see how he felt, but I personally wasn't so sure things would be all that much better for him in another state of consciousness, and anyway I wasn't about to go along with his wish to be off there, because I liked having him around in his present state of consciousness. He'd say yes, but on the other hand he was going to be the messiah and, as such, would be in a much better position to take care of things, particularly me. Then I could practically see myself sitting up there as Madame Messiah! I'd say that sounded very nice, and I appreciated his concern, but it really wasn't what I wanted. That was the way we would converse, night after night!

I wish I could really give you the flavor of those conversations, but I can't because I was so tuned out. All I can say is that we were talking rationally and calmly about completely psychotic ideas. Talk about folie à deux—I was really in one with him. It was like the "Jet Propelled Couch" with me in his fantasy too, talking as though those crazy ideas were not crazy ideas. I didn't have the strength to just say, "You are nuts!" Maybe it would have been better for him if I could have, but I couldn't. He knew I felt that way, but he also knew I was trying to understand his point of view. Whether he thought he was putting it across, I don't know.

There were some other little touches that seem funny now, although I can't say they did then—like his sending me the pawn ticket for his grandfather's watch. Even after he was dead, I was supposed to bail him out. I can talk about it now without getting too emotional, but it was a long time before I could. As a matter of fact, even now every once in a while something will touch me off and I'll burst into tears with no warning, just as I used to as an adolescent. The only difference is that now it's rather specifically related to all this stuff, and I know what it's about.

Dr. P. I think what you still have trouble seeing is that in their need to protect themselves your parents and Jingo were really very cruel to you. They couldn't take it any more, so they got out and left you with the whole problem.

A.C. They didn't mean to. That's just the way they were. As Mother used to say of Daddy, they just didn't think like other people.

Dr. P. Maybe not. But the way they were was pretty hard on you. You know it with one side of your head, but with the other you still want to deny it.

A.C. I guess you're right. However, if people make you a victim, you have to be a victimee, you know. I guess I was one. Fortunately my analyst protected me. He really saved my life during that period by helping me to make rational decisions when I simply couldn't think straight by myself.

Eliot gave all his paintings to me, and actually I was the only one who wanted them. Jingo had one or two that eventually came back to me, but they disturbed Mother, and I can see why. A lot of them disturbed me too. Unfortunately I burned quite a few of the most psychotic-looking ones. Right after his death I couldn't stand to look at them—all those women hanging on trees! I suppose I saw myself up there among them, but anyway, I didn't want them around. I did save a few of the less gruesome ones as well as the later ones that were beautiful and surrealistic, along with being just so many uteri. I have a lot of drawings of his architectural fantasies too.

He really didn't present himself as psychotic to most people, even fairly late in the game, and fitted in perfectly well at parties I gave and things like that. People would think he was a little strange, but it wasn't too obvious. Anyway, one time I had a group of architects, and he was talking about how he thought the nucleus of a whole new architectural concept was expressed by those buildings in Los Angeles shaped like a brown derby or an ice cream cone. He thought them indigenous folk art—forms emanating directly from the native core of a people unspoiled by alien European influences, and he felt that eventually Americans could go completely in that direction. The architects looked a little funny—well, it *is* funny. I can see the point, though, can't you?

Dr. P. Of course. What could be more natural than to have an ice cream parlor in the shape of an ice cream cone? There's something very direct about it. Anyway, Amy, there's nothing psychotic about that idea. Undoubtedly a lot of his ideas made sense, even though he did see himself as a symbol of all the wrongs in society. There are lots of people who aren't schizophrenic who see things the way he did.

A.C. Yes. That's one of the horrors. It's just like with Daddy—so many of the things he said made sense—and Mother too. That's what made everything so confusing.

Dr. P. How do you think living with someone who was schizophrenic influenced your own approach to life while you were going through it?

A.C. For one thing, I believe my involvement with my brother and his problems was really what kept me from marrying sooner. I was thirty-five before I finally made it, you know; I couldn't even begin to think seriously about any man until after his death. Right afterward, there was a sudden shift in the balance of forces inside me. Freedom from preoccupation with him and his troubles suddenly released a flow of potential for deepening other relationships and allowed me to perceive for the first time someone who for the past several years had mysteriously turned up whenever I needed someone. It was amazing enough to realize he must love me, but the most amazing thing of all was to discover that I could love him passionately after taking him so much for granted for so long! Actually, you know, we had been friends for a long time—had such a comfortable friendship nothing else ever entered my mind. Fortunately I woke up in time. I ended up with exactly the right man for me. That's the way I see it, anyway, and that's how it looks to everyone who knows us. Sometimes I can hardly believe it even now.

10

The Later Years

Amy's psychoanalysis had not entirely eliminated her tendencies to be fascinated and excited by men with an aura of ruthlessness, although she both recognized and guarded against such tendencies. It would not have been impossible for her to slip into a subdued version of her first love affair had sufficient temptation come her way. On the other hand, she was also aware that, in attempting to avoid such a situation, she might eventually settle for a relatively passive man willing to let her dominate him. A number of such men had been interested in her, and she had liked several of them quite a lot. As it happened, the ability to appreciate Bob for what he was enabled her to avoid both those pitfalls.

Bob was a man sure enough of himself and secure enough in his own profession to take pride in Amy's professional achievements without feeling overshadowed. Even more important, he was healthy enough emotionally to help her overcome certain residual anxieties at the beginning of their relationship without becoming emasculated by her inhibitions. Bob loved Amy and was both willing and able to give her time to adjust. Having lost a preadolescent child along with his former wife in an automobile accident, he was also able to forego further fatherhood without resentment. By the time they were engaged, both Bob and Amy felt too old for the need to adopt children and were able to concentrate on nurturing each other. Where she was weak, he was strong, and where he needed support, he could accept it without losing self-esteem. All in all, he really was just the right man for Amy.

With one side of her mind, Amy was a very rational woman. With the other side, however, she almost believed herself singled out for special protection and good fortune, and it would be hard to convince her completely that her good luck in finding Bob was not due to the planning and supervision of a very solicitous and efficient guardian angel. After all, she did need to account for the fact that just when she was ready to love a man, she found the perfect one for her right at hand, not only available but able to love her in return. Amy was smart enough to know that people don't get what they deserve, either good or bad, and she found it rather frightening to think that so many good breaks throughout her life might have come about by pure, blind luck. Nobody in her right mind would believe that luck singles people out, so she preferred to think somebody was watching out for her interests.

Amy was not without self-esteem, nor did she feel completely undeserving of Bob's devotion. On the other hand, the whole thing took a bit of explaining. Even though she didn't believe in miracles, Amy was never quite sure that a miracle hadn't happened to her.

Dr. P. In spite of all the horror, Eliot's death had its compensations as far as you were concerned.

A.C. Yes. I wonder if I could ever have been free as long as he lived. I really doubt it.

Dr. P. That would be hard for me to say. In any case, your future life would have been very different. Tell me, how did your parents adjust? Did your Mother ever give evidence that driving sad thoughts away by reciting poetry was not entirely successful?

A.C. I have no idea, because I didn't see them until a long time afterward. It was fascinating to me that, of the two, my father took it hardest at the time. Another one of those moments when something got through to him and really shook him. He collapsed completely and was ill for the first time in his life, I think. Perhaps the need to care for him kept Mother under control—that and her ability to find "right" in whatever happened. So far as I know, once that was over, they picked up their life as though nothing had happened at all. We slipped back into our usual pattern of brief communications, and it wasn't until a year later that I made my first visit to their new home.

Amy never told her mother about the operation. Why upset her when she had already been through so much? She tended to write only about pleasant things, knowing that Laura would remain relatively undisturbed if she thought her children were getting along all right, and although it was sometimes hard to explain the kinds of things she herself found satisfying, she made a point of mentioning happy events whenever possible. Now, a year after getting well again, there was really something good to tell—something so exciting, in fact, that a letter actually seemed inadequate. Amy was engaged to be married, and she decided to make her news the gala occasion for a long-anticipated trip to visit her parents' new home.

Although she did not exactly miss her mother from day to day, Amy periodically felt a real need to see her, and sharing her own happiness would be a treat for them both. She could hardly wait to go but nevertheless approached the visit with a certain amount of dread. How would everyone handle an emotionally loaded first reunion after Eliot's death? Her father, who had been so hard hit, would probably be more volatile than usual, and when he was wrought up, nobody knew what to expect. Although she had made a solemn vow to say or do nothing disturbing to either parent, Amy knew from experience how difficult it sometimes is to keep from letting out a word that gives offense, and she fervently hoped for strength to survive the three days without creating some kind of storm.

The meeting was as emotional as she had anticipated. As they hugged each other, all three shed a few tears, and for a moment Amy was on the verge of breaking down. Most of the tears were tears of joy, however—a few of momentary sadness, but most of love and joy and pleasure at being together. Her father beamed and beamed, reiterating the "Well, well, well!" that customarily expressed his wordless pleasure, and repeating several times how lovely she looked. "You have become a fine woman, Amy! A fine woman!" and then he bustled into a little kitchenette to prepare lunch and leave her for some girl talk with her mother. He had always dreamed of puttering around a kitchen and had now taken over the cooking completely, putting together meals of scientific nutritional balance, and seeing to it that Mother ate every nourishing bite put before her. "As you get a little older, it is particularly important to eat correctly and stay healthy. Your body has to have the proper elements, you know, if you want to keep your strength. Don't you agree?" Amy agreed and was glad to see that both of them really were looking exceedingly fit.

Her mother had by now proclaimed an end to sadness and wiped away her last tear. This was to be a completely happy occasion—so long since they had seen each other, with so much to catch up on. First, however, Amy must see their little home from stem to stern. A truly unusual "find" it had been, in the midst of an overcrowded city where attractive places in old buildings usually have prohibitive rents. Just by chance, she and Daddy had located this apartment with its lovely, high-ceilinged rooms and fireplace in a converted mansion, situated just on the line separating a still nice-looking neighborhood from "Blacktown." If you didn't know what was on the next street you would never suspect, because the marble foyer of this building was kept up so elegantly. They were, in fact, "very lucky to be right here," because shops just over the line were quite a lot cheaper than those in the other parts of town, and the black shopkeepers always very courteous, too. After all, there is no color line in the sight of God, now is there? Amy found it charming, as her mother's homes always were, and expressed her admiration with sincere enthusiasm. Her mother, very pleased, chatted all through lunch about the apartment, the shops, the available transportation to her clubs, and while Daddy became visibly restless, he managed to let "the girls" have their talk without interrupting. It was obvious that he too had made a vow and was manfully trying to keep it.

After lunch, though, it was his turn, and as soon as the gate-legged table was replaced against the wall, everyone settled down to listen. He knew Amy would want to hear all about his affairs, so without further ado he was off explaining them to her. Amy really did want to hear and tried very hard to follow, but as he went on, becoming increasingly violent, increasingly loud and bombastic and high-pitched, she found herself slipping into a familiar state of semicoma, which insulated her against electric charges building up in the surrounding atmosphere. The insulation would gradually wear away, she knew, leaving her exposed to waves of shocking current, but as long as humanly possible, she would try to maintain her composure in the only way she knew. When it became unbearable, she planned to plead fatigue from the plane ride and take a brisk walk in the cool October sunshine before renewed exposure to the "ordeal by percussion," but right now drifting off into a state of numbness offered blessed relief. As she sank to the lowest level of consciousness, Amy retained only enough contact with the outer world to nod her head occasionally and murmur something noncommittal during the rare moments when her father stopped for breath. That, of course, is all he would have permitted even if she had been capable of full participation.

Several hours later, as vibrations in her nervous system reached jarring proportions, Amy gradually began to emerge from her psychic cocoon. Gradually her mind reopened to stimuli from without, and she again became aware of the words her father spoke. Now she began to hear him commenting on the state of the world, putting forth his fanatical right-wing political stance, while at the same time decrying with fury the organized religions which serve as cornerstones to that very same right-wing philosophy. Amy felt her hackles rising, but she was used to contradictions and had prepared herself beforehand to tolerate this kind of conversation. It was, in fact, primarily to avoid arguments over just such a subject that she had pledged silence at all costs, so she bit her lips and let him continue.

At this point, however, she became aware of her mother, and suddenly Amy had a revelation. Laura had been sitting all this time on the couch beside her husband with a bright, encouraging smile on her face. She had been nodding agreement periodically, now and then patting his knee acceptingly as the diatribe continued, and she was still doing it when Amy returned to life. It was with a real sense of enlightenment that

Amy suddenly realized Laura was as far from the whole scene as she herself had been a moment before. She was completely tuned out and would have been making the same gestures, would have been purring the same soft, little noises to accent his points, and would have been patting his knee in the same way if he had been discoursing on the habits of the abominable snowman. Amy was suddenly hit by a wave of comprehension. Mother had been able to live with Daddy all the years she had because she simply didn't listen. Her parents, like nursery school children in parallel play, could live together in relative peace for a long, long time because neither of them ever really heard a word the other said. Tuning out was a pattern by which these two people managed to tolerate each other's chatter, and by some means it had been passed on to Amy as her single, most effective technique for self-preservation when in the presence of either one. Why this came as such a revelation is hard to say, but Amy felt it as such, although she was not aware until later how much relief the recognition afforded.

Actually, the three days passed very quickly. Amy went once to lunch at her mother's club, delighting the ladies with her wit and charm, and the whole affair came off as a magnificent triumph for Laura. Another day Amy took her mother to lunch at a fine restaurant to see the passing parade of beautifully dressed women. Evenings were no problem, because her parents retired before seven, leaving Amy free to dine again later with friends of her own. All in all she was having such a pleasant time that Amy almost forgot to tell her parents what she had come to tell them.

On the last day, however, she did manage to break the news at breakfast, and the sensation created was everything she could have hoped. Her mother flew up in delight to hug and kiss her, and her father beamed,

*repeating four or five times what a fine wife she would
make, and declaiming on the luck of any fellow who got
his little girl. He then left for the kitchen, perhaps to
give Mother a chance to tell her child the facts of life,
and Laura siezed the opportunity to broach a subject
that had obviously begun to disturb her as soon as she
heard the news.*

*"Amy, darling, I do wish we could give you a
beautiful wedding like Virginia's, but I just don't see—"*

Amy managed to keep a straight face.

*"I understand, Mother. Times have changed. But
don't worry about it. Actually, you know, things are
just a little different for me than they were for Jingo
twenty-five years ago anyway, and I hadn't really
planned on much of a whoop-de-do. In fact, I think we
will go quietly to a justice of the peace since I know you
and Daddy can't possibly get to California, and it would
be difficult for me to get east again for quite a while."*

Laura looked relieved but still rather wistful.

*"All right, dear, if that's what you want. But I feel
every girl should have a* wedding. *Perhaps we could do
something about a trousseau—"*

*"No, Mother. I really have quite a lot of clothes. As a
matter of fact, I have a very pretty dress to be married
in."*

*Amy described it in detail and her mother seemed
mollified, but something was still bothering her, and
Amy suspected what it was.*

*"I do wish, though, that you would pick out my
wedding nightgown for me. Nobody but you could find
just the right one."*

*Laura looked a little sly, but now delighted at being
given an important role in her daughter's marriage, she
launched into reminiscences about her own. For the
next hour or so Amy sat enthralled by descriptions of
those happy days—six sewing women covering yards and*

*yards of fine voile with tiny tucks, the flowing lace veil,
and her mother billowing in flounces, with a radiant
face above the bouquet of freesia and white roses. That
lovely, innocent face from her wedding photographs,
bright with joy and expectancy, once belonged to this
little aging lady, now so full of nostalgia after a lifetime
of frustration. For a moment Amy's eyes misted over,
but the moment passed, and then it was almost time to
go. Daddy rejoined them for the one last, well-balanced
lunch they would share for some time to come, and it
was all over.*

*Amy had had a happy visit and on boarding the plane
still felt the pleasurable glow of a mission successfully
accomplished. All had been peaceful, satisfying, and
loving. No disasters precipitated by a careless word, no
unmanageable sorrows. In fact, Eliot had not been
mentioned by anyone the whole time. It was not until
she was settled in her seat that Amy realized this fact
and simultaneously became aware of something else. In
all their talk about her marriage, in all the excitement,
the delight, and the planning, neither parent had asked
her a single question about the bridegroom-to-be. At
this very moment, while her mother and father were
probably talking about what a nice time everyone had
had, neither of them even knew the name of their
prospective son-in-law, and without a doubt they would
never stop to wonder unless Amy herself brought it up.
All they knew was that their baby was happy with her
life, and that is all they needed to know.*

*At the moment of this realization, Amy threw back
her head and laughed so loud that people turned to
stare. At that moment, once and for all, true understanding of her parents consolidated in her mind. She
accepted them for what they were, forgave them for
what they were not, and relinquished forever any hope
that some day they might really come to know their*

youngest daughter. At that moment, on a plane from fairyland back to the real world, Amy separated a lifetime of knowledge and true perception from a lifetime of wishful thinking and freed the love for her mother from the wish to have her be an entirely different person. From that day on, Amy enjoyed seeing her parents now and then, felt relatively comfortable in their presence, and placed upon them no burden of unfulfillable demands. She gave up worrying about them and in her heart gave full permission for them to lead their own lives in their own way.

A.C. It's just as well that I did, too, because they continued on happily for nearly fifteen years before finally dying in their middle eighties. Not even the tragedies of their two older children made more than a transient ripple on the surface of their life together after nearly a quarter-century of separation.

Dr. P. You say "their two older children," so I take it that Jingo's end was tragic, too.

A.C. The whole last years of her life were tragic, but of course my parents didn't know about that until the end.

For a few years after El's death, pandemonium continued to reign at the House of Usher. Jingo, now financially dependent on rents from the big house given her by Mother as a "management fee," lived alone in the garage apartment, crippled and in almost constant pain. Alex, living in a room nearby, had taken a hack-writing job but spent his days largely doing Jingo's errands and his nights arguing with Miriam. Miriam, who had finally been divorced by her husband, had expected Alex soon to replace him. However, this idea was as untenable to Alex as the idea of ceasing to keep her as a foil against Jingo. They therefore continued to live in a reluctant threesome, left strictly on their own by everyone they knew.

Friends had rapidly backed away from the whole complex entanglement in a state of embarrassed bewilderment. Mother didn't know how bad the situation was for the very simple reason that nobody told her. Jingo wrote, but she never really let her know how bad things were, and neither did I. What was the use of worrying Mother when there was nothing she could do anyway? That's the way I saw it then—it never occurred to me that she had a right to know—I only wanted to protect her, as always.

So far as deserting Jingo, I was just as bad as everyone else. I was beginning a new life with Bob and wasn't about to involve him in the family mess any more than necessary. Alex repeatedly hinted that Jingo would profit greatly from a protracted visit with us, but I pulled back in absolute horror at the idea of getting caught in a squeeze between two people who, when together, wanted nothing more than to be apart, and when apart, wanted only to be together. I was panicked at the idea of getting stuck with the responsibility for her life as I had been with El's. The only thing I felt I could do was harden my heart to all pleas for support, and I withdrew from Jingo even the amount of concern and affection I really felt and longed to offer her.

Dr. P. You really had to choose, you know—choose between self-preservation and compassionate self-sacrifice. There was nothing else you could have done without jeopardizing your own life and sacrificing Bob.

A. C. I know that, and I knew it then, but I hated myself for choosing as I did, and even now I sometimes wake in the night consumed with guilt feelings. In any case, I said no to Alex and all but severed connections with both of them.

Alex was left with responsibility for both his women and he assumed it. Although it burdened him as much as it increased his sense of importance, he assumed it because he had to. Both of them were cursing him by that time, but both of them were totally dependent on him and he on them. He was forced into the role of an Ethan Frome, and he played it bravely to the end.

Just about five years after El's death Jingo fell down the stairs and went into a state of shock her damaged liver couldn't handle. She only survived her fall by a few hours, but during that time, separated from everyone else who loved her, she had Alex constantly at her bedside. I didn't make it down in time, and nobody even thought to notify Mother and Daddy until everything was over. Everything happened so quickly, you know. Anyway, at the end Jingo still had the one who, having deserted her in all the ways that made her life worth living, still interacted with her and loved her throughout most of her life.

In the few lucid moments allowed her just before her death, Jingo dictated to a nurse a will in which she specifically disinherited Alex of her few remaining valuable possessions. Then, hugging to her breast the flowers he had brought, she pressed his hand to her lips in a last loving kiss and died with his arms around her. For years her heart had been filled with fury and disappointment, but as much as she had come to hate him, she never really stopped loving him. Alex never stopped loving Jingo either, in spite of his need to be cruel. He was truly devastated by her death, I know. However, that didn't stop him from threatening to make trouble unless he was given the cash value of her jewels, nor did it stop him from marrying Miriam six months later—Miriam who had by then become just as demanding and nagging as Jingo had ever been. At that point, he broke off all connections with our family, and I can't even imagine what has happened to him.

Dr. P. Did your parents come out for that funeral?

A.C. No, but I went east, and we had a little memorial service there.

Not long afterward, the House of Usher was sold and torn down. Fortunately Mother never returned to see the hideous pink ticky-tacky apartment building which now stands on the site of her parents' home, and could retain unsullied in her mind a proud memory of her House of Refuge.

She and Daddy continued on in their little apartment as cozy as two bugs in a rug. Looking at them, you'd have said they had never had a care in their lives. They were completely devoted to each other, and Daddy took splendid care of Mother. I think she just never thought about what he was up to—handled the whole situation as she had handled the deaths, I guess, just reciting all the poetry she knew whenever "negative thoughts" entered her head.

Dr. P. I've always been astonished by the number of marriages that turn out to be a kind of folie à deux—women putting up with the most bizarre demands and accepting them as perfectly normal in order to avoid seeing that their husbands aren't what they thought they were. Men, too, of course. In any case, your parents take the prize.

I wonder if death didn't save Jingo from going the way of her brother. Toward the end of her life, anger seems to have gained such momentum that she might well have crossed the line from extreme egocentricity into actual paranoia.

A.C. To me she seemed more and more like my father in her ability to twist anything she heard or read to relate directly to herself and support her point of view.

Dr. P. You feel your life was saved by analysis and by finding Bob at just the right moment?

A.C. Yes. Bob became my balance wheel, and we have had a long and happy marriage. By that I don't mean to say we've had no problems, because we have had many of them. We've run into most of the snags that everyone runs into and have needed as much compromise, forbearance, and forgiveness as any other two people trying to get along in a close relationship. As a matter of fact, in the beginning I wasn't at all sure I could give myself wholeheartedly to anyone and once or twice went back for some brief psychotherapy when I realized that some of my reactions toward Bob were irrational in terms of anything he was actually doing. I worked at it, though.

I'm not saying I had all the quirks either. Bob had his share, but he tried as hard as I did, and eventually we did manage to chip away at things that interfered with understanding one another. We really did want to make each other happy above all things, and I think we've succeeded pretty well, if I do say so myself.

Dr. P. You succeeded because to both of you marriage was the most important aspect of your lives, and you were willing to work at it.

A.C. Perhaps. I really was lucky, though, to find a man like Bob—someone who could nurture without being patronizing or restrictive, and who wanted pretty much the same things out of life as I wanted.

Dr. P. You certainly were. Only a few rarely privileged women get from their husbands the kind of acceptance and help necessary to attain both freedom and security. You were a liberated woman long before liberated women had a name.

A.C. Don't think I haven't realized it. You'll have to admit it really was a kind of miracle, don't you think?

Dr. P. You are determined to have your miracle, so I'll admit it was. And it was another that after all those years your parents lived long and happily together at the end. Did they ever become a problem to you and Bob?

A.C. No, I can't say they did. They furnished quite a few moments of drama throughout their last years, but for the most part Bob and I remained blissfully and purposely ignorant of much that took place.

Once a month or so, I wrote Mother briefly and superficially about what we were doing and on all appropriate occasions sent cards or flowers. Even less frequently I received brief notes in return, saying she and Daddy were well and busy with various activities. I never asked for details, and she never offered any. On periodic trips back east, either alone or with Bob, I carefully allotted to my parents not more than a weekend, and this usually passed pleasantly without my acquiring much information. At first I'd hoped that Bob would have the stamina I didn't—the capacity to listen to Daddy's orations and actually hear what he was talking about. When it became obvious that even he had trouble keeping his attention from wandering, we both gave up trying to understand.

What did manage to permeate was that Daddy had abandoned the idea of trying to found a church. Although lessons were still being sent out in fairly large numbers whenever requested, he no longer promoted them and was concentrating on battles with various groups of people who had caused him trouble. I knew the church funds had been used up in legal battles that were still continuing, again with the aid of volunteer attorneys willing to help in a struggle against forces that everyone involved felt had again illegally persecuted my father, and that everyone expected victory sooner or later.

Daddy was also busy plying taxpayer's suits to contest the right of religious bodies to hold property tax free. A lot of exciting episodes occurred periodically, and Mother was thriving on all the excitement. That's all I knew, and all I cared to know. I led my own life, and my parents led theirs three thousand miles away. Most of the time I didn't even think about them, and when I

did, it was in the way of recalling characters in a
play—interesting but fantastic. In fact, so removed was I
that when for the first time in fifteen years a long-
distance call came through from my father, I didn't
recognize his voice and took several seconds to understand what he was saying. By the time I did, he had
already hung up.

   "Is that you, Amy? Amy, are you there?"
   *"Who is call—oh, good heavens! I'm here Daddy. How
are you?"*
   *"Get on a plane, Amy. I think you will want to see
your mother as soon as possible. Get here as soon as you
can, Amy."*
   "I will, Daddy. What has happened?"
   *"Come as soon as you can, Amy. I will be expecting
you."*
   *When planning action, Amy's father was a man of few
words who told people what they were expected to do
and assumed they got the message. It would never have
occurred to him that some preparation for what she
would find might have helped to lift the load of lead in
Amy's chest during her speedy preparations and plane
trip. Why waste time talking over the phone when she
would be there in a few hours to see for herself? Had he
thought about how she might feel, he would have told
her more, for he would not intentionally have hurt a
flea, let alone his own daughter. It simply didn't occur
to him, so he didn't waste time on superfluous words.*
   *Of course, Amy was to some extent prepared for her
parents' death. Both were over eighty-five, and although
until now they had been completely alert and active, at
that age things happen rather suddenly. Without a doubt
Mother's time had come, but in what way? Was she in
pain? Was she in a hospital somewhere, full of needles
and tubes, ending her days without dignity or hu-*

*manity? Mother would hate that above all else, and
Amy could hardly bear to think about it. She worried
about her own reactions, too. How could she tolerate
seeing Laura in pain? By this time, Amy was well into
middle age, but feelings of oneness with her mother's
fear and suffering were as fresh as they had ever been.
The only way to keep them submerged had been to stay
out of range and think about something else, but now
she would be confronted. With what? There was no way
to anesthetize herself in advance, and it was an
agonizing plane ride.*

*However, things were not too bad yet. Her mother's
heart had been gradually failing, and for a week now her
brain had been failing too. She was in and out of
rational contact, and Amy's father had called her at this
point in order that she might say good-bye while her
mother was still to some extent her old self.*

*"There will be a few more weeks, but what would be
the sense of getting you here when things are all but
over? Now is the time, and from here on out the doctor
and I will have everything under control. There will be
no hospitals or operations—no tubes, needles, or heart
massage. Mother will be cared for peacefully in her own
home, by her own husband, with a little assistance from
the public health nurse. She has had a long life and a
good one. Now she is becoming like a little child again,
and we will make her happy until the end. We have a
doctor with good sense, even if he does take leave of it
on Sundays, praying to the Pope of Rome, and there
will be none of that modern nonsense of prolonging life
when one's number is up. There will be no nonsense
about funerals either. Everything is all arranged and will
go according to plan. When it is all over I will let you
know, but there is no reason for you to come again. Just
have a nice visit with your mother now, and I'll take
care of her for the rest of her days as I always have."*

With no more ado, her father retired to the kitchen to prepare a nice little lunch for them all. Mother was fond of walnuts, and through the closed door Amy could hear faint cracking sounds begin.

Laura had seemed a little confused while Amy and her father were talking only partly out of earshot, fluttering around the room with a vacant look, first hiding and then a few seconds later frantically searching again for the rings from her fingers. Alone with Amy, however, she became calm and seemed much as she had for the past few years, childlike and a little vague at best. Except for frequent moments when expression fleetingly faded from her face, she appeared placid and affectionate, holding Amy's hand and smiling as they sat together on the couch. Amy was obviously the only one feeling at all perturbed, and she was using maximum restraint to keep from showing anxiety. Attempting to maintain contact with Laura's fast-retreating mind, she began to recall the well-remembered stories from her mother's youth.

"Remember Maggie Maloney, Mother—and the time old Joe lost his queue? Remember when Grandfather brought Conchita home? Remember the attic and the Sleeping Beauty? Remember, Mother? Remember?"

Frantically she searched her own memory, giving back the stories with which Laura had brightened her children's early days. As little sparks glowed among the dying embers of her mother's mind, she nodded and smiled, occasionally indicating some recognition of the old names and places.

"Ah yes. Father brought her home in his pocket. She was such a little dog. Yes, Hattie was the wicked fairy, with her red hair sticking out from under that peaked black hat. Dear Hattie. I hope she is well. She was sick for a while, you know."

"Yes Mother, I know. And you all got to ride her new bicycle. Those must have been lovely days."

"Lovely days. Yes, lovely. How I wish you would be here all the time to talk about those days."

They reminisced for a while in quite a normal exchange, but then came the quizzical look again—the uncertainty and confusion, the slight air of suspiciousness.

"You are not my sister Amy! How do you remember all those times? You aren't—oh, of course—you were my baby Amy!"

Amy was shocked and furious with herself to recognize the surge of pleasure that shot through her—the gratitude that at least for this moment her mother actually knew who she was. Then, as the spark seemed to go out, she sat helpless in the ensuing silence, scanning her mind again for something that might bring it back. Sitting wordless, she suddenly saw a smile spread slowly over her mother's face and waited almost breathlessly for what might come.

"You were my baby. The smartest of all my children. At first I didn't expect you, you know, but after you came it was all for the best. Of all my children, you were the most—"

Silence fell again. If she says "the most capable" I think I shall die. I can't stand it, Mother! Say almost anything, but please don't say that! Laura paused for a long time, and it seemed she had drifted away entirely. After a while, however, she started again where she had left off.

"Of all my children, you were the most—loving."

With another slow, sweet smile, her mother looked right at Amy, and for that brief moment she saw her daughter. For almost the first and certainly the last time, there was real communication in her smile, and

Amy, rewarded after years of longing, held back with herculean effort the flood of tears threatening to dissolve her. Patting her mother's hand, she rose unhurriedly and made it to the bathroom where, in a rushing torrent of excitement, she urinated away a lifetime's accumulation of wishes to hear those words spoken.

By the time she returned, lunch was on the table, and her mother sat happily munching walnuts from a little pile stacked beside her plate.

A.C. Even now when I think about it, it makes me want to cry. There was so much about my relationship with Mother that makes me want to cry.

Two weeks after my visit, she died quietly in her sleep, and Daddy took care of her just as she had always known he would. As a matter of fact, he and she had talked together about that moment many times, each knowing exactly what the other wanted in case he or she went first. She would have taken care of him in the same way, he was perfectly sure. Fortunately, though, she hadn't had to. At this point she might not have been quite able to cope with the situation and would have been so terribly distressed. Of course, he was perfectly capable of handling everything without help and had plans for his own future laid out as well. Things had long ago been arranged with the undertaker, who had already been paid for Daddy's own cremation whenever the time should come. Money enough was saved to keep him comfortably in the apartment for the year or so necessary to wind up his current affairs, and he would not be a burden to anyone. Plans had been made for him to enter an old people's home recommended by his doctor when he got feeble. There was a lot of starch in the old bones yet, however, so nobody need worry. He

knew I had my job and my husband to think about and
should not consider another trip east for at least a year.
My Daddy was not one to sit and grieve when so much
wanted doing in the world, and he'd never been sick a
day in his life. So he said.

He had apparently forgotten what happened after El's
death—forgotten as completely as he seemed to have
forgotten he ever had a son—and for the moment, I
forgot too. Knowing he wanted things done according
to his own plan, I offered no resistance and assumed he
could manage.

*Two months later, however, Amy was again en route
to the East. Within a week of his wife's death, Eliot had
begun to run a fever without knowing it, and he now lay
dying in a hospital from complications of severe
dehydration. What's more, he lay in a religious hospital,
and Amy quaked at the very thought. Knowing all too
well the particular quality of vehemence with which he
freely excoriated religious organizations in general, and
the impact he had on people who felt the sting of his
attack, she was rushing to his bedside in a near state of
panic. Real fear for her father's safety, as well as shock
from another crisis so soon after her mother's death,
shook her with fits of trembling that even Bob's
comforting presence at her side could not quite still.*

*Again, however, her fears proved groundless. Even as
she neared the ward in which he lay, Amy could hear his
voice raised in a pleasantry to the student nurse and a
giggling response to "the Reverend" uttered in musical
brogue. The "Spirit of the Irish" was with him still, and
although three other patients shared the four-bed ward,
it became evident within a few seconds that Reverend
Carpenter was the major object of solicitude.*

*Amy had arrived almost simultaneously with the
ward inspection tour of a head nurse, accompanied by*

her train of subordinates, and beside a bed across the aisle everyone stood at sharp attention as the sister checked an order sheet and snapped out instructions in the crisp tones of a drill sergeant. Eliot was obviously so fascinated by the scene that he barely noticed his daughter's approach.

"Look at that woman, Amy. Isn't she a wonder? No nonsense around here, I can tell you that. Everything is shipshape and to the minute. She runs this place like an army. What an executive!"

The admiration in his tone was unmistakable, but his voice sounded strangely loud in the silent room. As usual under such circumstances, Amy shrank back with embarrassment, anticipating annoyance at her father's interruption of the quasi-military proceedings, but of course nobody else turned a hair. In all that battery of nurses, no eye deviated from its forward-looking position, nor did the sister look up from her examination chart. In every young eye was laughter though, and even across the set features of the "general" there flickered a faint smile. With softened voice she continued her inspection, and Amy, regaining her own composure, recognized again the magnetism with which her father exerted his influence. Right in the midst of the enemy's camp he had created a firm ally, one who, meeting him eye to eye, saw a kindred soul well versed in the knowledge of how things are done properly. What matter, then, an old man's ravings about the Pope? Even on his deathbed, Eliot had the situation well in hand.

As the afternoon wore on, her father seemed to doze off, but as Amy rose to stretch her cramped legs, he touched her arm, speaking the last words he ever spoke in a voice now faint and fading.

"Sit a little longer, Amy. It is almost over. In a few minutes I will be with your beautiful mother and very glad to see her, too. Fifty-five years is a long marriage,

but it was good all the way. We were never separated a day in our lives, you know."

That was all, before he dozed off forever, but Amy found her sadness almost overshadowed by the shock of surprise at her own reaction. He actually believes it. What's more, it may actually be true. Were they not really together all the time, if neither of them ever knew they were apart? Who can see truth written in the heart of another and call it a lie? Maybe all the rest of us were the deluded ones after all. Holding his thin hand for a few more moments, she felt a sudden flood of love for both her parents whose fantasy of life held more truth than their objective reality.

Even through love and sorrow, Amy also felt a touch of amusement at the odd turn of events in her own mind. Believing in no afterlife herself, and knowing that until the last moment of life her father didn't either, still his matter-of-fact assurance of imminent reunion with her mother afforded Amy a wealth of comfort. If Daddy wants to be with Mother throughout eternity, you can just bet he will find a way, and not even a host of angels will be able to come between them. Those two know what they want, and they will have it even if God himself thinks they are crazy. She left his side feeling strangely light with relief.

When the tears flowed later, they flowed largely because from now on there would be nobody left to worry about. The Carpenter family was gone—all but Amy, who remained with a vast, empty place near the center of her heart.

A.C. I don't cry much any more, but I feel a little like crying now, because the story is finished. Telling it has been a reliving—more painful than I expected, but also a great relief. It reopened some old wounds, yet I feel that for the first time I have it all in perspective. I didn't expect this to be a therapeutic experience, but it was and I'm doubly glad I did it. I wonder why I felt so strongly that I *had* to?

Dr. P. If I were to hazard a guess, I'd say you needed to cull something useful out of the tragically wasted potential in your family—that this is your way of giving meaning to their lives and in a sense restoring them to a place of honor in your own heart. By turning their tragedy into a learning experience for others, you have tried to make their suffering count for something after all, and you chose this way to say you loved them and recognize nobody was to blame for the tragedies that occurred.

Postscript

Amy Carpenter's story is a tale told retrospectively, with as much objectivity as possible, by a family member who was also a professionally trained student of human behavior and motivation. The description, through the eyes of one who was there, of the interpersonal environment in which a man who later became schizophrenic grew to adulthood, gives us an opportunity to examine from behind the scenes the way in which the Carpenter parents and children thought, communicated, and behaved toward each other. We can participate in interactions which might have been specifically instrumental in laying the groundwork for this particular kind of mental disturbance, and can try to assess the degree to which Eliot Jr.'s vulnerability to breakdown may be attributed to the interpersonal atmosphere in which his developmental years were spent.

In choosing to comment primarily upon this aspect of the material, I have no intention of trying to disprove the importance of other factors in the genesis of schizophrenia. Evidence of constitutional vulnerability to physical weakness or mental disorder on a hereditary basis is not prominent in an examination of either family line contributing to Eliot Jr.'s heritage, and there is also no evidence in his personal history that physical disease or injury to the brain played any part in the development of his psychosis. This does not prove that he did not carry a predisposing gene creating some metabolic or chemical abnormality. However, it does strongly suggest that some aspects of his interpersonal experience might have been major determinants in creating a predisposition for the breakdown that occurred, and that such factors are important to recognize regardless of what else might be involved.

Under pressure of severe anxiety some individuals tend to abandon ways of thinking that are considered logical in all civilized societies and revert to the more primitive forms of mental activity characteristic of schizophrenia. Under equally great pressure of anxiety other individuals may become neurotic or depressed but do not suffer a similar derangement of their thought processes. It has been suggested that from the beginning, and throughout their development, those who later become schizophrenic have been less deeply rooted in the capacity for logical thought.

In the Carpenter family, all the children had early experiences that laid a groundwork for emotional disturbance, and all were subjected to periods of severe anxiety throughout their lives. All of them developed some irrational tendencies, but only one lost complete contact with reality and suffered a schizophrenic type of thinking disorder. Why was he less well-rooted in the capacity for sustaining rationality than his sisters? In order to answer this question we must first examine briefly the ways in which a child acquires such roots.

Logical thinking is based on learning and experience. The human infant at first feels himself the center of the universe and manipulates his world by magical thought in which his wishes are the direct cause of all events. He must gradually learn to understand the true relationship between wishes and facts by constant correction of his omnipotent fantasies. This occurs through the development of a communication system with those who must at first be counted on to meet his needs when he makes them known. As the child becomes assured that the signals he transmits will be received and responded to in a predictable way, and that the verbal and nonverbal signals sent to him by others have predictable meanings, he learns not only to rely on those who care for him but to trust the validity of his own feelings and perceptions. Such firm trust in his own rationality is based not only upon unambiguous early mother-child communications but also upon continued reinforcement throughout his developmental years by clear parent-child communications. The meanings of words and other forms of expressing attitudes and emotions must be agreed upon by all, and the child's own perceptions must be validated by the consensual perceptions of others, primarily his parents. If either of these basic kinds of experience does not occur, or occurs in a distorted form, the developing individual's ability to experience reality as it is experienced by others will not be firmly established. If a child's perceptions are not validated by his parents' recognition that they are correct, or if magical thinking is not counteracted by realistic parental responses, the individual will not be firmly grounded in rationality and under stress will more readily revert to primitive modes of thinking.

What can we see in the Carpenter family interactions to explain the difficulty all the children had in sustaining rationality? In spite of their obvious differences, all the Carpenter children were strikingly similar in two respects. All showed strong sadomasochistic trends, and all gave evidence of intense conscious, as well as unconscious, ambivalence toward their parents and each other—a mixture of great love, caring, and

concern mingled with anger and disgust, of pride
mingled with shame, and longings for closeness mingled
with intense struggles to avoid the impact of each
other's problems. Although ambivalence and self-punish-
ing tendencies are commonly found in the families of
schizophrenic patients, they are also found in the
families of people with many other kinds of problems
and cannot be considered sufficient explanation for the
development of psychosis as a solution to conflicts and
guilts. On the other hand, great psychological tension
and anxiety can be produced by conflict between
opposing emotional forces, and at times such tension
and anxiety may be strong enough to push an individual
over the brink into insanity.

What was it about their parents that aroused such
strong conflicting feelings in the Carpenter children?

Laura was by no means typical of the so-called
schizophrenogenic mothers described in professional
publications, and she offered a great many very positive
values to her family. Although she was beset by
anxieties and distress which often made it difficult for
her to feel comfortable in a mothering role, she was
nevertheless experienced by all her children as warm,
lovable, and genuinely devoted to their welfare—a
mother who gave unselfishly to everyone, even to a
point of considerable self-sacrifice, without at the same
time assuming martyred attitudes that so often cause
generosity to be experienced by the recipients as a
disguised attack. Her own children, as well as her
sons-in-law, felt her to be remarkably unintrusive,
allowing each to pursue his or her own goals without
making them feel guilty about their choices and without
imposing her own views of what they should be accomplishing. They also considered her unrestrictive and
encouraging of their efforts to be free and independent.
During the first twenty years of her marriage, she clearly
did seem to need the emotional support and companion-

ship of her older daughter to offset unacknowledged
loneliness and unhappiness in the marital relationship,
but even then she did not prevent Virginia from having
friends of her own age, and actively encouraged her to
participate in school and social activities. During the
twenty years that her husband was gone, which encom-
passed the adolescence and early adult life of the other
children, their mother gave no hint of inability to
manage without clinging to them. While Eliot Jr. lived
with her in his grandmother's house, she actually saw
very little of him and made almost no demands upon his
time or his concern for her. Amy was convinced that her
mother would have been reasonably self-sufficient in
spite of her loneliness and would have been content
with the companionship of her friend Kate, and later of
her own mother, had she not felt that the children
needed emotional as well as actual support from her.
Even more importantly, the children felt their mother
to be both honest and fair in all but a very circum-
scribed area of her dealings with the family—one who
told the truth as she saw it, kept her promises, and
could be absolutely depended upon to help in whatever
way help was asked of her. Nobody felt pressured by
what they considered excessive demands for behavior
more perfect than that demanded by the mores of their
social group, and they felt that her standards were for
the most part reasonable and constructive. Finally, and
not the least of her virtues, this mother was often able
to joke and play with her children—naïve and childlike
in her humor to be sure, with a wit full of puns, jingles,
and silly riddles, yet amusing to her children and lending
support to their enjoyment of fantasy and the beauties
of nature. She created an atmosphere in which family
members frequently had a lot of fun together, and love
for their mother greatly outweighed other feelings that
the children had for her.

The only thing any of the Carpenter children had

against their mother was her intense need for self-deception—her absolute need to maintain self-protective romantic fantasies of an idyllic past that was never really idyllic, and of an uninterruptedly happy marital relationship which had never been really happy and had, for twenty years, been totally nonexistent. Everything the children fought and raged against fell somewhere into this area—their mother's tendency to moralize in terms of a religion based on a principle of refusal to accept the reality of any unpleasantness; the discrepancy between her sincere conscious beliefs and the nonverbally expressed, contradictory attitudes purposefully pushed out of her consciousness because they conflicted with an idealized self-image; the need to create a completely unrealistic image of her husband; and the masking of what really went on between people by incessant use of euphemisms, clichés, and stereotypes to protect herself from the knowledge that all was not good and beautiful. Coming from a mother who was unusually honest and reasonable about almost everything else, her need to rationalize and stubbornly deny to her children the reality of conditions and attitudes that they clearly perceived aroused them at times to violent pitches of anger and frustration.

All but one of the children also had positive feelings toward their father. Even the hatred which Jingo bore for him in her adolescence and adulthood can be seen as a sharp reversal of childhood adoration, resting on the psychological mechanism of unconscious displacement, by which she was able to use him as a focus of angers and disappointments from other sources. Both Eliot Jr. and Amy saw him as essentially kindhearted, with altruistic intentions toward those weaker than himself. They sympathized with him over the hardships of his youth, were proud of his extraordinary gifts of imagination and ability, and greatly admired his courage.

Although neither child could stand being subjected for more than a short time to his intensely aggressive and excitable manner, feelings of affection, recognition of his unusual personality, and conscious goodwill toward their father persisted throughout most of their lives.

Virginia alone, for reasons of her own, continued to insist that her father was consciously aware of exactly what he was doing and that he was simply a heartless crook who didn't care what happened to his wife and family. Eliot Jr. and Amy understood that he deceived himself as much as he deceived others and was fully convinced that what he did was right. So far as they were consciously aware, the two younger children really held nothing against him throughout most of their lives, recognizing at an early age that he acted as he did because he could not help it. This was simply the way he was, and although his impact on others was often devastating, he meant well and could not be blamed for things that were built into his nature. In their early years, his tirades at the dinner table drove them to frenzy. Later, they were enraged at his callous use of their mother for his own business ends and at the way he tantalized her with false promises of his imminent return for twenty years. However, before they were past early adolescence, Eliot Jr. and Amy realized that he simply had a different idea of morality than his children. Raised in a jungle of cutthroat competition and forced to support his whole family from the age of nine, he operated on a principle that anything legal was ethical and saw no other side to the matter. They also realized that, over and over again, year after year, he firmly *intended* to arrive a week from Thursday, just as firmly as his wife believed he would, and that he really thought something always came up at the last minute to prevent it. Although they could not have put a name to it, Eliot Jr. and Amy knew that their father and mother were engaged in a folie à deux, and that nothing could be done about it.

Why, then, was the situation so devastating to *all* of the children? Why could they not accept it for what it was and allow their parents to live in their fantasy without developing such intense anxiety about it? The answer is that in addition to the guilt and self-hatred engendered in the children by the severe tug-of-war between feelings of love and anger toward their parents, their parents' tendency to guide their own lives so largely by wishful thinking and their inability to validate the children's perceptions of reality tended to suck the children into the same pattern. It produced in them all a strong pull toward irrationality which they thought they were fighting, but which only Amy overcame to some degree.

The extent to which Virginia's pattern of thinking, and the whole pattern of her life, paralleled that of her mother has surely become obvious in the course of this story. In spite of her violent rejection of irrationality in both her parents, wishful thinking, unrealistic ideas about the nature of her husband's character, and extreme egocentricity governed her own thought and behavior in nearly the same way that they governed theirs. Eliot Jr., of course, lost his grip entirely on the logical system which controls so-called normal thinking, and it is interesting to note how greatly the self-image which evolved in his psychosis recreated in a caricatured form his childhood fantasy image of an all-powerful father who ruled the world single-handed—a fantasy which his father seemed to share and to try living out in actuality. Amy managed a little better than the others to escape being engulfed by the prevalent trend toward magical thinking, partly because in the earliest years she had, in effect, been raised by a foster mother with whom she lived mostly in isolation from family interaction, and partly because throughout the whole of her later developmental years she had access to much trusted, rational parent-surrogates who constantly corrected in a loving and caring manner her temptations to lapse into diffuseness and tenuous logic. However, even she had to fight these tendencies on a conscious level all through her life.

Why was Eliot the only one to lose contact with reality so completely? Was he less well grounded in a reliable communication system at the earliest stage of his life, less well reinforced in rationality by clear communication all along the line, or was he simply pushed to the breaking point by a far more intense pressure of anxiety? In attempting to answer these questions, we must consider whether he was subjected to greater pressures because he was a male, or whether individual personality characteristics and particulars of his life experience created in him a special vulnerability to breakdown.

Previously I pointed out that the mother-child relationship showed no signs of being disturbed in the earliest period of Eliot's infancy, and that the conscious attitudes of both parents toward him were strongly positive. If that is true, we have to assume that a reasonably firm basis for a sound mother-child communication system was established. As tangible evidence that the "divine mind" of his mother's new religion was, in fact, "infinite truth," and as his father's first son and heir, he had a special position in the affections of both parents. As the son of a favorite daughter, he also ranked high in the affections of a maternal grandfather who lived nearby at the time. Although intense rivalry toward him can be assumed on the part of his five-year-old sister, she had little contact with him during his infancy, and neither he nor she later remembered any particular difficulties between them in the toddler period. It would seem that at stages of life most important for the formation of basic trust in himself and others, Eliot Jr. had every reason to feel loved and secure. His retrospective autobiography indicates that at least consciously he did, and that troubles started for him at a later age.

We have also heard that by the age of five he had already begun to react to pressure from his father, which tended to make him feel inadequate as a male, and was withdrawing into a world of fantasy and dreams where he could achieve without fear of failure.

Except for a brief reference to the fact that his mother could always be called upon to join in butterfly hunts and creative play, Eliot Jr. gave no autobiographical clue to the nature of his relationship with her at that age. His sister Amy felt that in childhood he had not been particularly infantilized by his mother or discouraged from fighting back if attacked by his peers. However, it seems clear from the material that Laura could neither counteract her husband's pressure upon the boy nor allow herself to give any sign of disapproval of what went on between them. At the same time, there is evidence that the situation was upsetting to her and that most probably she unconsciously gave nonverbal messages to the effect that, although she admired and supported her husband, she really did not want her son to be like him.

At very early ages, all Laura's children knew how much she had admired her dreamy, artistic brother Charley, and although such sentiment was certainly never verbalized, they also knew she felt that, by enforcing harsh demands upon his sons for "manly" strength, her own father had been almost directly responsible for Uncle Charley's death. He had been a "gentle" soul, and gentleness was a quality she constantly extolled to her children. As a matter of fact,

although intense aggressiveness was her husband's most
striking quality, she frequently pointed out that this was
"just his manner" and that underneath he had "an
unusually gentle nature." Throughout her life Laura
frequently commented on the temperamental similarity
between her son and her brother, and there seems little
doubt that mixed messages from her about the desir-
ability of "manliness" as defined by her husband in
some way got through to increase Eliot Jr.'s conflict
over accepting his father's professed values. Thus, by the
age of twelve, the boy obviously had a firm conviction
that, no matter what he turned out to be, he was bound
to displease one or the other of his beloved parents.
Whether his accident at that time simply gave him "time
to digest the poison his father had fed him," as
described in his autobiography, or whether it took on a
symbolic significance solidifying unconscious feelings of
castration, as psychiatrists will claim, it certainly served
as a focal point for the final establishment of a totally
negative self-image.

By the time Eliot Jr. left his parents' direct influence
and reached the world of "finest development" at
boarding school, he was faced with a source of even
more contradictory messages. Up until then, everything
he had ever heard expounded came out loud and clear as
a simple statement that to be a man meant to be like his
father—aggressive, ruthless in business, and headed
straight, unequivocally, and unquestioningly toward
acquisition of the almighty dollar. "Take no wooden
nickels, dream no dreams, and brook no interference.
There is one way to go, and a Man takes it unfalter-
ingly." Suddenly, at the age of thirteen, it was asked—in
fact it was demanded—by this same father that his son
turn about-face in his point of view, that he identify
with and adopt the values of people at least two
generations away from the rough-and-tumble market-

place where their fortunes had been acquired, people who were now in a position to be more "gentle" and to scorn those still forced to attain wealth and power through violent competition and business ethics which so often differ from the private moralities professed by a good many businessmen in highest repute. Such people looked down on and derided men like Eliot Sr., even though they were too polite to sneer openly in his face, and in order to adopt their values, Eliot's son must of necessity look down on his father and reject most of what he stood for. In addition, to attain the "finest development" that his father wanted him to attain, Eliot Jr. must reject the entire concept of manhood which had been drilled into him since earliest life. He must reject the idea that his father was a great man, which his mother fervently proclaimed, and adopt the gentleness and good breeding which she really admired but could not acknowledge wanting for her son without making a mockery of her admiration for her husband. Eliot was thus in a "double bind" with both his parents and could not possibly choose a way to go that would be right.

The ethically questionable structure of Eliot Sr.'s business, which came to light at the time of The Case, and all his other affairs which made front-page news off and on over a period of twenty years, was a source of great shame and conflict for all his children. Belief in their father's honest intent, belief that what he had done was not too far out of line with the loophole-finding tactics of big businessmen in general, belief that he was indeed being persecuted, and great admiration for the courage he displayed in fighting his enemies conflicted sharply with the knowledge that "refined people" would deplore the whole situation, and that it was among "refined people" that they were supposed to live their own lives. Virginia probably suffered most visibly from this shame, not only because she did not share belief in her father's honest intent, but because her whole world was most directly threatened by fear of social stigma. Amy suffered least, because for a long time she knew little about what was going on, having been removed from the scene of action before the age of ten and brought up among people who for the most part did not even know she had a father and certainly did not connect her with the noisy problems of someone fighting battles a thousand miles away. While she went through a period of hating her father for other reasons and did not approve of his business tactics, particularly his involvement of her mother, she never believed him to be purposely dishonest, and she suffered most from empathy with a mother whose need to remain "socially acceptable" she perceived only too well and shared, in spite of her disgust at having such a need. Eliot Jr. suffered in a different way. Although he was geographically removed from the city where his father's activities were being spotlighted and was never directly subjected to social stigmatization at boarding school or college, the shame he felt struck viciously at an already weak possibility of identifying with his father, undercutting the whole structure of his manhood and feeling of capability.

Even though he became an adult, Eliot Jr. never really reached psychological adulthood. He remained pretty much at a late adolescent level, confused in identity and helpless without support from the outside. He could not tolerate awareness of anger and aggression toward his father, but the existence of such feelings deep in his unconscious mind was clearly demonstrated in dreams and symbolic artistic expressions. Although he managed to cope with conflicts to some degree by becoming an artist, he could not really handle his intensely mixed feelings without becoming completely passive and essentially dependent upon his mother to furnish him a sense of self. At one point in his autobiography he wrote, "for many years, Mother was the only spine I had." Repeated failure to gain a sense of manhood through the artistic success valued by her, or monetary success valued by his father, caused a continually progressive erosion of self-esteem from the time he left college on. However, he managed to function in some measure until that spine was abruptly withdrawn. When, after so many years of caring for her son, Laura returned to her husband, clearly indicating that in spite of everything that had happened he was, in her mind, the better man, Eliot Jr.'s rational mind finally cracked.

From all this we can see that as the only son in the Carpenter family, he was subjected to pressures creating intolerable anxiety—pressures which were particularly related to the fact of his sex—and that he suffered other pressures derived from the nature of his individual temperament and life experience all along the way. Most important is the fact that of the three children he was the most direct target for veiled and contradictory demands from both parents, and that the extreme confusion in his thinking was a direct outcome of the ambiguities in theirs.

Eliot Jr. was the only grandson of Abner Carpenter to bear the family name, and his death without issue ended one branch of the line brought to America by Deacon Thomas Carpenter in 1635. He was also the last grandson of Thomas Scott to die childless, ending that line of descent through the male too, although the Scott name from Thomas's branch of the family had perished a generation earlier with the demise of Laura's two brothers. Thus the development of schizophrenia and the suicide of one descendant at the confluence of two family lines hitherto without known mental illness brought an end to both. We have seen something of what happened to him and have looked briefly at some sources for the anxiety that caused him to make a break with reality as others know it. Many of those pressures arose from the personality characteristics of his parents who, in their turn, had developed problems rooted in the personalities of their parents, and other parents before them. Perhaps there is no real answer to the question of how it all came about, and we are only left with one final question. Where did the end begin?